ISLANDS APART

ISLANDS APART

■ · ■ · ■ ■ ■ · ■ · ■

A Year on the Edge of Civilization

Ken McAlpine

TRUMPETER
Boston & London
2009

To Kathy, Cullen, and Graham
And to everyone who strives
to make this world a better place

Trumpeter Books
An imprint of
Shambhala Publications, Inc.
Horticultural Hall
300 Massachusetts Avenue
Boston, Massachusetts 02115
www.shambhala.com

9   8   7   6   5   4   3   2   1

First edition
Printed in Canada

⊗ This edition is printed on acid-free paper that meets the
American National Standards Institute z39.48 Standard.
♻ This book was printed on 100% postconsumer recycled paper.
For more information please visit us at www.shambhala.com.

Distributed in the United States by Random House, Inc.,
and in Canada by Random House of Canada Ltd

Designed by James D. Skatges

Library of Congress Cataloging-in-Publication Data
McAlpine, Ken, 1959–
Islands apart: a year on the edge of civilization / Ken McAlpine.
p.   cm.
ISBN 978-1-59030-530-0 (pbk.: alk. paper)
1. Channel Islands (Calif.)—Description and travel.
2. McAlpine, Ken, 1959– —Travel—California—Channel Islands.
3. Natural history—California—Channel Islands.
4. Outdoor life—California—Channel Islands. I. Title.
F868.S232M35 2009
917.94'910454—DC22
2008051930

Contents

ISLANDS APART

Introduction

. . ■ ■ . .

IT IS A FINE THING to sit and watch seas, shadows, and stars shift, but it is no longer easily accomplished.

We live in wondrous times, astoundingly fast times, Blackberry and instant-message times, humankind accomplishing a swelling tidal wave of feats that would have scared Leonardo Da Vinci witless. With a finger's touch, palm-size devices play music, provide news as it unfolds, and even tell us where we should go, a feat formerly accomplished only by spouses and the Oracle at Delphi. Another touch and we see, from space, our home's precise location on Earth, right down to our car in the driveway. When such things become routine, it is astonishing.

Of late, I often step out into our front yard at night just to breathe. Standing in the dark, dandelions underfoot (for I am a chronic ignorer of chores), I look up at the stars. I never miss their beauty, but I also notice they are dim. Nowadays two-thirds of the population of the United States and about half the population of Europe can't see the Milky Way. Man's ongoing rush to illuminate everything now dims the stars themselves.

Still the muted stars feel good, and the darkness and the stillness too, though the stillness is underlain by the steady rush of
passing cars on a nearby freeway. I pretend the sound is wind
blowing through a canyon. It is a trick, but why not? Today's
world is filled with magicians' sleights, why not a simple one
of my own?

As I stand there in the darkness, I sense that I am missing
something.

I doubt I am alone. Almost every day I encounter people
who, like me, do not feel empowered by these abundant times.
Some are mildly unsettled; others near to drowning.

A woman says, "There's so much change in this world. I feel
so insecure," her words nearly a bleat.

A friend says, "I thought chips were something you ate."

Someone else says, "The more they talk about being 'con-
nected,' the more isolated I feel."

On the Web a teenager I will never know—for now we are
accustomed to hearing the innermost thoughts of strangers—
blogs, "I'm scared. Some days it feels that the world is moving
much faster than I am."

Author Maggie Jackson claims information overload is crip-
pling our ability to think deeply; like the stars, what matters is
now veiled. We are entering a new dark age, she says. I think,
perhaps this will make it easier to see the stars.

People do what they can to keep up. "To do two things at
once is to do neither," proclaimed Publilius Syrus, a Roman slave
who lived in the first century B.C.E. But to do six things at once,
ah, that is seizing the day. On the road, I look at other drivers talking on the phone, jotting down notes, eating lunch, and checking
(and changing) their look in the mirror, a combination of activities my high school driver's-ed instructor never considered. I read
about an actress who says she likes to read and talk on the phone
while engaging in intercourse, forever attaching a new, and sad,
meaning to the term *phone sex*. One of our son's friends crashed
on his bike while text messaging.

This is the communication age, but it seems to me that when people talk with each other, often no one really listens; even as we stand there, we are mentally lighting on some future task. And so a conversation might go something like this.

"Say, have you noticed that your pant leg is on fire?"

"I might be able to find time on Thursday."

I am an optimist at heart. Humankind, after all, has produced the poetry of Alfred, Lord Tennyson and the Sistine Chapel. But increasingly my optimism is sorely tested. Often I am certain we have lost something essential; at times I am certain we have lost our minds. A celebrity's half-eaten egg salad sandwich (plus a companion's partly gnawed corn dog!) sells on eBay for $520. On Wikipedia more people chime in regarding Michael Jackson than they do Islam or Christianity. The entire staff of Congress is banned from making Wikipedia entries after some staffers were caught sabotaging profiles (*Representative Joseph Pendergrast, D-Iowa, likes to play with naked dolls*).

On pickanyblog.com people tell me they are clumsy, they are watching *Fight Club* and baking bread, they are sorely dissatisfied by Northwest Airlines customer service, and I wonder if they have anyone at home who listens. On the Web people snort spaghetti up their nose, and dozens of critics weigh in on the quality of said snorting, and I wonder if anyone ever leaves home. Wrote Tennyson,

The ghost in man and the ghost that was once man
Are calling to each other in a dawn
stranger than the earth has ever seen.

Events whip past in a torrent, at least for those not suffering from them. Wars, famines, floods, financial disasters, political peccadilloes, floods again; they all tumble past. Thirty-three people are murdered in a mass shooting at Virginia Tech in Blacksburg, Virginia, by a student killer who signs into English class with a question mark. Soon thereafter, callers on a radio talk show debate whether the shootings should be the show's topic.

"It is a tragedy," says one caller, "but everybody will forget about it next week."

Standing outside in the dark, taking slow, measured breaths, I wonder if in drifting away from certain things we have lost a part of ourselves.

The stars are dim, but they tell me what to do.

From Ventura, California, where I live, on most days you can see the blue hummocks of Anacapa and Santa Cruz islands. Our beach town rises into sloping foothills. The effect is like seats in a movie theater; from the bank, pumping gas, negotiating traffic, running late for pretty much everything, I see the islands, rising from the Pacific Ocean, stoic and lovely. Anacapa and Santa Cruz are stoic because they are rocks perhaps seventeen million years old. What matter is it to them that we are late for our nine-thirty appointment or that we can get cell phone reception in more places than ever? Anacapa and Santa Cruz are lovely because, though they rest a mere eleven and nineteen miles, respectively, off the southern California coast, like the rest of the islands that comprise Channel Islands National Park—San Miguel, Santa Rosa, and Santa Barbara Island— they are almost wholly bereft of people. These five islands rest within sixty miles of eighteen million people. They remain a wild place, right at the edge of our property line. Anacapa and Santa Cruz loom like omnificent beings, radiating serenity, beckoning with something more.

I had been to each of the Channel Islands before, traveling by boat from our local harbor for day trips. There I briefly walked their trails, climbed high crests to stare out at a dizzying spread of blue, stooped to admire poppies bobbing in the wind. Gulls wheeled and shrieked, sea lions leaped from churning waters, and waves thumped ashore, their mist hanging in the sunshine for a beat before swirling crazily up the empty beach. If the season was right, migrating whales exhaled misty spouts that hung briefly in the air like phantom sails. Everywhere, I breathed the sea, and the beating wind teased with a whisper I should hear, but always I turned my back, hurrying back to catch the boat. Hurrying is what we do.

What if I stayed?

It would not be difficult. Anacapa and Santa Cruz islands were quite close, and Island Packers, Channel Island National Park's official concessionaire, frequently runs boats out to the two islands from harbors in Ventura and nearby Oxnard. Santa Rosa, San Miguel, and Santa Barbara islands are farther afield, but Island Packers shuttles lucky visitors, albeit less regularly, to these islands too. All five islands offer camping. Standing beneath the stars, I thought, *What if I leave the rush and cacophony behind? What better place to breathe slowly and think clearly, to examine how we live, and what we live for?*

It was a simple premise, filled with lovely complexities, a chance to use Henry David Thoreau's cabin-in-the-woods method for getting to the bottom of things. I would not pretend to be Thoreau. The man was a philosopher, a naturalist, and a poet: but even if timeless rumination was beyond me, I knew one thing: On the islands I would be able to see the stars, and maybe even the Milky Way. I might watch the sun rise, my ears ringing with quiet.

Thoreau understood. "It would be well perhaps if we were to spend more of our days without any obstruction between us and the celestial bodies . . . ," he wrote in *Walden*. He also understood, as we all do, what we reach for. *Walden* again: "What is the pill which will keep us well, serene, contented?"

In Thoreau's time this was a metaphorical rumination; no doubt today more than one pharmaceutical company promises a pill that does exactly that. But snake oil salesmen have been with us since time began, Valium not quite so long, and even a pill that might be beneficial eventually wears off and you have to take it again, and what kind of life is that?

I was no Henry David Thoreau, but we did share some things in common. Thoreau loved the natural world, and I do too. Still, he was wise enough not to follow the lead of truth seekers past, disappearing into some hellish wilderness for forty years to emerge with enlightenment and a rib cage upon which one might rap out "Over the Hills and Far Away." Thoreau didn't go far away at all—his cabin was less than two miles from his hometown of Concord, Massachusetts—and he emerged, two years later, still soft to the touch, perhaps because he scampered into Concord almost daily, and his mother delivered weekly goody baskets to his Walden Pond door. I, too, planned no harrowing pilgrimage in my search; on some of the islands, at night, through my tent flap, I could see the pinprick lights of civilization flickering like the campfires of some tremendous army. Thoreau dedicated himself to the fields and waters of his hometown. I would too. The best place for each of us is where we stand.

I also hoped to apply many of Thoreau's actions—or, to be more exact, inactions—as a template. On certain summer mornings, Thoreau sat in his doorway from sunrise to noon, looking and listening. He did not consider this wasted time, nor did I. Was he not doing two things at once?

We would diverge too. At times Thoreau did his utmost to distance himself from his fellow man, who, he felt, distracted him with shallow thoughts. Though I would ardently seek solitude on the islands, I also planned to engage my fellow man, in part because he might have a nicer camp stove or a spare marshmallow, but also because I might learn from him too.

I did not see my plan as one of escape. Escape is for those who wish to wash their hands of the world. I care deeply about the world. For one thing, it is home to those I love. For another, it is all we have. My two sons will inherit it, and then, if things do not go too far awry, their children will inherit it from them. It was not just my family tree that mattered. I am fond of all children. I want them all, in their time, to be able to lie in an empty meadow washed by a salt breeze and listen to the wind. So I was not interested in escaping. I was repairing to a quieter place where I might hear myself think, using the solitude of the islands for reflection, examining our busy world, and our place in it.

In between my solo journeys to each island, I decided I would continue to look deeply at our world. Back on the mainland in southern California I wanted to explore experiences that spoke of our current world and times past too, for we are creatures of repetition. Religion, war, poverty, fame, kindness and ignorance, despair and hope—they have been with us since our first breath. I would chose experiences on the mainland that reflected these grand themes, with a human face in the mirror. I would eat lunch with the homeless in Beverly Hills; sit in the desert with a ninety-eight-year-old Benedictine monk; stand among the wood crosses of a war memorial with loved ones come to honor the dead. I would choose these and other venues, then let serendipity, like life, take its course.

Reaction to my idea was mixed.

Ignoring the premise, a host of friends offered to accompany me out to the islands. They had tents, they had headaches from their runaway lives, they had an afternoon free in—poke, poke, poke at the Blackberry—July. I patiently explained that I planned on spending a week on each island. This winnowed the queue considerably.

I also hoped to experience the islands during their quietest times. Most people visit the Channel Islands in summer. I would visit the islands over the course of a year. Keeping things meteorologically simple, the weather on the Channel Islands is not the weather of the southern California mainland.

"You're going in the winter?" one friend said. "What are you, a complete idiot? Have you ever heard of wind and rain? I've heard that people's tents have blown right off the island. With them inside."

This is not true, but, as I was to see, it is not far from the truth either.

My wife Kathy, who is caring and sweet beyond measure but often distracted by the world's rush, said, "What are you going to do out there? You can't use a computer."

Only to anchor down the tent.

Many questioned how I would handle being alone. Apparently spending time alone is a fearsome affliction fraught with potentially intriguing consequences.

"At the end you'll be smearing seal blubber on yourself and running around naked," opined one prophet.

A neighbor said, "Solitude as a concept is something lots of people want, but then it's like, 'When is the fucking boat coming?'"

Perhaps this was a proverb.

One evening, our home reverberating with ring tones, a churning washer, and the shouts of our sons conversing from opposite ends of the house, Kathy said, "Aren't you just a little bit afraid of being alone?"

"Not really," I said, and this was a white lie, but only partly because I didn't want my wife to worry.

A friend gave voice to my real fear a few days later.

"What if you like being alone?"

When I explained to people that I was going to try to slow down, that I hoped to use solitude to perhaps find something deeper in a world that often raced along the surface, they furrowed their brows with serious intent, reached into their buzzing pockets, and said, "Mind if I take this call?"

Oddly, even in California many people didn't know these islands existed. But some people did know, and a few of them spoke in hushed and wistful voices of their magic. They described a wild and wondrous place where housecat-size foxes scampered through fields of Seuss-like flowers, and elephant seals bellowed challenge, and moon and sun shone down upon the feral and untamed while, on clear nights, Los Angeles made its own sooty light known on the horizon.

At a three-year-old's birthday party, a weary mother said to me, "I remember once sailing out to the islands in my twenties."

She paused. Children ran around us. Microwaves beeped. Teens sat side by side, texting elsewhere. People talked, and perhaps they listened.

"Sailing back, I could hear humanity," she said. "It was like a wall. It was then I realized I'd never heard silence before."

Twenty years later she still looked surprised.

And I knew I was right to go.

Santa Rosa Island

. . ∎ ∎ . .

I visited the Channel Islands in no particular order, for they all offer solitude and so, in these chaotic times, a chance to see things more clearly. It's true, some of the islands offer more opportunity for quiet reflection than others. Mostly, this is a matter of distance. Of the five islands comprising Channel Islands National Park—Santa Rosa, San Miguel, Santa Barbara, Santa Cruz, and Anacapa—Anacapa Island, only eleven miles off the southern California mainland, is the most visited. Americans like convenience. Anacapa can be wrapped up in half a day; boat out, traipse about the island, and be home in time for *Oprah*.

But as the Channel Islands edge farther into the Pacific, the degree of convenience falls off and, not surprisingly, so does the number of visitors. Santa Rosa Island sits over twenty-six miles from the mainland; only one Channel Island—San Miguel—strays farther west. Fogbound, windswept, and weather-scoured, Santa Rosa's remote attitude whispered alluringly. It seemed as good a place as any to start reflecting.

Santa Rosa is roughly forty-six miles by boat from Ventura Harbor, under good conditions a two-and-a-half to three-hour boat trip, but conditions are not always good. Those who regularly ply the Santa Barbara Channel and the Pacific beyond are well aware of this.

And so, on a sunny April morning, Dwight Willey, captain of the National Park Service's hundred-foot *Ocean Ranger*, stood inside the cabin, giving a safety talk before the vessel left Ventura Harbor.

"Big swell today," said Dwight. He had the easy smile of an accomplished seaman, or someone quite comfortable with the prospect of a long swim. "Make sure you hang on to something when you're moving around the boat. If you're feeling a little under the weather, grab a trash can, don't go to the rail." Dwight held up a life vest. "Everybody seen these before?" Just as quickly, he stashed it away. "Hope you never have to see them again."

Dwight's briefing was, well, brief because, with one exception, the folks he addressed—scientists, researchers, and National Park personnel—made this boat trip regularly. A goodly number of Dwight's passengers had skipped the briefing entirely. Stepping aboard, they had immediately hustled below decks to score a bunk so that they could sleep during the trip out. True professionals, they realized it is best to be well rested when a boat begins to founder—thus ensuring one has the requisite energy to strong-arm all comers and clamber into the lifeboat first.

I sat at one of the cabin's tables and listened attentively to Dwight's discourse, partly because I wanted to be polite and partly because slipping away to a bunk was awkward since Dwight was talking mostly to me. Members of the public do not ride aboard National Park Service boats, but the park service had kindly made an exception for me because I was writing a book that involved their Channel Islands. A flood of public trips (offered through Park concessionaire Island Packers) churn out to the park islands in summer, but in spring, fall, and winter, the number of public boat trips dwindles, and, in the case of Santa Rosa, stops completely in winter.

Hopping aboard the regular Tuesday morning park service run to Santa Rosa (with a stop at Santa Cruz Island too) ensured that I would be the sole camper on eighty-four square miles of island. On Friday, Island Packers would send out their first Santa Rosa boat of the season. Distance, and impressive storms, made public trips to Santa Rosa in winter both daunting and pointless. In terms of economic feasibility, the number of people willing to pay to puke and pray for five Victory at Sea hours is far outbalanced by the masses willing to cling to the stability of dry land.

The beginning of spring had changed conditions—slightly.

Finished with his briefing, Dwight spoke to the man seated across the table from me.

"Just talked to Earl out there," Dwight said. "He said it's bikini weather."

Mark Senning, Santa Rosa's head ranger, nodded to Dwight, but he smiled at me.

"The weather's good now, but things change fast out there," Mark said. "If you'd gone out last week, it would have been, well, I won't say miserable, but it would have been challenging for you. It was the way Santa Rosa is typically in the springtime. It blows like hell."

In my years spent in the great outdoors I have learned many valuable lessons, one of them being that I am no great outdoorsman. It is a harsh lesson absorbed by many a dilettante—some of them no longer with us—but a heartfelt love for nature does not equal survival skills. In the wild, I am capable enough. I can build a fire and filter water, and, should I find myself at a loss for something essential, I know how to ingratiate myself with someone who packed extra chocolate or knows the way out of the damn look-alike woods. But I have also spent enough time in the wild to notice that, just when I start to feel competent, nature bites me in the posterior. This is not a random choice of phrase. In remote Outback Australia I once tended to my backside with an ideally textured leaf, the underside of which was smothered in soon-to-be unsettled ants. Nature teaches humility faster than anything I know.

One thing I do well is read, and in our information age there are cyber libraries bursting with helpful information. I had read up thoroughly on Santa Rosa Island. The island sounded impossibly beautiful and equally unique, but it did not sound like a place to be trifled with. Santa Rosa is home to many things quiet, rare, and enchanting—endemic oaks (among the rarest in North America), the housecat-size island fox, and one of world's last two groves of Torrey pines—but the weather is not one of them.

Consult a map of the California coast and you will clearly see that Santa Rosa rests beyond the lee of Point Conception, the prong of California mainland that offers a degree of shelter to the islands of Santa Cruz, Santa Barbara, and Anacapa (not to mention all of balmy southern California). No such umbrella for Santa Rosa; the island throws its arms wide to the full brunt of every hellish weather system from the north. Even on a good day, thirty-knot winds are not uncommon. Nautical types will recognize thirty-knot winds for the impressive blow they are. Thirty knots is the equivalent of 34.6 miles an hour. Something called the Beaufort Wind Scale defines such a wind as a "moderate gale; whole trees in motion; inconvenience in walking against the wind." I could only imagine the foot speed required to chase down a tent.

These winds blow across cold Pacific waters. I had done what I could to prepare. I had packed plenty of warm clothing—two duffel bags full—and enough canned soup to ride out all of April and possibly most of May; certainly enough for my planned week's stay. Our family owns a dome tent, but I had borrowed a low lying tent from a friend instead. One does not need a degree in aeronautical engineering to see a dome tent's capacity for lift when placed before a willing wind. Happily, I had also read that the campground on Santa Rosa had recently undergone extensive improvements. Among other amenities, park service personnel had constructed windbreaks for each campsite, placed so that their three sides offered some protection from the prevailing winds.

I had neglected to pack a bikini, but other than that I felt reasonably prepared. I had garnered much of my information from Channel Island National Park's very own Web site.

From across the table, Mark smiled again.

"People can visit the Web site, they can read all the materials, but they still don't understand what they're getting into," he continued. "You have to actually be out there to understand the place."

Mark had worked as a ranger for Channel Islands National Park since 1987. He had rangered on Santa Rosa for the past nine years, generally alternating a week on the island with a week on the mainland. Though he would not say it, others told me so: Santa Rosa was Mark's island. His word, based on intimate experience, was the final one. He had advised plenty of visitors on Santa Rosa's challenges. Given that listening is a skill fast being winnowed from humanity's gene pool, he had also rescued a fair share of them when they did precisely what he had advised against.

Mark took no pride or satisfaction in these rescues. As an enforcement ranger, he wears a badge and a gun. Along with these items he carries a natural air of authority that made me sit up straight and listen. But with time I would come to see that, more than anything, Mark was simply a good Samaritan, clothed, by necessity, in the federal government's insipid and intimidating storm trooper uniform.

As we made for Santa Rosa atop shimmering swells, I knew Mark wasn't trying to frighten me with his stories of idiocy, accident, and even death, but he was succeeding mightily. In a mildly sad tone he spoke of campers who came to these wild islands equipped only with coolers of beer. Truly sad, two summers earlier, a young woman, just graduated from Stanford University, died when her kayak capsized off Santa Cruz Island. She and six friends had been briefed by the island ranger before they paddled off the small beach on the eastern end of the island, the ranger advising they paddle a route that would see the wind and waves at their backs on their return. They headed in the opposite direction. The wind and seas rose. Two kayaks capsized. The woman died of hypothermia.

"Ill prepared for the ocean's power and unpredictability," Mark said very softly. "This girl was in the prime of her life. Smart, bright woman. Gone. Such a waste."

Excusing myself, I stepped out to the open deck on the stern. One of the researchers on board was a friend. A field biologist, Andy Day was wrapping up a research stint working with bald eagles on Santa Cruz Island. These regal birds were making a remarkable comeback, both on the Channel Islands and on the mainland after nearly disappearing from the islands, and this earth, due to hunting and the heavy use of the pesticide DDT, which causes the eagles to lay thin-shelled eggs that break in the nest. Eight months earlier, the bald eagle had finally been taken off the endangered species list. Andy and his girlfriend, Karen, also a biologist and also on board, were monitoring the eagles' comeback on Santa Cruz. They would be dropped off there, after the boat deposited us on Santa Rosa.

I had met Andy, a laconic Georgian, four years earlier on a rafting trip down the Colorado River. On that trip he had impressed me with his knowledge of the local biota and his limitless reservoir of lewd jokes. I was on that the trip for a magazine assignment. Whenever I turned my back, Andy pilfered my notebook, returning it with his own entries. *I continue to stalk Andy, a man like no other, a man who's made me question my already tenuous heterosexuality, a man of searing intellect and smoldering good looks.*

I note this entry verbatim because I made the mistake of

handing him my notebook when I went to use the Ocean Ranger's head.

Andy was a potential PEN/Faulkner nominee, but I mostly appreciated him for his no-frills assessment of humanity's relations with our planet.

"We're always fucking things up, and it's even worse on islands," he said, the sea breeze tousling his smoldering good looks. "Islands are generally pretty sensitive ecosystems. If you throw things into them that are nonnative it generally screws them up."

Humanity, albeit unwittingly in many cases, has, in Andy-speak, done much to fuck up the Channel Islands. Now humans are trying to restore them.

Andy was familiar with many of the restoration attempts on the various islands. We discussed a few of them, including an ongoing effort on several, Santa Rosa included, to return the diminutive island fox to its former glory. A descendant of the mainland gray fox, the tiny island fox—standing roughly a foot tall and weighing four to five pounds—is found nowhere else in the world but on the Channel Islands. They had scampered across Santa Rosa, San Miguel, and Santa Cruz Island by the hundreds, but when the bald eagles vanished from these islands, a strange thing happened. Suddenly the foxes were dying faster than campaign promises in February. The reason was quickly apparent, though not to the island fox, a creature not instinctually hardwired to protect itself from aerial attacks. With the dominant bald eagles gone, golden eagles assumed dominion of the islands' skies. Bald eagles normally eat fish, but the golden eagles were only too happy to gorge themselves on the hapless island foxes, who wandered about in the open like fuzzy take-out dinners.

And so golden eagles were slowly and painstakingly trapped and transplanted to remote mainland locations, as bald eagles, due to equally painstaking work, slowly made their comeback on the Channel Islands and elsewhere.

All should have ended well, but for a series of recent surprises.

"They just found three dead foxes on Santa Cruz last week," Andy told me. "They were sort of peeled inside out, so it's likely a bird."

"Are the golden eagles back?" I asked.

"It's possible they were killed by golden eagles," said Andy. "But a few of us think it might possibly be bald eagles. They can learn new behaviors. That would suck for the foxes."

Nature—or at least what survives of it—is adaptable. These adaptations don't always assume man's moldings.

That we cannot orchestrate everything in this world is a fact ably understood by scientists and researchers. Perhaps because of this I have found them to be a patient and good-humored lot, more adaptable than most to nature's rhythms, and life's exigencies. That most of us are compelled to control our world— or have it controlled for us—may explain why many Americans are incapacitated by an unfamiliar dose of latte.

Clark Cowan was also standing out in the breezy sunshine. A botanist, Clark was conducting an ongoing study of several rare endemic plants clinging precariously to their final hope of existence on a single block of loamy slope on Santa Rosa. He had been studying the plants for four years.

"We've been trying to figure out what makes for a good year for them and what makes for a bad year." Clark gave a wise grin, which was easy for him because he looked a bit like a weather-roughened Santa Claus. "We still haven't figured it out yet."

By his estimate, Clark had been out to Santa Rosa on some fifty occasions, usually for a week at a time, though he had once stayed on the island for nearly three weeks.

"At first I thought, 'Oh my God, three weeks is going to be a long time.' And then, all of the sudden, the time was gone."

The boat rolled. I snatched drunkenly at a ladder. Clark deftly shifted his feet.

"You get very much into the moment. You're here on the island and the mainland is over there and things are going on."

He went silent for a moment. Perhaps he considered some of the things going on, because he grinned and shook his head. "People ask, 'Don't you miss the mainland?' It's simply not there. It's not in front of me. The island becomes your world."

He looked away, and this time he did not smile, and I did not bother him with any more questions.

The researchers and park service personnel would spend their week inside tidy little homes, linked together by equally tidy sidewalks. I knew this because I rode with them from the landing pier, up a dirt road, to their small neighborhood atop a flat expanse of hill. They unloaded propane tanks for their grills, Tupperware containers, and coolers filled with goodies. There were satellite dishes and antennas atop the roofs; from somewhere I heard canned laughter. Cheerily nodding to one another, everyone toted their supplies into their respective quarters. I felt like Ishi, with his face flattened against the glass of the Ritz-Carlton.

Unable to bear the sight of coolers and camaraderie, I walked around to a garage. Two ATVs were parked out in the sunshine. Each bore a small red plastic flag, waving high above the vehicle. Both flags looked as if they had been inserted into a shredder. The wind whispered lustily in my ear, *I'm going to kick your ass.*

I felt a queer unsettling in my stomach, not quite nausea, not quite fear, but pretty damn close.

The campground on Santa Rosa is sequestered within the folds of Water Canyon, about a mile and a half from the landing pier, and some two miles from the cozy park service enclave. Fortunately Mark needed to check on the campground, sparing me a long, hernia-inducing hike: I had not packed a cooler of beer, but my two duffel bags, bulging with Chunky Soup cans and mounds of woolen undergarments, probably weighed more. We bumped along the dirt road to the campground in a park service Suburban. On Mark's recommendation I chose the site tucked at the far back of the campground. The campground sloped gently upward so that this site rested alone above the others. Directly behind the windbreak there was a small hill; a softball toss away, a creek, occupying a narrow ravine, ran purposefully toward the sea.

From its high vantage point the site offered both privacy and a lovely view of Santa Cruz Island six miles to the east, today a blue mountainous mass beneath a cheery sunny sky.

"We call this site the lovers' campsite," said Mark, politely ignoring the obvious. He nodded to the abutting hillside. "The hill also blocks some of the wind."

Mark walked around the windbreak, giving it a professional once-over.

"I'd pitch the tent inside the windbreak. If it really starts blowing hard, there's really no place to hide. Once you get in the twenty-five-to-thirty-knot range you get this eggbeater effect." He made vicious little circles with his hand. "The wind just comes wrapping around the sides. And don't leave stuff out, because the birds will get it. As can the spotted skunks and the mice at night."

Suddenly it was very, very quiet.

"So it's all yours, man," Mark said cheerily. "Have fun."

And with that he left, his truck dropping down off the backside of a ridge like Columbus's ship falling off the horizon.

I set up my tent, carefully counted out my freeze-dried meals, trooped down to the shockingly upscale bathrooms (two flush toilets, vanities, a shower, and soft-to-the-touch toilet paper bereft of ants!), returned to my campsite, tied the tent to the windbreak (if the windbreak failed me, it was coming along too), sat down at the picnic table, and worried about what I'd left behind (knife, flashlight, matches—all present and accounted for). Then I walked back down to the bathroom to change my jeans (why?), scanned the surrounding hillsides for signs of life, wondered what my family was doing, and, in making various trips back and forth through the dry, crunchy grass, nearly sprained my ankle twice.

"The music of the world," observed Albert Camus, "finds its way more easily into this heart grown less secure."

In my heart, a symphony played.

Travel is, to varying degrees, a process of searching. My journey to Santa Rosa certainly qualified. I was searching for quiet, open spaces that would give me a better perspective on things and perhaps some peace of mind. But searches do not always provide clear answers.

"Anything you may find through seeking," Rinzai Zen foretells, "will only be a wild fox spirit." This is meant as a warning, but I would come to see it as both warning and gift.

If we are honest with ourselves, solitude takes some getting used to. Henry David Thoreau once wrote to a friend, "I have an immense appetite for solitude, like an infant for sleep, and if I don't get enough for this year, I shall cry all the next." I'd wager that the majority of us, left suddenly alone, will bawl just as long, but for the opposite reason. Thoreau was probably telling the truth about himself, but I believe even in his time, when solitude was easier to attain, he was the exception and not the rule. In his writings Thoreau repeatedly noted that though he entertained visitors at Walden, he often spent much time alone, and this was a puzzle to his fellow townspeople, who were always asking him *how* in the world he managed without their company.

This question, I believe, is posed as much out of fear as curiosity, and never more so than now. Most of us are irreparably bonded to the noise and clamor of the human world, the opportunity to flick on the TV and observe explosions, sirens, and storms; the ability to instant-message from Chapel Hill to China; the chance to bemoan the mindless nattering of our times and then plop down in front of the computer and watch a

You Tube video showcasing the world's largest ball of yarn (to date). No age is louder than ours. We have reached a crescendo of clamor, and it is both curse and comfort. Solitude, in our times, is rare and, for many, profoundly unnerving.

When I am on edge, I move. I prefer this phrase to "when I am afraid, I run," because the latter implies unseemly coward-ice, whereas the former suggests man-of-action fortitude.

Faced with no sane reason to change my pants again, I hiked down to the beach. Santa Rosa's campground rests about a quarter mile inland from the vast curve of Becher's Bay and the white-sand strand of Water Canyon Beach, and if there is a more heaven-sent stretch of beach, I have yet to see it.

It was, indeed, bikini weather, so I took off my hiking boots and walked barefoot over the sand, its surface soft and pleasing. There were no other footprints. Ferried by the wind, sinuous sand contrails ran down the beach. I kept looking for people—maybe a researcher squatting over some rare clam, or, better still, a ranger checking in on me—but there was no one. The waves expended themselves against the shore, whispering their approval.

Near the end of the beach, where it ran up against a steep escarpment of cliff, a large rock jutted from the sand. I sat in the rock's lee to escape the wind. My mind refused to sit. First it spent some time worrying about various unfinished obliga-tions at home. Then it considered whether I should use the current circumstances to run about the beach naked. Finally, with nothing else to do, I looked at the rock closely. Walking along the beach, I had been struck by the sensuous curves and slopes of the unblemished sand; the architecture of their sine curve was perfect, as if each grain had been lovingly tucked against the other by a doting mother's hand. Now I saw that the sculpted beach had been one-upped. Resting along the rock's ledges were sand dunes in miniature, no longer than a thumb, their ridgelines razor-edged, their flanks sleek as taut silk sheets. Their perfectly crafted rightness sent my spirit soaring.

Being alone is about highs and lows. Back at camp I burned

my thumb trying to light the flammable fire starters that pur-
portedly, once lit, would cook my dinner. But the wind, performing precisely the eddies Mark had described, kept snuffing
the damn things out so that finally, driven to desperation, I risked
a week of sleeping with the skunks and mice and fired up a cube
inside the tent, waiting until it achieved a healthy flame before I
squirmed back outside. It took two cubes to boil a cup of water.
While my freeze-dried foodstuffs softened under the influence
of boiled water, I re-counted my fire starters. I had eighteen left,
nine of which I had haphazardly tossed in at the last minute,
since I had misplaced the box they came in. Note to outdoor
self: on a windy island, regarding fire, one cannot overdo.

Spooning down bits of pork and broccoli, I watched the
shadows begin to creep slowly down the canyon walls. I looked
at my watch. Six P.M., time for the evening news. The news here
was simple: deepening shadows, with no chance of letup in
the wind.

In the creek, frogs began to sing.

Mark had told me he would pick me up early the next morning.
He needed to check on a few things. In the process he would
drive me out to the trailhead at Lobo Canyon, in his opinion
one of the prettiest hikes on the island. Again, this was not standard park service procedure. The park service has better things
to do than shuttle visitors about the islands, but in this particular case I was the only one on the island, Mark has a soft heart,
and, more important from a bureaucratic standpoint, he was
in charge.

"There's no way you'll get a good look at the whole island
unless I help you out," he said as we bumped out toward Lobo
Canyon. "This is a huge island, eighty-four square miles."

I didn't have to look at the Beaufort Wind Scale to know that
this was a very large piece of ground, and I was very grateful
for Mark's kindness.

Before coming under the ownership of the national park in

1986, Santa Rosa Island had a long history of ranching, focusing primarily on sheep and cattle. Several ranch buildings remain along the bluffs edging Becher's Bay—the barn was built before the Civil War—and here and there in the island's interior, collapsing corrals and rusted tractors are slowly succumbing to wind and weather. First on horseback, and later by truck, ranchers had to access the island interior to check on their ranging cattle. Consequently a handy latticework of rutted dirt roads lace the island, the important ones maintained by the park service, and the others going rapidly to seed.

We bumped along one of the main roads, rising slowly up into the island's interior. After a time, Mark stopped the Suburban.

"That's the fox recovery program main site," he said, pointing down into a tucked-away valley where a collection of low-lying buildings hunkered into the landscape. "The principal captive breeding goes on there."

It seemed like a fine private place for romance.

"How is it going?" I asked.

"We started with about fourteen foxes six years ago and now we're approaching one hundred," Mark said. "We've sent a lot of them back into the wild. There're more in the wild now than in captivity."

I asked Mark about what Andy had said, that bald eagles might now be preying on the foxes.

"It's possible that bald eagles could predate foxes; however, it's pretty universally agreed that their principal food source is fish, so it's highly unlikely," Mark said. "As the bald eagles grow to maturity, they're an opportunistic species, they'll eat anything, but as they mature, they focus on the ocean. It's been a long haul relocating the golden eagles. We haven't shot any of them. You have to trap them, and they're smart. The last ones are hardest to catch for a reason."

And sometimes the last ones are simply hidden away. Gazing down into the enclave of the low buildings, I was suddenly struck by how very much like a military field hospital it was, a brave and desperate attempt to keep life going.

Mark looked out over the tawny hills rolling away into the distance.

"There used to be thousands of these foxes out here, and then we were down to fourteen." He sounded mildly surprised, like an English professor, reading aloud before a class, who had suddenly come across a forgotten passage he himself had written.

"Wait until you see Lobo Canyon," he said, pulling back onto the road. "Your mind will be blown."

Mark was right. Lobo Canyon was beautiful and the sea at its foot was even better. There are no wolves in Lobo Canyon—it is named for sea lions, which Spanish speakers aptly call *lobos del mar,* wolves of the sea—but there were lovely butterflies, and alligator lizards that disappeared in a flick, and a peregrine falcon riding easy on the canyon updrafts. The park service had hewn a path alongside a stream that was at times narrow, at times wide, at times gin clear, and at times filled with wind-blown grass that made it seem as if the stream still flowed. Slot canyons ran up and away, their sandstone walls carved by wind and rain into countless shapes—here a flaring cobra, there a breaking wave. Wind and birdsong flew down the canyons, electric-blue dragonflies mated in midair. Trail and stream made for the sea.

And a glorious sea it was. At the canyon's mouth the stream spat out a thumb of detritus, a small gravel beach abutting the sea, but I ignored the beach and climbed the path that rose to the top of the craggy bluffs. Sunshine still basted the island behind me, but out over the Pacific, gray clouds with fiercely bruised bottoms carpeted the sky, bestowing on the ocean a wintry hue. The wind had strengthened. Far out to sea, large breakers frothed and jumbled, their white implosions indicating some shallow reef; it was not hard to envision a proud Spanish galleon coming to a wicked end. The bluffs on which I stood were composed of rock worn smooth and scattered patches of sand; behind this initial buttress rested flatlands of equally storm-pummeled grass. Here was a raw place. It was like being at the edge of the world, and it was stirring because of it.

Turning away from the sea, I spied a small dark slash in the side of a sloping cliff. It was too much to resist. I climbed up the grassy steep. Stooping low, I shuffled into the cave. It was quiet out of the wind. The cave went back only a few yards, but I was glad I had come. Atop a small mound of sand at the rear of the cave, the delicate claw prints of *Urocyon littoralis santarosae* made their indelible stamp. One island fox had removed itself from aerial threat for at least a moment.

Reversing my path, I hiked back out of the canyon, and then continued back to camp on the road that Mark had driven me in on in the morning. It was a pleasant walk. The sun was out again. Here atop the hill the world was only blue sky and a vast wavy, wheat-colored sea of more hills that ran away into the distance: most of Santa Rosa is now covered with what science calls nonnative grassland, but just because you're invasive doesn't mean you can't be beautiful. To be afoot and look ahead at a distant cluster of hills and think, *I'm going there*, is a pleasant thing.

I took my time; anything else made no sense. It was late afternoon by the time I arrived at the cluster of ranch buildings and their surrounding pastures. I stood for a moment outside the white picket fence that runs around the main ranch house, believed to have been built by one Alpheus Basil Thompson in the late 1850s. The ranch house and a nearby bunkhouse are still used now and again when the ranch owners (in an agreement reached with the federal government, they are allowed to stay on the island until 2011) and visiting hunters come to stay on the island; periodic hunts are allowed on the island to cull the population of nonnative mule deer and Roosevelt elk, introduced originally by ranch owners for hunting. Some things change, and some things stay the same.

Just away from the main ranch buildings I spied two men

standing in a pasture. I was about to hail them when I recognized the implements in their hands.

One of the men, already hunched, swung his iron. Jerking upright, he issued the golfer's eternal refrain.

"Awwwww fuck!"

Next his opponent swung. He must have made a similar shot, for he too spoke rudely to the sky.

In their defense, the course they played redefined the word *rough*. The grass was long, and in some places it exploded in great tufts. There were bushes everywhere and the wind blew like hell. Tiger Woods would have wept.

Focused on their challenges, the two men, who I would later learn were ranch caretakers, ignored me. Leaning against the fence, I watched. They took turns, first one, and then the other, swinging at balls I never did see, sending them, with colorful exclamations, to places it took them a long time to see. But the men cursed happily, and why not? Theirs was a course more exclusive than Saint Andrews, and they no doubt wasted little money on greens fees. I imagined them, round complete, watching with great satisfaction as their clubs looped lazily into the Pacific, backlit by the setting sun.

Not in the mood for cooking my thumb, I opted for an early dinner of peanuts and granola bars. Next I wallowed in the joy of a hot shower. When I was done, I left my towel hanging proprietarily on the towel rack. I owned the place.

The sun had dropped behind Santa Cruz Island, but there was still plenty of light in the sky. Remembering the frog chorus of the evening before, I walked down to the creek that bordered the campground.

Walking along the creek, I saw no sign of frogs at first. Then slowly I began to find them, tiny things that flopped off rocks with infinitesimal splats or made vague, disinterested breast-stroking motions.

The Pacific tree frogs brought me both light and darkness. When our sons, Cullen and Graham, were younger, the three of us would disappear for hours into an arroyo near our home. The frogs there were harder to find than the frogs I saw now, what with the nearly black stagnant water and moss and garbage, but small boys don't care, and if they don't, their father doesn't either. Using those small nets you get at the fish store, we scooped the frogs up gently, placing them in a hand-size plastic terrarium that had once housed tomato caterpillars. When the container brimmed with frogs, we returned them to the stream precisely where we had found them, for who would want to be uprooted from their home and placed amid Styrofoam cups and rusted beer cans they didn't know?

Those were magical times, squatting beside my young sons, their nets darting sure and quick into the water (and sometimes their whole bodies too); only magic, too, can explain how none of us contracted a single itch from the swathes of poison oak blanketing the place.

But as the boys grew older, somehow they grew very, very busy. Standing beside this creek, fat with frogs for the temporary taking, I could not recall the last time we'd gone frogging, or wiled away an afternoon engaged in a similarly joyous version of absentminded nothing. There was schoolwork, and guitar lessons, and Cotillion, where for an obscene fee America's young men learn that it is not proper to pull your date's chair completely out from under her—just a little bit will do—and that women are served their chocolate chip cookie first, leaving the broken-up bits, not surprisingly bereft of chips, for you. Both boys now also played club soccer, "club" being a euphemism for weekend tournaments played in the far reaches of Transylvania.

Several years ago I interviewed a straightforward psychologist named Alvin Rosenfeld. The topic was overscheduled kids. The science of overscheduled children was still nascent, Rosenfeld told me, but already alarming facts were emerging. Over the past two decades, he said, unstructured children's activities had decreased by 50 percent; kids in 1950 had two and a half times more free time than kids today. Yes, today's parents spent more time with their kids, but at least one study pointed out that most of that time was spent in the car schlepping them around. One does not need a degree in psychology to conclude that negligible quality time is fostered with the back of the head.

Rosenfeld also said that only in recent years had science begun to ferret out the truly critical importance of free play in fostering everything from imagination to the ability to cooperate with others. No quantum leap to see that these traits don't just come in handy in childhood. Already the brains of certain world leaders are sorely stunted in these respects; to think that these skills might dissipate further conjures up a bleak future.

Free time, said Rosenfeld, was essential. "Boredom is not necessarily bad," he said. "It can stimulate kids to think, create, and hear the soft murmurings of their inner voice, the one that makes them write the unusual story, draw the unique picture, or come up with the unusual thought."

Had Edison and Einstein been part of a car pool, our world might have been a much different place.

In Rosenfeld's honor I sat beside the stream as night fell. It was a cloudless night. When the moon cleared the canyon wall, it threw patches of shimmering silver onto the dark water. I conjured faces from the morphing puddles of silver. The nearby canyon wall was pocked with caves, dark slashes in the wall's light surface. An odd number of them turned upward in grins. Ken Kesey would have been proud.

On closer inspection some of the grins appeared sly, mocking, the kind of grin you saw in grade school just before someone kicked you, simply following through on the order taped to your back. Suddenly I was struck by a vision of spotted skunks and mice making merry with my supplies, feasting on my beef jerky and getting amped up on powdered drink mix—hold the water—leaving me to survive on my outdoor wits, a frightening prospect indeed.

I confess I fairly vaulted out of the ravine. There were no creatures on my picnic table, but there was life on the far ridge of the canyon. Three mule deer bucks stood like dark cutouts against the night sky. They watched, antlers poised attentively, as I sat down slowly at my picnic table. I remained still, and they did too. They stood on the ridge for a long time, backlit by the evening stars, and then, on some signal unseen by me, bounded away as one.

When I woke at dawn the next morning the mule deer were back on the ridge. As I walked groggily down to the bathroom, I flushed a pigeon from the grass, the sudden whirring explosion nearly rendering my trip to the bathroom unnecessary. Frog song turned to birdsong. At any minute I expected Snow White to come prancing along surrounded by woodland denizens.

Today Mark was heading in the direction of a spot called Clapp Spring. He would drop me off there and I would hike to East Point, where I would rendezvous with Clark Cowan and fellow researcher Kathryn McEachern, who, when they were finished with their work, would drive me back to camp on their way home. By Mark's reckoning, the hike would take me three to four hours, allowing for plenty of time to meet up later with the researchers, who would be heading home around six.

Mark dropped me off at Clapp Spring at noon. I stepped from the truck. North, south, east, west—all was oak-threaded valleys, chaparral, and grassy sward, and streams twisting their way to the sea between folded hills.

It was wonderful, but I noticed something else too. There are times in my life when I want to run screaming from all the noise; even when the noise is being made by my own loving family. I don't mean run as Paul Gauguin did—disappearing forever to a faraway tropical isle (though a few weeks might be nice)—but I do mean slip away, at least for a few hours, to a place where the sound of humankind is as rare as, well, silent humankind.

Now, faced with just that opportunity, I wanted human noise. So I dawdled beside the truck.

"How hard did the wind blow yesterday?" I asked Mark.

Hiking back to camp from Lobo Canyon, there had been times when the wind nearly lifted me off my feet. With a slight jog and a moderate downslope I might have matched the Wright brothers' initial attempts.

"Yesterday was a little windier than normal," Mark said. "What time?" Mark, I had already learned, was precise.

"About three in the afternoon."

"It was honking then. It's blowing about twenty-five to thirty knots today. How was it last night at the campground?"

The wind had walloped my tent all night, making a ripping sound alternating with a resounding *whump,* as if some petulant, tireless, and amply booted child stood outside demanding admission. The wind eddies had turned into whirlpools. Sleeping had proved difficult, to put it mildly. But no one wants to look like a cry baby.

"Kind of windy." I heard the faintest peep of whimper in my voice. I think Mark heard it too.

"Let's just say last night's wind was typical for spring," he said casually. "It's not for everybody. Without the windbreaks it would be very grim."

For a long moment my mind worked out what day it was. Thursday. I was barely into my second full day. A great deal of cyclonic eddying awaited.

"The campground will be full tomorrow," said Mark.

This provided me a mild shock. Friday, I suddenly remembered, was the day the Island Packer boat was scheduled to arrive.

"Full?" I said, as if I had suddenly been rendered both lonely and deaf.

"Yep."

The wind blew cool, but I still felt the sun on the back of my neck.

"It's a gorgeous trail," Mark said slowly. "Precipitous drops right down to the water."

I did not miss the hint of envy in his voice. One does not become a park ranger without some feeling for the great outdoors.

The two of us stood looking out over the emptiness.

Mark said, "I suspect every year we're going to have more and more people here."

The wind carried this thought away.

"Our job is to encourage more visitors and minimize the impacts on the islands," Mark said. "Kind of at opposite ends."

He tried a wry grin that didn't quite work.

I suddenly remembered something Mark had said the day before, just before I slid out of the front seat to hike in Lobo Canyon.

I didn't join the park service to make money, he'd said. *I joined because I wanted to do a small thing to improve the world.*

Sometimes we are forced to make mixed improvements.

I had all day, but Mark didn't. Mark gave me one of his water bottles, and a last bit of advice.

"Look for a white pickup," he said, getting back into the truck. "And don't go too slow. You shouldn't risk missing your ride back."

It was twelve thirty. I had nearly six hours. Yertle the Turtle could have done it, in cement boots. I also noticed that the wind was pushing gently at my back. I wasn't quite sure this was coincidence. I looked at Mark. It might be that the man was a living Irish proverb.

And so I hiked off into a windy veldt-of-a-world. The trail rose and fell, sometimes gently, sometimes precipitously. Once or twice it rose so steeply I felt as if I would continue climbing on into the blue sky.

Mark was right. The hike was gorgeous. The thick grass flowed up the summits as if hurrying to catch the view; from the summits, I looked down on sheer cliffs plunging a long way down into the sea. I swayed slightly. Upon the ocean's surface, thick strands of kelp did the same. Here and there as I hiked

I came upon fences. They looked small, futile, and mildly humorous—*now remember, this side belongs to you, and this side belongs to me.* Other than the trail, and the vast prairie of invasive grass, there was no sign of humankind.

I reached the stand of oaks at two thirty. It was a small stand, and I mean this quite literally, for it was a stand of Santa Rosa's rare endemic island oaks. They weren't much taller than me, and I trooped in among them feeling a bit like a giant, but, working together, their mottled trunks and half-size fluttering leaves provided shelter from the wind and sun. I stretched out under an oak and ate lunch, the wind making the distant sound of passing traffic and the leaves over my head dancing giddily because the wind lied. A few days later I would find myself at sunset, in another grove of island oaks, this one atop Black Mountain. In the falling light, the shadows appeared reluctant, and the leaves fairly glowed, and where shadow had not yet reached, the sun dappled the canopy of fallen leaves with the softest gold. It was an ethereal place, a place of elves and fairy creatures, and one man too, for I felt wholly at home, felt it with a surety and serenity as deep as it was beyond doubt. And I thought, *Everyone should have a place like this.*

Once I saw the Dalai Lama speak in Santa Barbara. In almost every written account of him writers note—along with his kindness and sense of humor—an unshakable serenity. I don't know the man, but he certainly has his worries—the horrific Chinese oppression of Tibet, for one. Yet I remember, the instant he entered the auditorium, feeling a palpable sense of calm. It didn't come from the crowd; they erupted in frenzied applause as soon as the first fringe of his orange robe appeared. Taking his place behind the podium, the Dalai Lama folded his hands and stood easily. Though he was very much in the present—even from my nosebleed seat I could see him acknowledging people in the crowd—I had the distinct sense he was somewhere else too. It is presumptuous to predict the inner workings of a man purported to be a living buddha, but I'll do it anyhow. He looked out into the maelstrom of noise and flashing cameras as if he was gazing upon a quiet oak glen. And then, when he spoke, he spoke of things equally simple—of compassion, of choice, of personal responsibility.

War and disease and poverty and oppression—our problems are Big and Complex and impossibly difficult to solve, so it is all the more important to keep sight of the simplest things, like a silent oak grove. The Dalai Lama understood. Nothing is impossible to solve, for the bridge between the complex problems and the simple solutions is, in truth, nonexistent.

We humans often remain largely confused, this man in particular, which explains why, despite Mark's very specific directions, when I reached the dirt road that runs the length of Santa Rosa's eastern flank, I turned left, hiking back in the direction of camp. Had I turned right, I would have come across Clark, Kathryn, and their white pickup only ten minutes down the road. But I didn't, and by the time I realized my mistake, I had hiked for nearly an hour, so I decided it was smarter to keep heading back toward camp, for that led to the ranch, and just above the ranch the small suburbia of park service personnel— in short, the chance to encounter some human being so that I might inform them that I wasn't lying twisted and broken at the foot of a cliff, or gored by an elk, or crushed—well, maybe just slightly flattened—by a miniature oak.

So it was that six thirty saw me fairly running down the road, screaming many un-serene things. Mark had trusted me with a simple exercise, follow one path and make one turn, and I had gotten it wrong. I knew exactly why Clark and Kathryn hadn't yet come bumping up behind me in the white pickup. They were now out looking for me, and pretty soon the whole damn park service, and maybe even the National Guard and the Girl Scouts too, would be doing the same thing.

As soon as I had realized that I had missed my rendezvous, I recalled something Andy had told me on the boat trip out. His searing intellect—or perhaps the fact that he had already

witnessed my propensity to take the wrong trail during our ad-
venture in the Grand Canyon—led him to believe I just might
wander off.

"You know, they take it pretty seriously if you don't show
up at your campground," he had drawled. "They send out the
helicopters. It's a big search and rescue."

He had grinned as if he already knew I'd be paying the bill.

Well, I didn't need any choppers, I knew exactly where I was,
and that was pathetically half running, half sobbing along a dirt
road bereft of any sign of human life. I prayed for a sign of humanity. Where were all those damn researchers? Weren't they
getting paid to be out saving something? Curse Andy. Hadn't he
said he spent a lot of time on the island playing Ping-Pong? All
I wanted was one measly soul. I had already been on the island
long enough to see that pretty much every soul on Santa Rosa,
except me, carried a radio. One short, crackling message, and
the choppers would be throttled down and the world righted.

I will be the first to admit I worked myself into an apoplec-
tic frenzy. Sam will be the second, because he had the dubious
honor of bumping up behind me in his pickup, at a little before
seven.

As he would tell me later, when I had gathered enough of my
senses to start comprehending things again, "Shit, you *charged*
the truck. I wasn't sure if I should help or back away."

Fate being what it is, a park service truck came down the
road the other way about thirty seconds later. Dirk Rodriguez,
a park botanist, was driving, and as soon as he brought the
truck to a standstill, I was fairly slobbering apologies through
his window.

Having ascertained that I was OK, if not a trifle frothy and
addled, Dirk got on his radio.

"We have him here," he said.

I heard Mark sigh.

"Thank God. Does his health look all right?"

Dirk gave me an amused look and then spoke into the radio.

."He looks fine."

As easy as that, it ended. Sam, who I later learned was the ranch caretaker, and one of the golfers I had seen earlier, offered me a ride back to the campground.

It was another mile and half back to camp. I'd been walking for seven hours, and jogging and shouting like an escapee from a mental institution for the last two.

Proving that was indeed where I belonged, I said, "I'll walk back as penance."

Sam gave me a sly grin.

"Do you know where the campground is?"

Dusk was falling as I stumbled up the slight rise into the campground, staring at my tired feet. Something made me look up. An island fox stood in the middle of the trail. We looked at each other, disheveled man and curious beast. I know I imagined it, but for a brief instant the fox gave me Sam's sly smile. An instant was all I had because the fox cocked its head and then disappeared, just like that.

The wind was blowing again. For all I know, it kicked at my tent like David Beckham on amphetamines. I slept like I was in the presidential suite at the Four Seasons.

The next day civilization did indeed arrive, in its full and glorious spectrum.

I welcomed my fellow man by leaving camp before they turned up. I spent the day at East Point with Clark and Kathryn. Before they started their work, Clark told me they had indeed gone looking for me. He harbored no grudge.

"We walked up the ridge and found some more *Dudleya,* so it was worth it," he said. To the casual visitor Santa Rosa is a windswept island with great bathrooms, but to the botanist the island is a rare and very special place. Of the seventy-five plants endemic to the Channel Islands, forty-two occur on Santa Rosa. In a sense, these plants are escapees from a world in which they can no longer survive. They are making a last stand in a harsh, salt-splattered place, sending their optimistic roots down into soil with very few nutrients; hence these plants are small.

Dudleya is a flowering succulent—it looks a bit like a miniature artichoke, peeled open and sprouting tiny daisylike flowers—and Santa Rosa is home to two types of *Dudleya* that grow nowhere else on earth but East Point. These plants seem to have searched the world over for a place where they would be out of the way—they are not the competitive sort—but now these tiny plants are being overtaken by introduced weeds and grasses. For some species, sharing ground is a very hard thing to do.

So today Clark and Kathryn planned on spraying the invasive grass with a goopy blue mix of poison.

"The blue is just a dye so we know where we've sprayed," Clark explained. "Last time I had a really weak solution, so it was hard to tell where I had sprayed and where I hadn't."

Sadly we are all aware that species are vanishing from our planet at an alarming rate, but even as you stare at a tiny flower holding to its very last square foot of soil, the concept is still hard to grasp.

"Do you find it anywhere else on the island?"

"No."

Clark was bent over, concentrating on his poison mix.

Sound journalism is about repeating a question idiot-savant style until you're certain you understand the answer.

"So this is the only place on the entire globe that you'd find it?"

"Uh-huh," said Clark.

"The only place?"

"It's a subspecies of a mainland species, but it is distinct from the mainland population genetically and morphologically."

I thought about asking Clark one more time to see if he really was as calm and jolly as Santa Claus, but I decided against it. I didn't want to return to camp with a blue face.

Clark screwed down the lids on the spray canisters and we schlepped them up the steep sides of a ravine to the grassy knoll above. Actually I schlepped. Clark and Kathryn bounded up like mountain goats.

The view from the sloping bluff was stunning. From up on the knoll we looked down at the sand spit that is East Point, jutting into the water like an enormous snow-white arrowhead. The Pacific was a deep blue. Most surprising of all, there was no wind. This was very good.

"We don't want to spray the *Dudleya*," said Kathryn. "It's the first time something like this has been done, spraying a known poison inside a population of endangered plants."

The invasive grass was everywhere, and it resonated a robust green that any homeowner would have killed for. The *Dudleya*, and also an equally delicate flowering plant called *Gilia*, held on to a smattering of thumbnail-size patches that the grass had not yet overrun. Here and there tiny flags of yellow and orange stuck up out of the soil, marking the valiant survivors.

"It looks like David and Goliath," I said, perhaps a trifle pessimistically.

Kathryn smiled.

"It is a daunting prospect, but you certainly have to try."

The battle was wholly one-sided, and I was affronted. Who could have been so mindless and self-centered to allow this takeover to happen?

"The invasive grass is called *Brachypodium distachyon*," said Kathryn. She nodded at my feet. "All that stuff that you're picking out of your socks."

That I was wantonly dispensing *Brachypodium distachyon* like some malevolent Johnny Appleseed was humbling, but in my defense the seed of destruction can be nearly imperceptible. Eco-tourists visiting the Galápagos Islands lament the goats, dogs, and cats that we humans have brought to the islands, because these introduced species have razed native vegetation and gobbled up everything from turtle eggs to iguanas. Nighttime lectures on board tour ships decry illegal fishing and the machete slaughter of ancient tortoises. The ship is anchored off an island for the night. Its blazing lights attract insects. When the ship pulls anchor the next morning, those insects travel to the next island, adding new imbalance. The eco-tourists sleep soundly.

Scientists understand this multiplicity. They don't rant about it. They simply do what they can.

"We've all probably done things," said Kathryn. "It's hard to point the finger, because it's hard to know."

Clark and Kathryn spent most of the day stooped double, spraying carefully.

At one point I heard Kathryn talking to herself.

"They're all doomed," she said. "They're going to die."

I hoped she was talking about the weeds, but I didn't have the heart to ask.

By the time I returned to camp, it was dark. The frog chorus had been replaced by loud laughter. Mark had been right. Each and every windbreak cupped campers; groups of two, four, and possibly more. It was hard for me to tell because as I walked past the first windbreak, someone shone a flashlight into my eyes.

I find it hard to approach strangers in the dark. It seems more invasive than approaching them during the day; plus they might not be wearing any pants. So, with my eyeballs giving off flash-cube pops, I made directly for my haven on the hill. I ate dinner, cleaned up, and then crawled into my tent. No doubt some of my new neighbors respected the fact that canyon walls give off a substantial echo, but as always the considerate mass was drowned out by the loudmouthed few. Our little valley reverberated like the Great Hall of Henry VIII. A basso voice roared, "More Jägermeister!" to which someone responded, "Fuck you!" This was followed by much laughter. Similar incisive witticisms and laughter continued unabated. Apparently there was plenty of Jägermeister, and maybe even a megaphone.

Tucked into my sleeping bag, I adopted the realistic outlook of the scientist. There was nothing I could do; trying to shut up drunks is like pouring gas on a fire. Plus, Mother Nature was already at work. The wind was starting to pick up. The drinkers had staked their tents out in the open.

The next morning as I was eating breakfast, a woman approached me deferentially.

"We all heard about you," she said. "We didn't see you last night. We thought maybe you'd scurried off into the backcountry."

She didn't look like one of the drinkers. She was young and clear-eyed, if not a trifle intense.

She was looking at me. I realized it was my turn to speak.

"Quite the party last night."

She looked disgusted.

"There's this group of eight. They were drinking on the boat ride out. I mean they started at seven thirty in the morning. They were saying insulting things about other people on the boat."

Unless they had fallen overboard, no doubt the revelers of the previous night.

She told me that the park service was taking them out to hike in Lobo Canyon.

"We don't really want to go with a group of twenty." She turned up her nose. "It's not really a nature experience then, is it?"

I wasn't sure if I could define a nature experience tidily, but it struck me that it was not simply a matter of numbers. Twenty quiet hikers were likely better than one hiker still feeling the happy jolt of Jägermeister.

At eight thirty, two Suburbans appeared at the campground entrance. Mark was driving one of them; my current position as the island's unofficial Jeremiah Johnson apparently allowed me the front seat next to him. Apparently Mark had not mentioned my directional debacle of two days earlier.

We bumped out toward Lobo Canyon, two vehicles filled with strangers. Here let me present an obvious, but rarely mentioned, fact. In the course of our brief time here on this planet, *Homo sapiens* has wrought a long list of miracles: the harnessing of fire, penicillin, the printing press, car seats that warm your bottom in winter. These are astonishing advancements, inventions to which single-celled organisms and certain members of Congress could never aspire. Yet there is one advancement that consumes humankind.

"What about those bathrooms?" someone said.

There was a collective murmuring behind me.

"I've never seen nicer bathrooms," someone else said.

Now we were rolling.

"They're nicer than my bathroom at home."

"Shit, there's room for two more toilets and a couple of bidets in there."

"I'll bet you've already gone through all the drawers."

It took me a moment to realize this last comment was directed at me.

"I thought about it," I said.

Neglecting to continue on does not constitute a lie.

Fortunately someone noticed that we were driving across a lovely island.

"How many deer are out here?"

"Deer?" said Mark. "Probably in the four-hundred range."

"What about elk?"

"The elk, closer to seven hundred."

"Seven hundred?? We haven't seen *any*. Shit, Richard, will you keep your mouth shut?"

Richard, I surmised, was Mr. Megaphone. I also surmised that Richard was sitting next to me. He was the one who had mentioned the bidets, and asked me if I'd rummaged through the bathroom drawers. He was not shy.

Mark said, "After the hike, everyone needs to check for ticks."

"I'll check you if you check me," said Richard.

Since I had already hiked Lobo Canyon, Mark drove me out to Carrington Point, a fat thumb of land on the northeastern edge of the island.

Our relations with our own kind are a flip-flop affair. Two days earlier, I would have cut off my left arm (OK, well, maybe Richard's tongue) for any sign of humankind. Today I wanted to be as far away from humankind as possible.

I was also excited. Carrington Point has a wonderful prehistoric past. In 1994, on a bluff on Carrington's west side, paleontologists dug out the most complete skeleton of a pygmy mammoth ever found. Like the *Dudleya* and the island fox that would follow, this mammoth, given the limited resources on the island, did not grow as large as its, well, mammoth relations on the mainland. Only four to seven feet tall at the shoulder and weighing roughly two thousand pounds, these mammoths were unique to the Channel Islands, cavorting, in two-thousand-pound fashion, over the islands' grasslands and forests during the Pleistocene Epoch, which ended about ten thousand years ago.

Lovers of the past will also be interested in something else on Santa Rosa. Digging in Arlington Springs, on the north side of the island, archaeologists discovered the oldest human remains unearthed so far in North America, a radio-carbon-dated thirteen-thousand-year-old woman they imaginatively named Arlington Springs Woman.

Now, anyone who has ever seen those old movies with swarming cavemen jumping about as if being goosed while the mammoth they are hunting, moving like a Claymation figure, tries to stomp the innards out of them, knows that mammoth and human coexisted.

And so, hiking the lovely flower-edged trail out to Carrington Point, I entertained myself with an intriguing scenario: our ancient ancestor, walking out to this same point to do whatever she did and glimpsing a woolly, not quite puppylike bulk rumbling across the grassland. This is conjecture of the wildest sort, with no basis in science, only personal observation, but it is my guess that Arlington Springs Woman—even then a soul of a higher plane—probably let the mammoth go its own way, whereas Arlington Man, assuming he existed, probably succumbed to testosterone and leaped upon the animal's back. This may be why there is no skeleton of Arlington Man.

Carrington Point was just as I had hoped it would be: fog-wrapped, wave-pounded, and devoid of JägerMan, though not of wheeling gulls and drifting pelicans and industriously plunging cormorants. I sat in the grass—first scanning for *Dudleya* just in case Clarke and Kathryn were wrong—and simply looked about. I had nothing else to do. I watched the large waves roll out of the fog, the biggest breakers drawing back the water before them, exposing the foam-edged tops of craggy black rocks. Nearby on a rocky bluff, gulls strutted about shell piles in their vaguely psychotic, indecisively greedy manner (*Should-I-fly-away-should-I-stay-where-I-am-whatever-I-do-what's-in-it-for-me?*). A few yards from where I sat, a bleached bone rested in the sand, a big bone by island standards, a femur, possibly six inches long in the sand, perhaps a remnant of an unlucky island fox. This was the same body part, a femur, that Arlington Springs Woman left as her legacy. Unlike the mammoth, she did not bequeath us her entire remains; most of them were long gone by the time she was unearthed. Ashes to ashes, dust to dust, quicker than we know.

I had brought Henry David Thoreau's *Walden* with me. After a time I opened it up and read a little, including a comment by a long-dead reviewer for *The Yale Literary Magazine*, who opined that "Thoreau's communion with nature divorced himself from the study of mankind." I disagree. The behavior of animals, the physics of nature—first on Santa Rosa and then on the other Channel Islands I visited—again and again made me think of people. The antic gulls, always looking over their shoulders, always looking for more. The waves, rolling in from the distant horizon, proud and powerful, rearing up, crashing, dissipating into nothing, followed by another wave, unique, but really little different, the Mongols, the Greeks, the Persians, the Romans, the United States of America. The mindless spread of weed and human.

I spent several hours lolling about at Carrington Point. Finally I began to hike back, marching up a steep slope and passing between two hills shaped like rounded breasts (not everything reminded me of man). The fog that had enveloped Carrington Point now enveloped the highlands too. A cold, stiff wind blew in my face, and as I leaned into it, great gray balls of fog tumbled past me like wraith mammoths.

I was distracted. I regarded the trail absently, only to make sure I didn't plunge off a cliff, and so, yet again, I was surprised by *Urocyon littoralis*. This little fox stood right in the middle of the trail, head up, looking directly at me, the *Waz-zat?* posture of its head mirroring mine. Its body swayed back and forth as if it were trying to hypnotize me. We stood looking at each other for almost a minute. Then I, of course not satisfied with the gift I had, stepped forward. In the snap of a playing card, the fox turned and ran. This time, though, I saw it go, bounding down the track, until its backside disappeared into the fog.

This fox had looked a little bedraggled. Later one of the fox researchers would tell me that the fox I had seen at Carrington was likely an older female.

"She looks kind of ragtag, poor thing," the woman said. "She's had a rough life."

The island fox, of course, is not cute at all. This is just a superficial judgment applied by us. What the island fox really is is adaptive. *Urocyon littoralis*, the munchkin *Dudleya*, the (now extinct) giant island mouse, and the pygmy mammoth each did what they had to do. In a world of dwindling resources, they learned to do more with less. An adaptation humans have yet to accede to.

When I returned to camp, events were again in full swing. This time it was still light, so there was no slinking away. As I had surmised, many of my fellow campers were pleasant, quiet folk come to enjoy solitude and nature, but somehow—perhaps because, when I was little, I was always the first to see just how hot that griddle really was—I ended up amid the gang of eight.

They were friendly but in the antic fashion of people who are either drunk or wound tight or both. Several women in the party seemed nice, but they didn't talk much, drowned out as they were by the boisterous men.

"What in the hell do you *do* out here?" said a ruddy-faced man named Ron.

I didn't have to answer, because Richard interrupted.

"You're a writer? You got a screenplay going?" He laughed. "Marc brought Wild Turkey to the island." He turned to Marc. "Get me a beer, bitch."

Richard apparently had skipped Cotillion. Having placed his drink order, he informed me that he was a fourth-generation Californian, and then he stared at me as if daring me to one-up that. This is not an uncommon challenge in California, where over half the residents, including me, come from another state. I was neither impressed nor unimpressed with the depth of Richard's roots. My take on lineage is simple: We have nothing to do with where our ancestors coupled and gave birth. It's how we act in the present that matters.

Marc had indeed brought Wild Turkey to the island, and right away he shared one of his last two tilts with me.

Marc said he had a wife and two teenagers at home.

"Why do you think I'm out here?" he said, tilting the bottle and sending Wild Turkey into extinction. "Plumbing pipes broken, wife yelling, kids driving me crazy. Time to go."

Night fell. We sat around a picnic table tucked inside the windbreak. The polite women politely insisted I help myself to nice cheeses and other delicious hors d'oeuvres. Richard drank Jägermeister and made various loud and unrelated proclamations. People came and went.

At one point—I'm pretty certain of this, though it's true everyone was talking at once—a man named Norman said, "I had a Mars infection on my penis. It was really big."

Later Richard looked at me and said, "Where the hell is all the wildlife?"

I told the table about my fox encounter at Carrington Point. Marc grinned.

"There was one right here in camp. Crapped on the table. It was here when we got here."

A woman—Eva was her name, I think though with all the dark forms coming and going I wasn't sure—gestured toward the moonlit cliffs rising up beside the creek.

"In all those caves, the foxes used to live with their pups. You could hear them yelping. They sounded like coyote. It was nice."

Eva gave a bitter laugh, not unlike a yelp actually.

"There are people who were born in southern California who actually have no idea these islands are out here," she said. "People go, 'Oh, where are they? In the Caribbean?' I think it is kind of sad."

"No," barked Norman. "It's good. Otherwise they'd be out here like crazy."

Norman scowled.

"Having showers and toilets out here is ridiculous."

Norman was grizzled and whippet-lean. If I understood him correctly, he had been coming out to the islands since about the time of Arlington Springs Woman. Now the park service had ruined the place with windbreaks and toilets.

The talk turned to our era's technological advances.

Marc, who, like most of the gathered, was fifty-something, said, "The technology today is amazing. Think of all the changes we've seen. Remember our parents yelling at us not to fool with the tuner?" He went quiet for a moment. "If we don't kill each other off."

Norman allowed he was not the least bit impressed with today's technological whiz kids.

"Show them a rotary phone," he shouted, "and they won't know how to work it!"

Unless they're applying for a job as curator at the Smithsonian, why should they? I thought, but I said nothing because, though he appeared to be twenty years my senior, tangling with Norman looked like an uncomfortable prospect.

Eventually I excused myself, and went to bed.

The next morning, when I went down to use the bathrooms, Richard was standing outside waiting.

"The park service probably commissioned a multi–million-dollar study to find out something I found out for free," he said, dispensing with the conventional Good Morning. "People take a whole lot longer to take a dump in a fancy bathroom." He banged on the door. "Somebody in there?" Somebody, of course, mumbled. He looked at me triumphantly. "See what I mean? My toothbrush is in there. In the old days with the pit toilets, people didn't stay that long."

Creature comforts have changed us all. In the old days, people didn't leave their toothbrushes in pit toilets.

Marc was up too. At dawn his smile was softer. It was Sunday, and everyone was leaving on Island Packers' 3:00 P.M. boat.

"I'll bet you'll be glad when all us assholes are gone," Marc said. I told him a half-truth.

"I like people," I said. "It's nice to have company sometimes."

Marc was more perceptive in the morning too.

"I hate people, and I like them too."

No doubt people have been a mixed blessing since their dawn, though in the not-so-distant past you still had to encounter them while hunting mammoths, or attending neighborhood Christmas parties, or shopping in the grocery store. Today mammoths are gone, and in most places neighborhood parties have followed them into extinction, and you can have your groceries delivered to your home.

Returning to my site forced me to pass within a few yards of two men eating breakfast at a picnic table tucked inside their windbreak. Though there was nothing to be done about it, I felt bad fairly walking across their cereal.

"I guess that's why people build houses with four walls," I said apologetically.

"That's OK," one of the men said. "I now know you better than I know some of my neighbors. I wouldn't know them at all if they hadn't gotten some of my mail."

That afternoon I walked up among the Torrey pines to see the boat off. The grove sits high on a slope overlooking Becher's Bay. I hiked up through the cool canopy of twisted pines until I found a spot that allowed me to see the landing pier, from this distance a Tinkertoy appendage jutting into the Pacific.

The ground was soft with pine needles. I was careful not to sit directly under a tree, for great floods of pinecones already poured like migrating armadillos across the ground. Hiking up, I had bent and picked one up, noting both its softball-like heft and the fact that I could not get my hand around the thing. The Torrey pine may not be a large tree, but its cones take a backseat to none. Judging from the deluge already on the ground, the Torrey pine also jettisons these seedlings at a rate only barely outpaced by passengers leaping from the Titanic. Getting knocked unconscious raised the possibility of another chance to call out the choppers, something I did not want.

Torrey pines once existed as vast swaths of forest during the Ice Age, but now there are only two small groves left, the one on Santa Rosa and one some two hundred miles away in a small preserve along the coast just north of San Diego.

Again I felt the weighty sobriety that comes with being amid the last of a kind. Everything on this earth, of course, passes, and with this comes some sadness, but that sadness is usually lightened by the fact that some progenitor remains behind, whether a pinecone seedling or a bright-eyed child. In this grove there was little light; this family gathering was sadly intimate. The view from the hillside was breathtaking, a sweeping panorama any army would kill for, but the Torrey pines weren't at war with anyone, though they were making a final stand.

I checked my watch. Two-fifty. By now everyone was boarding, kicking their grimy gear into a corner, ordering hamburg-

ers and cold Cokes from the ship's galley and, if there were any
drops left, likely hoisting a few Jägermeisters too

I thought about Richard. Maybe I had been too hard on him.
It was true he was loud and obnoxious, and he genuinely seemed
clueless about the fact that his mouth alone had frightened all
the wildlife off to a far corner of Tibet. But it was also true that
he had made me welcome at his table and had offered me his
Jägermeister, and when I was with him he had insulted no one,
other than his friends, directly. We dislike and distrust people
who aren't like us. It is a trap old as time, from which it is hard to
escape. The ancient Greeks may have been the original snobs.
The word *barbarian* comes from the Greek *barbaros,* meaning
"someone who doesn't speak Greek," but instead something
unintelligible and, so, by inference, something inferior.

I dawdled away the afternoon beneath the pines. When I returned to the campground in the evening, it was empty but for
a solitary raven, swaggering about, justifiably, as if he owned
the place. A chunk of ice and a piece of plastic—two of our
greatest inventions—sat in the grass beside the camp's spigot.
I picked up the plastic. I left the ice so that the nonnative grass
might drink it down.

That evening Richard's deer appeared on the skyline, shadows beneath the stars. I watched the moon climb slowly above
the ridge of the canyon wall, the orb itself preceded by smoky
bluish light.

As the moon broke free from the ridge, the frogs sent up a
resounding chorus.

The following day was my last full day on the island and I
resolved to spend it well. In a parting gift, the day dawned
without wind and stayed that way. Without the wind it was
cathedral quiet. Hiking out of the campground, I paused for a
moment to consider the joy of hearing wings beat one hundred
yards away.

I hiked with no intention. First my feet led me back up among the Torrey pines and then they continued on up and over the ridge to a hilltop of birdsong with a valley below and, rising on the far side, hills running away in fold after fold.

One pine had broken free of the grove; it sat by itself at the edge of a downward sweep of grassy hill. I sat beneath it. It too had littered the ground with stiff needles, and I watched a fuzzy caterpillar with a dark splotch of face negotiate this minefield, inching out to the end of a needle and swinging the upper half of its body out in open space before redirecting and, eventually, arriving in a place where it had to do the same thing again. It was a Byzantine maze nearly without end, but the caterpillar proceeded without stopping, or, as far as I could tell, complaining to someone in public works that the street sweepers were taking some serious lunch breaks. I felt a kinship with the fuzzy creature, for its wanderings ably mirrored my life. I encouraged the caterpillar, and at one point it may have returned me some affection by ascending my pant leg, making its gentle fuzzy Ewok way across a strange patch of denim, before descending again into pine needle mayhem. It was a dogged and admirable display of patience, persistence, and regrouping.

My feet then led me to a grassy promontory overlooking the sea, where I took off my boots, leaned up against my pack, and spent my own lunchtime and then some watching the curious flights of a group of black and white birds. They would shoot suddenly from some hidden cleft in the cliffs like a mass of arrows, veer wildly here and there, and then, in ones and twos, start crashing abruptly into the water as if they had never landed in water before. After bobbing there for an unspecified amount of time—perhaps regaining their stunned senses, for their landings were violent—they would slowly drift together again. Then one or two of them would lift from the water, and suddenly—*Hey, where in the hell is everyone going?*—the rest would follow. Airborne, they would again veer as one, before performing their individual crashes into the sea.

But as I continued to watch them, I slowly saw that their landings, though abrupt, were actually extremely efficient. None of the extended braking, flapping, and caterwauling of say, geese; they simply landed without taxiing. You got the impression that had the Pacific been suddenly reduced to the size of a thimble, they would land precisely on their heads. Nobody could have beaten them at musical chairs. Some would disappear beneath the surface for what seemed like minutes at a time. Later I would learn that certain seabirds that frequent the Channel Islands not only crash through the surface, but they continue down, possibly as deep as two hundred feet searching for foodstuffs like zooplankton and krill.

As I watched the birds, a small lizard scurried from the grass. At first he explored one of my discarded boots, disappearing into the dark interior before darting back out to have a look at me, his breathing marked by rapid-fire leathery inflations and collapses. I stayed still. After a time, deciding I could be trusted, he dashed down my pant leg and insinuated himself atop my foot. From there he watched the birds with me, perhaps also enjoying the hypnotic hiss and fadeaway of breaking waves. After a time a bird cry reminded him that he was exposed; performing five quick push-ups—I know because I counted them off for him—he bolted away. Before I left the bluff edge, I thanked the lizard for his company and then I turned to the sea and applauded the birds, who surely didn't care since nature's denizens do what they do for their own reasons and not to impress others.

At the last, my feet took me back down to Water Canyon Beach, where I had taken my first exploratory steps a week before.

The sand was velvet smooth and without secrets. My own footsteps followed me like a neophyte stalker until I stopped beside a small rise of dune near the bluffs. The dune was peppered with tiny paw prints. The tracks swung apart and then mingled together, roving back and forth across the dune; possibly a single fox padding schizophrenically about. But I preferred the alternative. The previous night had been silvery bright; it made me smile to think of a fox pair cavorting alone on this beach, and then it made me miss my wife. The sound of the waves came to me like a whisper you have to lean into.

And so I passed the day. Some of my behavior might seem strange, perhaps even a tad insane, but I will tell you this. It was one of the most rewarding days I have ever spent, filled with beauty, freedom, adaptation, and shining example.

The next morning, I boarded the park service boat, headed for home. I was suddenly, desperately keen for company.

I addressed one of the fox researchers, a young girl with her hair in pigtails.

"Did you have a good week?"

She gave me a weary and slightly sad smile.

"It was a long week," she said.

In that moment I was struck by how quickly my own week had passed. Stepping on to the pier a week before, I had been frightened by the great expanse of time stretching before me; to be a bit more honest, a part of me had considered getting right back on the boat. Now that my time had ended, I was already starting to miss it.

The fact that I had tackled a week largely on my own, and, with the exception of the eggbeater wind, thoroughly enjoyed it, produced an orgasmic flush of happiness.

But it is rude to focus on your own orgasm when someone nearby has not had one.

I put on a sympathetic face.

"Why was it a long week?"

"We lost two fox pups. The male ate them."

Returning to the mainland, we stopped at Santa Cruz Island, picking up the researchers there, Andy Day among them.

When I told Andy about the cannibal fox, he shrugged.

"Captive animals do weird shit," he said.

Kathy picked me up at the dock. She drove home, which was a good thing, because everyone, my lovely wife included, drove very, very fast. A man in an enormous white Suburban cut off a car; there was a squeal of brakes, and the driver nearly skidded off the road.

The man in the SUV didn't even look back. He was busy shouting into his phone.

Crosses in the Sand

· · · ■ ■ · ·

IN NATURE A SPECIES sometimes attacks its own, but no species engages in this pursuit with the relentlessness of the human race.

The original Arlington National Cemetery in Arlington, Virginia, received its first body on May 13, 1864. William Henry Christman, age twenty-one, was laid to rest upon a gentle slope above the south bank of the Potomac River. Christman was buried there for a simple reason: with the Civil War in its fourth year, so many dead bodies were coming into Washington that there was nowhere else to put them.

In Santa Barbara, too, the dead have already outstripped the capacities of the living. On a pale blue morning, late September's sun soft upon the beach, Frank Schmidt shuffled backward, dragging a rake through the sand, creating smooth furrows between the rows of small white crosses that comprise Arlington West. There were close to thirty rows. Fifty yards away the Pacific sparkled.

"We had to stop putting out crosses," Frank said, padding

carefully backward. "The van was full and the trailer was full. We would have had to get another vehicle."

Frank's feet kept moving, but his gaze went to the last row of crosses, the ruler-straight edge of a diminutive cornfield. Arlington West was full: three thousand regimentally spaced crosses in a rectangle 141 feet wide by 310 feet long.

"In the beginning it was just a little quadrant," Frank said.

Frank addressed this burgeoning matter-of-factly, in a tone you might use to describe a weed infestation to a fellow gardener. Even death, to a degree, gets to be old hat. Arlington West has been part of Santa Barbara's waterfront nearly every Sunday since November 2003, when the local chapter of Veterans For Peace first placed 340 crosses in the sand, one for each American soldier killed in Iraq. Now each Sunday, a little after seven in the morning, a group of roughly thirty volunteers—sometimes more, but often less—arrives at the beach beside Stearns Wharf. The crosses and assorted accoutrements arrive in the van and its accompanying trailer. The crosses go into the sand. They stay there until late afternoon, at which point, to accede to city ordinance, they are pulled up, and the sun sets on jumbled sand.

On this fall morning I had arrived as setup started. I watched from the foot of Stearns Wharf, where the wooden pier angles a few feet above the beach. The volunteers moved about casually but efficiently, erecting the temporary monument while Johnny Cash crooned softly over the loudspeakers. Someone said, "It's always nice to hear some other kind of music while we're setting up."

The work was done by experienced hands. The volunteers charged with placing the crosses walked slowly across the beach, bent only slightly, half dropping, half tossing the crosses in the sand, each toss performed with the practiced wrist flick I recognized from summer days spent idly tossing a penknife into the ground. If a cross required additional straightening, they bent and did so, but most crosses buried themselves straight and true on the first try. I would later learn that many of the volunteers, no longer in the prime of life, did not bend in order to save their backs.

The memorial formed quickly. The work was not perfect. Here and there were gaps between crosses, like an old man who has missed a belt loop. After the crosses were placed, tiny American flags went into the sand in front of each cross. They fluttered halfheartedly in the sea breeze.

There is another Arlington West, in Santa Monica, California, but the Santa Barbara memorial has the dubious distinction of being the longest running. Visit Arlington West and you will see that the atmosphere is an odd mix of respectful solemnity and family gathering. The volunteers laugh, sip coffee, eat sweet buns, and share their week. Meet someone every Sunday for forty-six months, and you get to be friends.

Frank had come every Sunday for the first three years, but then that got to be too much. But he was here to help today, dragging the rake to smooth the sand, sweating slightly, and enjoying the fine morning.

"I feel like I'm going through life backward," he said with a soft smile. "It's kind of meditative."

It was. As we shuffled, heels first, the rake left hypnotic furrows in the sand. The rows of crosses drew equally hypnotic lines alongside them. Nearby, a little girl laughed.

"Did you see the number up front?" Frank asked.

I had seen the wooden sign standing before the field of crosses. The sign faced the pier, which would soon be flooded with visitors, couples, families, locals, tourists from all around the world, who had come to stroll out on Stearns Wharf, peer out at the forest of sailboat masts in the harbor, eat at the restaurants on the pier, and buy knickknacks at the tourist joints. The sort of thing the living take for granted.

I looked at the notebook in my hand. I confess, I had already forgotten.

"Three thousand seven hundred and ninety-eight," I said. *Dead* was not necessary.

Frank nodded and continued his furrowing.

Many crosses bore names on laminated placards, each placard affixed to a cross with rubber bands. But just as many crosses were blank.

Had they been forgotten?

"They used to put the names on every cross," explained Frank, "but when we got so many crosses, putting something on every one of them got to be too time-consuming. Now we just put a name on a cross if someone comes to visit them."

Frank handed the rake off to another volunteer.

The two of us crouched before a cross.

"I haven't read this one," said Frank.

We read the placard, tidy and efficient: name, age, rank, hometown, and a few personal notes, penned small and neat, by visitors to this small monument to Chief Warrant Officer Ian D. Manuel.

September's chill wafted off the ocean.

Frank stood.

"When I was nineteen, I didn't know anything," he said softly.

On November 11, 1921, the first anonymous soldier was placed in the Tomb of the Unknowns at Arlington National Cemetery. Attendance was so large it created a massive traffic jam. There was much pomp and circumstance. During the ceremony President Warren G. Harding said he hoped the day would mark "the beginning of a new and lasting era of peace on earth, goodwill among men."

He was mistaken, and this is one reason why I visited Arlington West.

I had glimpsed Arlington West many times. Santa Barbara is only forty minutes up the road from Ventura, and, local or tourist, its palm-lined beach promenade is a fun place to visit. Like other families, the four of us had wandered out on Stearns Wharf, glancing down at the crosses and feeling, for a moment, the brief darkening and guilt that comes with the realization that your life is blessed while other lives are not. And then we walked on.

I have been to Arlington West's namesake too. My parents live outside Washington, D.C., and I had visited Arlington Cemetery several times to see the Tomb of the Unknowns, the Eternal Flame, and also to visit the headstone that marked the resting place of my grandfather (an army colonel) and later my grandmother (a loyal army wife who would have made a good colonel). I was a boy then. Mostly I remember that you couldn't kick off your shoes and run across the soft grass, and how the endless headstones rose up and down the hills in a way that made you feel queasy as if you were actually at sea. There was also something about the place that made me wish I wasn't there. I was always happy to leave.

Today Arlington National Cemetery, despite several expansions and concessions, is fast approaching carrying capacity. They have already reduced the size of the graves (from six by twelve feet to five by ten) and conducted "tiered" burials—caskets buried on top of each other like berths in a ship. Beginning in 1967, the government made it harder to get in—you earn a plot if you die while on active duty, if you are highly decorated for valor, or if you're a spouse of such—though the honor of resting in Arlington's dark ground is likely lost on successful applicants.

Despite these belt tightenings, it is estimated that the current grounds of Arlington will be full by around 2060. There was the Civil War, the Great War to end all wars, World War II, the Korean War, Vietnam, the Gulf War, and now the wars in Iraq and Afghanistan. At these current crosshairs of history, one in ten soldiers killed in Iraq are buried at Arlington, a higher percentage than from any other war. Between (and during) wars, the grounds are further filled by deaths of natural causes (my grandfather died of a heart attack), assassinations (John Fitzgerald Kennedy is Arlington's most famous resident), and, of late, terrorism. Sixty-four of the 184 people killed when American Airlines Flight 77 crashed into the Pentagon on September 11, 2001, are buried in Arlington, the plane having passed directly over the cemetery on its way down.

Of course, not everyone dies in war. Dan Seidenberg, along with a handful of others, is responsible for starting Arlington West at Santa Barbara under the auspices of Veterans For Peace, a group whose stated aim, written out on another sign in the sand is, at face value, simple: "We, having dutifully served our nation, do hereby affirm our greater responsibility to serve the course of world peace."

Dan was pointed out to me on my first visit to Arlington West. Another Vietnam veteran gestured toward him as he stood in the shade of the canopy tent also erected each Sunday. "A rocket went through his head in Nam," the man said. "He died twice."

Actually, the medic who saved Dan's life later told him that his heart had stopped three times, but whatever the number, Dan is the only one who will never be certain. He remembers the date: March 2, 1969. He remembers the circumstances leading up to the moment, tucking into his customary position in the front corner of the landing craft. ("That way," he explained, "you'd have armor on two sides, and when you hit the beach, you'd be one of the first guys out, because if the action was going to happen, they would go for the main body of men.") He remembers the landing craft moving slowly down a narrow river, without the protection of the chopper that usually accompanied them spraying ordnance at anything that moved along the banks. The rest he has pieced together from other people's accounts, military records, and dreamy memory, occupied as he was with falling in and out of consciousness and fighting for his life. The grunt next to him, cut in half by the RPG (rocket-propelled grenade), the shrapnel peppering his own face and neck like steel-wool chunks, the knee-deep blood, his rifle, struck by shrapnel, cooking off, firing on its own until someone yanked it from his hands and threw it overboard because Dan himself had already been rendered incapable by the fragment of rocket that sliced through his helmet and lodged in his right temple.

The end result—though there never really is an end result with things like this—is that Dan is blind in his right eye and hears only ringing in his right ear. When he pushes back his now gray hair, you see a small indentation, still the size of a large marble. The ringing leads Dan to now and again lean forward slightly and politely say, "I'm sorry. What did you say?" He looks like you and me, but he is not.

Dan was very, very lucky. Years later, at a reunion, he pulled the medic aside. Hey Mike, did you make it through your year tour? *Yep.* Did you get injured? *No.* How many of our severely wounded were you able to save? *Just you.*

"His whole year in the infantry unit, he gets to save one fucking guy, and that's me."

When Dan told me this, he shook his head, smiling with unabashed amusement and appreciation. "Life is one fucking haphazard puzzle," he said.

I liked Dan. He was honest. The very first time we met, he told me that when he was drafted, he fled to Canada, but then he had come back. I asked if he did this because his conscience had bothered him. He could have said yes. He knew I was writing a book; at that moment, I was jotting down everything he said. Though the military is ruthless with documentation, I doubted they had any record of what had been going on in Dan Seidenberg's head almost forty years ago. It was an easy lie, impossible to uncover.

"You're up there, and you're all alone," he said. "I knew nobody. The thought of never going back again was scary."

It was just how a nineteen-year-old would think.

Dan called a friend in the army. *Come back*, the friend said. *Nothing will happen to you.*

Dan does not miss the humor in this either. Standing on the beach beside the crosses, he gave a sly smile.

"It was nobody's fault," he said. "It was my decision."

Given humankind's long-running history of warfare, one man's war does not a comprehensive synopsis make. In my visits to Arlington West, and my talks with Dan and others, I knew that I wasn't going to be able to get a complete understanding of war. I was only hoping to take the smallest first step toward understanding how war affects us, and why it is so often with us. It was true, I could spend the rest of my life talking to Dan and every other war veteran I could find and still not really understand what they had experienced on the battlefield; my generation slouched by between wars, a happenstance for which I still feel oddly guilty. But it was also true that this division between soldier and civilian was part of understanding war too.

"I'm hearin' the same thing now as we knew it in Nam," drawled one Arlington West vet. "What bothers them the most is they're over there in Iraq, and they're hearing all this stuff about how they're fighting for America, and they come back here and everybody's screwing around like nothin's goin' on."

But even the ignorant can grasp certain things by listening, and so listen I did.

Along with being honest, Dan is also funny and very wry, and when he is with his fellow vets, he lapses into a sort of foxhole patois—"Maaaan, you gotta' roll me one of those fuckin' cigarettes"—though as Dan points out, large parts of Vietnam were so fucking muddy that foxholes were out of the question. But Dan is also introspective and smart. He no doubt has his flaws, but he seemed able to peer over the rim of the metaphorical foxhole many of us dig for ourselves. War had given him a perspective I found more realistic and clear-sighted, perhaps even more adaptable to an increasingly violent world. As you read this, somewhere people are fighting and dying. Dan and his fellow vets understood the field of play, the total lack of rules of engagement. Dan's own experience endowed him with a dark clarity you are not sure you want.

Dan carries repugnant memories, alongside the enticing thrill of an adrenaline rush bordering on the Divine.

"There was nothing more spiritual to me than my experience in the war," Dan said, and he did not smile.

War always accompanies Dan, even when the act is simple. One morning we drank coffee at a table outside a coffee shop in Santa Barbara. Dan sat with his back to the sun.

"They say in chess and combat, you always keep your opponent's eyes in the sun," he said.

Dan spoke openly about deeply personal matters. Was a time when Dan didn't talk to anyone about these things, but my timing, forty years after the fact, was good, and Dan talks now in the hope that what he has learned might play some small part in putting humanity on a different track.

Composed of flesh and blood, with a sprinkling of shrapnel, Dan is no different from the rest of us when we are truly honest with ourselves. He is both hopeful and hopeless. Life is gray, not black and white.

When I asked Dan if he thought war was inevitable, part of our fabric, he told me no. "I think war has been imposed on us," he said. "Don't get me wrong. I'm not against war. There's nothing wrong with an honest defense against a foreign invader. I'm against war for resources. Most wars are fought for money. That is not a cause worth dying for. I think, regardless of context or current history, we have the ability to learn from our mistakes. Take slavery. Today most civilized countries say, 'No, we don't do that, that's wrong'. All we have to do is get war pushed into that category. We've been taught that the theme is survival of the fittest. That's wrong too. If you look at natural history, the species that survive over evolutionary time, they not only adapt, they cooperate with the other species and among themselves. The ones that only compete, they tend to die out."

I thought of the tiny *Dudleya* on Santa Rosa Island, asking only for its small slope, making the rest of the globe available for others.

When I asked Dan if he foresaw a day when humankind would pack up war with slavery in the box marked mistakes, he said, "That's the hope. The fear is that most of us will have to perish first."

War was now stitched into Dan's fabric, and most of us don't have to look far to know that Dan is not alone. I have an uncle who is a decorated war veteran, Korea and then Vietnam. He commanded men, met the likes of General Westmoreland. He now lives quietly in a small town in upstate New York, the kind of town that sits beside a lake and, on the Fourth of July, celebrates our country's independence with pancake breakfasts, modest fireworks, and an old-fashioned parade. A few years ago our family celebrated the Fourth of July in my uncle's town. The town asked my uncle to be in the parade. He is a quiet man, not inclined to center stage, but he agreed. They assigned him a car to ride in, and festooned it with balloons. When he saw the balloons, he became more agitated than I had ever seen him. He refused to participate in the parade, and he refused to give a reason. That evening, fireworks exploding over the dark lake, he sat silent, with his family, and alone with his thoughts.

Such incidents are commonplace for those who have fought in war, and bewildering for those who haven't, and no amount of reading, talking, or *Letters from Iwo Jima* will help the peacetime civilian understand, though impartial listening might. Seeing a fellow human being killed is a corner turned, with no hope of turning back.

One day I listened as Dan and a fellow Vietnam vet named Louis tried to explain the impact of watching people die.

"The first time it happens in combat, you're kind of rendered ineffective for the first split second, and that's very frightening," said Dan.

"You're shocked," said Louis. "You're just shocked."

"You can't be that way," said Dan.

"You got to pull out of that space quick. They're not going to stop the battle so you can cry," added Louis.

"I looked the first three or four times," said Dan, "and then I stopped looking. You can't get emotional. I wanted to be crystal clear, ready for anything."

"Numb," said Louis. "Or you're fucking dead."

And so you deal with death and killing by other means, and this isn't so good either.

Dan and Louis forgot about me. Smoking in the warm sun, they talked about soldiers they knew who could and couldn't turn things off, the things they had seen, and the things they had avoided seeing. Louis had been very successful at turning things off. Upon returning from Vietnam he had found a construction job. While he was working at one site, he had watched two boys on a dirt bike shoot out of an irrigation ditch and into an oncoming car.

"Got nailed right in front of me," said Louis. "I went out there, man, and drugged 'em out of the road, cussin' em' the whole time, both of them lost their legs, but what they did was stupid and it pissed me off. The driver of the car, he's freaked out, he's crying, and I told him to shut the fuck up, it's not your fault, the fucking kids didn't look. And then when the ambulance came, I walked back over and went back to work. And then when I went home from work, I didn't even mention it to the wife."

Louis smoked. Traffic slid past.

Louis said, "These kids in Iraq, it's the same shit. This marine girl came up here from [Camp] Pendleton. She looked like she'd been livin' on the streets. Old. Tough. She knew some of the soldiers. She broke down a little bit, but then, *pow*, she's on her way back to Iraq. Tour number three. She signed up for it, man."

Louis shook his head.

"Most people, they don't get it," he said. "They just don't get it."

Dan laughed.

"Here's why they don't," he said. "It's a very punishing subject. Why punish yourself with this stuff? If you mentioned Vietnam in a crowd of civilians back in the sixties, it was like yelling a curse word. They didn't want to hear about it. It's no different now."

Dan's hand went up, two fingers lightly brushing his temple. The motion was absent, without intention.

"Anyhow," he said, "there are really no words you can say that mean that much. That's why we have the crosses out there. That field of crosses, it has more of an impact than anything we can say."

It is also true that you don't have to go to war to learn to turn things off.

Another Arlington West volunteer was not so certain of the memorial's impact.

"After a while it all just fades away, like any story," he said.

Perhaps what makes cemeteries so poignant and mesmerizing is that they call all of us, we just don't know when. I read that John F. Kennedy, on surveying the serene oak and maple grounds of Arlington National Cemetery, quietly remarked, "I could stay here forever." Later that same year, he got his wish.

The problem with assassination and war is that they send us there too soon, and no matter what your take on the war of your time, the sadness of moments lost is deep beyond measure, and politics, states of red and blue, and whatever affiliation we ourselves choose, in the honest light of loss is rendered inconsequential and silly. Weddings that will never be, children that will never be, accomplishments that will never be. At Arlington West, every cross marked opportunity lost.

Wandering between the crosses was sobering and enlightening. Crouching down, I read the laminated placards. A father of three killed on Easter Sunday, a soldier killed on his father's birthday, a soldier killed on his last helicopter flight before coming home. A soldier killed by hostile fire, in an ambush, by an IED (improvised explosive device; IED, RPG, d-e-a-t-h), by a heart attack, by bacterial infection, by a vehicle crash on an oil-soaked road. So many ways to die.

Almost immediately, I began seeing connections. Some were universal. Crouching before Paul T. Nakamura's cross, I saw it was peppered with photos; a happy baby, a little boy in a crisp Scout uniform, a smiling young man, his arms around a pretty girl. Later an Arlington volunteer told me, "The whole family would come and sit in front of the cross for hours."

Other connections, arriving with equal speed, were more specific, and mildly unnerving. A soldier killed on our wedding anniversary; four crosses down, a nineteen-year-old killed on our youngest son's birthday. These personal connections, of course, were not a matter of eerie coincidence. They were the result of sheer numbers.

Approximately 116,000 American deaths in World War I; 405,000 in World War II; 36,000 in Korea; 58,000 in Vietnam; 382 in the Gulf War. These numbers mark only the American dead. The field of crosses at Arlington West, halted at 3,000, was 141 feet wide and 310 feet long. At the time of my visits, a memorial for the Iraqi dead would have been 141 feet wide and 13 miles long. Opportunities lost but unnoted, at least by us.

Dan said it was impossible to put the impact of war into words, but plenty of people had tried. At the foot of the pier, Veterans For Peace had assembled a series of panels, plastering them with photos, newspaper clippings, statistics, bar graphs measuring losses and costs, quotes from famous pacifists ("An eye for an eye leaves the whole world blind."—Mahatma Gandhi). There were quotes from war heroes too. Dwight D. Eisenhower proclaimed in a speech in 1946 in Ottawa, Canada, "I hate war as only a soldier who has lived it can, only as one who has seen its brutality, its stupidity. War settles nothing."

There were also blank pages that welcomed visitors to write down their thoughts, and they had.

God bless you all. We may never fathom as human beings what you do for us on a daily basis. You are truly heroes.

Live and let live. That should be the motto.

Thank you for reminding . . . . As an Israeli I find it very sad and weird that Americans have memorial "sales" for remembering their dead. Good to see something else.

Not everyone was supportive.

This is not being done to honor the ones who have died in Iraq—this is only political—a statement against Bush. They would spit in the faces of you who stage this "Arlington West" were they to come back as you use them for your own political aims.

You could see the anger in the letters, big and hurriedly scratched. This didn't bother me. It was the sort of free expression that makes our country great, free expression that many had fought and died for. And though Arlington West's organizers deny any political aim, to deny any possibility of ulterior motive in war or peace is foolishness. Among Arlington National Cemetery scholars, though not among those of us who have forgotten large blocks of history, it is well known that William Henry Christman was buried on the confiscated grounds of the Confederate commander Robert E. Lee. By the time the war ended a year later, thousands of headstones salted the grounds, ensuring that the Lee family would never reoccupy their estate.

There are those who are still beyond politics and selfish motive, though this time what I read did darken the day.

On one page a child's hand had scrawled, *I am always sad and afraid.*

Lane Anderson, another Vietnam veteran, was well aware that Arlington West was not a boon in everyone's eyes. Lane preferred to leave the memorial open to interpretation.

"It's the eye of the beholder," he said one morning. "To some it's the cost of war. To some, it's patriotic. I don't like to challenge anyone's beliefs. You don't accomplish anything by doing that."

It was also true that Lane had a button pinned to his ball cap: *I took Bush's Place in Vietnam.*

Taps now played from the speakers. Once the crosses are in, there's no more Johnny Cash. Taps is a stirring anthem. It is also twenty-four notes in all. The military knows what it is doing. Currently at Arlington National Cemetery there are six thousand funerals a year; most graveside ceremonies last ten minutes or less. An Arlington Cemetery guide advises clergy, "Please remember that time is our enemy at ANC." Death is not something the living want to dwell on; this holds equally true for the military. And the backhoes need to get started.

Lane strolled up and down in the sand at the edge of Stearns Wharf, passing postcards up to tourists who were willing to take them. The postcards briefly explained the history and purpose of Arlington West at Santa Barbara. The last sentence read, "We must never forget the true cost of war!"

Lane allowed that some people had cursed at him. Louis had been spit at. Dan told me he had been cursed at too, though his wife had to tell him, because the epithets had come at his right ear.

Other volunteers joined Lane, engaging those tourists inclined to be engaged. From what I saw during my visits, all the volunteers adopted Lane's nonconfrontational approach. There had been enough confrontation already.

Between postcards, Lane told me about Charlie Liteky.

"He was a Catholic chaplain, a captain in Vietnam," said Lane. Lane gestured to the sign, tallying America's Iraq-War dead. "He just stood right by that sign all day asking people, 'What do you think?'"

Liteky's approach seemed to me as right as any. He was only asking people to think.

"He was awarded the Medal of Honor," Lane continued. "He once dragged something like twenty-two injured men to the landing zone. He's the only recipient ever to turn the Medal of Honor back. I don't think anyone else knows this story, but he was called on the carpet for giving last rites to the Viet Cong. He said, 'God can't tell the difference.'"

Lane was a fixture at Arlington West, but several weeks later Dan told me Lane was leaving.

"He's sailing off tomorrow," said Dan.

Sprawled in a chair in the sand in front of us, Lane confirmed this. I recognized the same satisfied smile he'd given me when he recounted Liteky's rebuttal to military authority.

"When are you leaving?" Dan asked.

"Whenever the wind blows."

"Heading for Mexico?"

"Yea, but I'll avoid the towns."

Out at sea, my Channel Islands floated. I was fairly certain I knew what Lane was thinking.

"There's a lot of room to camp and explore on the Baja Peninsula," Lane said.

He was headed eventually for a spot called Ensenada de los Frailes. The Bay of Monks.

This war in Iraq may have seemed distant to many of the folks thumbing through sale-price T-shirts and eating soft-serve ice cream on Stearns Wharf, but it remained front and center for some.

One afternoon a young man ducked under the canopy tent. He sported dark, close-cropped hair, equally dark glasses, and a solid assemblage of muscle. There were others with him, including two more clean-cut men, and a blond woman who looked too young to be a mother of a twenty-something son, but, given the way she anxiously watched the soldier, she most certainly was.

"You know someone?" Louis asked politely.

"Yea. Five of 'em."

I listened from a distance. I did not want to intrude. I could not hear clearly, but Louis and the soldier spoke for a minute. The soldier gave Louis a name, and Louis consulted the book that listed the American dead in Iraq.

"He's not out there," said Louis.

The soldier gave Louis the other four names. They too had yet to be visited, and so were missing from the crosses.

From a nearby table, a woman discreetly produced five small plastic vials, each containing a tiny bouquet of flowers.

She handed them to the soldier, and he walked out among the crosses with his friends and family.

I asked the mother if I could join them.

She looked at me for a moment.

"No problem," she said. "Both my boys just got back from Iraq. Chris lost five friends."

I felt guilty for eavesdropping.

Chris Witt walked among the crosses.

"Vietnam, huh?" he said to Louis.

Louis nodded.

The boys' names had already been printed on placards, just in case. Now each placard went on a cross. Chris squatted before each cross, carefully pushing a flower vial into the sand.

His mother wore dark glasses too, but her hands shook. Hands rarely lie.

"They were all in your unit, right, baby?"

"Yeah, they were all in my platoon."

Chris produced a digital camera and took a picture of each cross.

His mother was not doing well.

"Tanner was only twenty-one?"

Her voice mimicked her hands.

No one spoke. The answer was on the cross.

In three minutes it was done.

Chris Witt is a career marine. When we stepped away from the crosses, his mother introduced us. Chris shook my hand politely, but he spoke and looked as if he were at inspection, and the half smile he produced for my benefit dissolved quickly into a face without expression.

"Tanner was the first combat-related death in our unit," Chris said. "He was sweeping for IEDs, making sure it was safe. He just stepped on it, and it, uh, killed him."

Chris cracked his knuckles.

This was enough, but I asked just the same. I was deeply sorry for my intrusion, but I had to be certain.

"Is it hard?"

"It is definitely hard. It's the right thing to do. To pay your respects."

No one said anything. Chris's mom fidgeted, and I felt worse.

"We didn't have time to grieve out there," said Chris. "We had to do what we had to do. It sucked. We had a service back at Pendleton, and we met their families. It is hard, yes."

And then Chris remembered, and the smile below the dark glasses reappeared, only this time it was genuine.

"Knowing these guys, they wouldn't want you just to be sitting here bummed out, hanging your head," he said. "They all had a sense of humor."

Chris's brother picked up a handful of sand, slowly releasing it so that it spilled across the crosses. Someone said a prayer, and then they left.

I went back out to the five crosses. Kneeling in the sand, I read the placards. Twenty-two, twenty-four, twenty-six, twenty-two, and Tanner, twenty-one. Columbus, Georgia. Wayne, Oklahoma. Malvern, Arkansas. Longview, Texas. Mount Dora, Florida. Cause of death was kept necessarily short. Tanner's read, *Killed August 29, 2007, when a roadside car bomb exploded near him in Al Anbar Province, Iraq.* The other four inscriptions were almost identical. *Killed September 6, 2007, in Anbar Province when a suicide bomber drove into a security checkpoint.*

It was the most horrible kind of repetition.

All the veterans I met at Arlington West were searching for reasons, so they recommended books, poems, and scholarly dissertations that addressed war. One poem was called "Bury Me with Soldiers" by Father Charles R. Fink. The words were simple, and therefore all the more beautiful. I read the poem several times. Each time one stanza stood out.

Yes, bury me with soldiers, for
I miss their company.

We'll not soon see their likes again;
We've had our fill of war.

I will continue to visit Arlington West. It's close to home, and I agree with Chris. It's the right thing to do. Veterans For Peace plans on putting out the crosses until the war in Iraq ends, and one day it will. It remains to be seen whether another war will take its place. The drumbeat of war has sounded throughout history, but evolution has produced its share of surprises and, in the matter of war, our incentive to change is great. As I write this, I see the young mothers on the pier standing close to their strollers, and through my office window I hear laughter, my own sons playing outside.

Anacapa Island

· · ■ · · ·

EACH TIME I ANNOUNCED my intention to spend time alone on the Channel Islands, I was offered a range of opinions. People were, at turns, fascinated, jealous, baffled, and mildly alarmed.

Anacapa Island was no exception. When I called to make my camping reservation, the National Park Service reservationist responded zestily, "Well, that will be a fun weekend!"

"Actually I'd like to stay for a week."

"Oh. Well, then, how many in your party? The maximum allowed is four."

"Just one, please."

"Ooooh-kay. That will be nice and quiet." All zest was gone.

When I booked the boat trip with Island Packers, the woman on the other end of the phone was blunt.

"A week? That's a lot of time staring at blue water and dodging bird poop."

Many people exhibited an odd ambivalence regarding my escapes. On the Friday morning of my departure, as my wife,

Kathy, readied herself for work, I told her I wished she could come along.

My wife is sweet and understanding beyond measure, but now her laugh resembled a sharp bark.

"A week? On Anacapa? I don't have the luxury of having nothing to do."

For a moment she was quiet, attending to some womanly ministration.

"I kind of hate you," she said.

With a total land area of just over one square mile, Anacapa was the smallest island I would visit, and even this acreage was misleading. Anacapa comprises three islands—East, Middle, and West—but for *Homo sapiens* this is a moot point, for there is no way to clamber up the sheer basalt cliffs of Middle Anacapa, and West Anacapa is off-limits unless you are a California brown pelican, in which case you may revel in the largest nesting ground on the West Coast. Because Anacapa is only eleven miles from the mainland, it is a popular destination for day-trippers, who traipse East Anacapa's one and a half miles of nature trails, stopping to admire various oceanic panoramas and holding up their cell phones to see if they get reception before hustling back to the snack bar on the boat. Overnight campers usually confine their stay to the weekend, which, for the analogously inclined, is roughly equal to dedicating an afternoon to hiking around your bedroom.

Once again, I packed up my gear, making a few additions and, more important, a substantial number of deletions. Humping two duffel bags, each filled with the equivalent of Jimmy Hoffa, to the campground on Santa Rosa had taught me an important lesson. Anacapa was much smaller, the hike to the campground was only a half mile, but, thrust from the sea as lava about sixteen million years ago, Anacapa is sheer-walled. To access the island, visitors must first ascend 154 steps that switchback in fire-escape fashion up from the landing dock. Many a visitor's first view of Anacapa is the ground between their knees as they collapse at the top of these steps.

I left from Oxnard's Channel Islands Harbor on a Friday afternoon, accompanied by two dozen day-trippers. Island Packers has been running visitors out to the islands since 1968, long before the islands became a national park in 1980. Their naturalist guides are friendly and knowledgeable, and the boat captains are first-rate, a handy thing given that the weather in the Santa Barbara Channel separating the mainland and the islands can change faster than a pop star's latest peccadillo. I had experienced these changes firsthand once before, when I'd headed out across the channel upon pond-still waters with a merry group of revelers and returned home with a chalk-faced, slobber-stained lot, exhausted from a purgatory at the commode.

Today's waters were milky calm, and they remained so during the fifty-minute trip to Anacapa's landing cove. Water is a glorious buffer. Within fifteen minutes of our leaving the harbor, the mainland had been reduced to a charming Tinkertoy town, the world naught but the throbbing of the boat's engines and a sweep of sun-bright Pacific. As if to celebrate our escape, a pod of common dolphins joined us, their dark shadows rushing in to ride the boat's wake. Everyone ran to the railing and began madly snapping pictures with their cell phones.

Eventually the dolphins tired of us and swam off.

Beside me a squinting man scrolled through his photos.

"Looks like I've got about thirty shots of water," he said.

We sat again, listening politely as our naturalist guide, a chipper English transplant named Patricia Turner, relayed various facts regarding the island we would be visiting. Patricia was cut from the same cloth as many volunteers. She was friendly and very enthusiastic, her enthusiasm enhanced by her chipper accent and jaunty floppy hat. Among other things, Patricia told us that a blue whale's spout rises three stories while a humpback's ascends only two (spout envy?), and that Anacapa is one of

California's most important seabird rookeries, with California brown pelicans, western gulls, and three species of cormorants (double-crested, pelagic, and Brandt's) all finding the island's isolation from predators and man appealing.

Patricia beamed.

"When you see gulls on the southern California coast? They probably all hatched on Anacapa Island."

This avian windfall is evident long before one sets foot on the island. Before we went ashore, the captain throttled us slowly past the distinctive rock arch rising from the water off the eastern tip of the island. A bracing ammonia-like scent wafted across the water. There was no doubting its source. The base of the arch retains its basalt darkness, but the whitewashed summit is a paean to gastrointestinal regularity.

The Chumash Indians who first came to Anacapa aptly dubbed this arch the House of the Pelican. Unable to let things be, modern man recently renamed the arch Cabrillo's Rock, in honor of Juan Rodríguez Cabrillo, the conquistador who accepted the offer of New Spain viceroy Antonio de Mendoza to explore the northwest coast of New Spain and proceed on to China. Sailing north from what is now Mexico, Cabrillo came upon the Channel Islands, making the acquaintance of the Chumash Indians, who already inhabited most of them. Cabrillo's relationship with the Chumash quickly turned contentious, understandable given the man's penchant for striding ashore, taking a hack at a nearby tree with his sword, moving rocks from one place to another, and then pouring seawater on the land in a ceremony designed to indicate, not mental instability, but New Spain's possession of the land. Proving that in the end no one owns anything for long, Cabrillo fell while coming ashore at one of the islands. Infection from his injuries killed him. Historians believe he is buried on one of the Channel Islands, though precisely which island no one is sure. Bobbing off the guano-stained rock, I wondered if there might have been at least one Chumash descendant on the honorary naming panel.

Even back in Cabrillo's day, the Chumash didn't live on Anacapa. The island has no streams and so no reliable source of water, and even in Chumash times there were no trees to provide firewood. The Chumash used the island as a stopover on their journeys from the mainland to the other Channel Islands. When weather was propitious, they'd come ashore and, making good use of the plentiful supply of fish and shellfish in the surrounding waters, enjoy a mouthwatering bouillabaisse. Here and there collections of ancient shells (deemed so by carbon-dating) still lay alongside the trails of Anacapa, the Chumash equivalent of discarded wrappers. The Chumash dubbed the island Ennepah—"mirage"—because the islands appeared to change shape in the summer fog or afternoon heat. Despite these temporary morphings, for most of the year it remained a harsh, waterless place.

Patricia informed us that descendants of the Chumash still lived in southern California. She had recently been to one of their gathering spots, where she had observed a piece of antiquity nearly as old as Cabrillo.

"Some of you have probably been to the Chumash Casino." Patricia beamed. "I was there two weeks ago to see that fantastic Englishman Tom Jones performing."

As we drifted along the backside of the island, watching sea lions and admiring the deluge of guano on Cabrillo's monument, I again felt the curious constriction in my chest. It was the same trepidation that had assumed me as I rode out to Santa Rosa Island on the park service boat. It wasn't fear, at least not in the life-and-limb sense. The apex predator on Anacapa is the deer mouse. Ax-wielding psychotics were unlikely to charge from the woods, since they weren't apt to pony up forty-two dollars for the boat ride, and, as previously mentioned, Anacapa has no trees. My anxiety was something different, something deeper-seated and harder to pinpoint. But there was no doubting its presence. The thought of a week on Anacapa turned me dry-mouthed and mildly light-headed.

Anacapa's landing cove is a small elbow of water: bordered on three sides by sheer cliffs, it offers a certain amount of protection from the open sea. Competently easing into the concrete landing stern first, our captain held the boat in place with subtle throttlings while we clambered up a short, rusted ladder to the dock.

Since I had plenty of time to unpack, I left my gear down on the landing. I wanted to tag along with the day-trippers and listen in on Patricia's tour of the island. But as a newly arrived camper, I first had to be briefed. Yancey Goins, the island ranger, was waiting on the landing dock. I liked Yancey immediately. He kept his briefing brief. He told me I should stay away from cliff edges, or risk falling to my death. He also said I should avoid sleeping in mice feces, as evidence of hantavirus—airborne organisms that had, in certain instances, proved lethal—had been found in some of the island's deer mice. He pointed out that no visitor to the Channel Islands had ever actually contracted hantavirus, and left it to me to reason that I didn't want to be the first. And that was it.

I caught up with the day-trippers, most of whom were still at the top of the steps, gasping like beached guppies. Right away, we all noticed that the island was very, very brown. As promised, there were no trees. The only vegetation, and I use this term in the broadest sense, was a ground cover of wind-whipped plants that only just raised their cowed and desiccated heads off the ground. There were also five white buildings, four of them low-slung, each with a Spanish-style red-tile roof. The largest building, perched on a rise above the others, resembled a church.

"Christ," someone whispered. "The whole place is dead. There's nothing here but rocks and dirt. What time does the boat leave?"

It's true, no guidebook is required to get the lay of East Anacapa. On the western tip there's aptly named Inspiration Point, with a spectacular oceanic panorama that includes Middle and

West Anacapa in the foreground and, in the watery distance, the great looming bulk of Santa Cruz Island, the largest of the Channel Islands. On Anacapa's eastern tip there's a lighthouse, built by the Coast Guard in 1912 after one too many captains showed an unerring ability to plow into the island, the lighthouse foghorn bemoaning these calamities day and night. Between eastern and western tips rest the bunched buildings, four pit toilets, and a five-site campsite, most of which is easily observed from any piece of ground higher than a speed bump.

Patricia moved briskly along the dirt trail bordered by ice plants and assorted squashed shrubs. Only one plant species stood tall, and only waist high at that; they looked as if they had been roundly punished for their chutzpah with a substantive burst from a flamethrower. Picture a menorah turned into a plant and then staked out in the desert for far too long.

"Giant coreopsis," said Patricia gaily, as we gazed at the limp, withered stalks. "They're dormant now. Waiting for the winter rains so that they can bloom into lovely yellow sunflowers."

As we walked, Patricia discoursed on the Chumash Indians, on the DDT that had nearly seen to the demise of the brown pelicans that now strafed the island in droves, and on the need for continued vigilant preservation. Glancing down, I noticed that the trail was littered with small bones, as if a horrific battle between two Lilliputian tribes had recently taken place.

Patricia nodded knowingly.

"Can anyone tell me where these bones come from?" she asked.

We hemmed and hawed as people do when no one has any idea.

"Kentucky Fried Chicken, among other places," said Patricia. "The seagulls on this island have discovered that there are a lot of garbage cans eleven miles away."

Seagulls are, in ornithology-speak, consummate generalists, gobbling up whatever foodstuff is available. In this, they are not unlike many humans. Researchers who have the honor of witnessing such things have seen gulls regurgitate chicken bones, onions, spaghetti, casserole, carrots, chips, dog food, and mince pie—and kudos to the researchers for being able to distinguish between the last two. After returning from Anacapa I would read a newspaper account of a Tasmanian researcher concerned by the outsized gulls waddling about Hobart like Pillsbury dough birds. Not only were the gulls fat, but measurements of their blood biochemistry showed higher cholesterol levels and their offspring were less healthy too. Whereto man goes, nature, sadly, often follows.

The mention of fried chicken aroused the curiosity of at least one naturalist in our group.

He turned to a friend.

"Do you think they sell beer on the boat?"

It was interesting eavesdropping on my companions' conversation. They had all paid to be here, and they listened like good schoolchildren when Patricia spoke, but they filled the silence between Patricia's discourses with complaints about their neighbor's ostentatious new addition, the evening's dinner plans, and a coworker's resemblance to the gulls of Hobart. When we reached the breathtaking seascape of Inspiration Point, a man in a Caribbean Joe T-shirt took out his phone and started text messaging.

Even Patricia seemed unable to disconnect from the mainland. At one point during our tour she began vehemently patting herself. At first I wondered if one of the island's deer mice had scurried up her pant leg.

"Oh my," she said, looking mildly aghast. "I don't seem to have my wallet. My identification, my money; I don't have anything."

I soon parted with the tour. Returning to the landing dock, I gathered up my gear and marched it to the campground. After staking down my tent, I looked out toward the mainland. On the blue expanse of the Channel, the Island Packer boat had become a Tinkertoy too, ferrying everyone home in time for their dinner reservations.

There were eight other campers on the island, three groups in all. They had arrived on an earlier morning boat. No doubt they had also come to East Anacapa for a dose of solitude. For the rest of the afternoon we kept to ourselves, each group hiking off discreetly in different directions like divorcees occupying the same room. As evening fell, the sunset hidden behind fog, we kept to our own dirt squares, fixing dinner and puttering about as campers do.

I still had company. With the gloaming, the deer mice appeared. Scuttling out of the surrounding scrub, they dashed around the perimeter of the picnic table like mindless windup toys. Driven mad by a chance at something other than insects and shrubs, several mice dashed rashly beneath the picnic table. There was an odd hollow plunking sound. Looking beneath the table, I saw one deer mouse again run headfirst into one of the gallon water jugs I had brought with me. I shooed him away, or at least I thought I did. When I settled myself back on to the picnic table bench, he attempted to use my leg as a means to ascend the table. I would have screamed if not for the indignity of it. Instead I stood as fast and as quietly as I could and, like some angry cheerleader, gave a single, spasmodic kick, sending the defenseless rodent pinwheeling off into space. Perhaps his companions glimpsed his flight and my inferred dominance. After that the scavengers kept their distance.

As the world slowly turned dark, I discovered what would become one of my favorite island pastimes. Across the water, civilization appeared low on the horizon, tentatively at first, a glimmering light here, a sparkling pinprick there. As my fellow Californians turned on headlights and threw switches, the lights strung together until, by full darkness, they assumed a single continuous twinkling line, like the campfires of a spurned Viking army whose ships were riddled with leaks.

I knew the sounds of evening well, the rushing drone of commuters driving home, on their arrival televisions, iPods, microwaves, and computers flicking on, an indistinguishable symphonic blend of mindless beeps and chatter, the white noise of the twenty-first century. A fitful sea breeze slapped lightly at my tent. Now and again my fellow campers laughed, and from the eastern edge of the island the lighthouse moaned. When the breeze paused, I heard the deer mice scurrying about in the scrub.

That night it rained lightly, the drops crackling on the rain shield of my tent. Inside the tent it was warm and dark as a womb.

Man is a social creature. The following morning we made ourselves known to one another. First I met Tyler and Kathy. Engineers from L.A., they had been to the islands before, a planned visit to distant San Miguel that had been turned back and rerouted to Santa Cruz Island by rough seas.

"The boat was going up and then dropping ten feet," said Tyler. "Everybody was yakking."

They were going to cut their current stay on Anacapa short too.

"We're supposed to be on the five-thirty boat this afternoon, but we'll probably leave on the twelve-thirty boat," Tyler said. "We're planning a trip to New Zealand, and we're running out of time. We've still got a lot of things to do."

It struck me as funny, and a trifle sad, that often even our recreation is rushed.

Heidi and Jane didn't plan to get on the boat until Sunday afternoon, when they were scheduled to depart, though Heidi immediately questioned my itinerary.

"You're out here for *how long?*"

"A week."

Heidi looked around. I didn't need to; I had already seen everything.

"What are you going to *do?*"

I felt vaguely lost.

"I don't know," I said. "I'm open to suggestions."

"Leave Sunday."

Jane listened. She was short. She stood, stooped slightly, her posture one of quiet submission. She reminded me of the deer mice.

"I could stay out here for a week," she said softly.

"Well, then, give me the car keys," Heidi said.

I would learn that Heidi and Jane had both come to Anacapa for a respite from various responsibilities, but it was immediately apparent which woman was best suited to Anacapa's charms.

Heidi rubbed her chin.

"I wonder how long I could stay out here. Let's see. . . . Two days is plenty. I need more things to keep me busy. I like to be busy."

Jane said, "It's been quiet and peaceful. And nobody's been angry at me. I love this place. I don't know why. There's nothing here."

"I thought it was going to be bigger," Heidi said.

Later that afternoon, Heidi and Jane returned to my campsite. Another boat had arrived, disgorging day-trippers. Sitting at the picnic table, we watched them far below, milling about at the top of the landing steps. Slowly they made their way toward us in dribs and drabs. They passed by the campsite wordlessly, disappearing in the direction of Inspiration Point.

In short order a man returned, walking briskly. The path he took brought him close to us. It would have been rude to ignore him.

"That's a pretty view out there at Inspiration Point, isn't it?" I said.

He nodded, but he kept walking.

"Yes, but I have to get back to the boat."

He sounded mildly worried. Perhaps he knew what Heidi was going to say next.

Smiling winsomely, she whispered, "Let's draw you in with a siren song and eat your liver."

"Don't turn your back on her," said Jane, grinning at me.

That night Heidi and Jane joined me for dinner, walking down from their home—"Number Seven Dirt Lane," said Heidi—to mine. They brought dinner, which to my relief consisted of Dinty Moore beef stew without a hint of liver.

It was true I had come for solitude, but it was also true that I sorely yearned for company. I had already surreptitiously pulled my cell phone from my pocket at several points around the island, discovering that, in high areas, I got reception. I hadn't yet buckled under and called home, but I had already listened to the same saved message—Kathy thanking me for something and sweetly professing her love—three times, a pathetic compromise.

I liked Heidi and Jane: Jane for her thoughtful, slightly abashed manner, Heidi for her honest and unapologetic lack of finishing school. Over dinner we talked about our lives, our families, and other trips we had taken. Jane had been to Anacapa twice before. Heidi had once been to a Cracker Barrel in Kentucky, where a stern-faced manager had staunchly refused to serve her a cocktail before noon.

"You go east of the Mississippi," Heidi said, "and you can die of dehydration."

The previous night had been overcast. Tonight stars filled the sky.

"Hey," said Jane. "The Milky Way."

There it was, above our heads, in all its vaporous riverine glory.

I thought of all the nights I had stood in our backyard and looked up at the stars.

"In twenty-two years I've never seen the Milky Way in this sky," I said.

Heidi threw her liver-eating glance toward the mainland.

"All that light, screwing things up."

Jane proved as open as Heidi. She told me she had a fourteen-year-old daughter.

"She's bipolar," Jane said matter-of-factly. "Sometimes she's very, very angry. You just have to let her break things. My husband is with her now, giving me a little rest. With a bipolar child you don't have much free time."

Jane nodded toward the upper end of the campground, where Dirt Lane rose past their campsite to a high bluff. I had been up there that afternoon. The bluff provided a vertiginous view of the backside of the island, cliffs plunging into a sparkling ocean where sea lions barked and leaped free of the water.

"The last time I was here alone, I walked up there to see the sunset," Jane said. "All the seagulls were all sitting down, facing the sun. It was like some weird animalistic ritual. It's funny the things you see when you have the time to look."

We sat quietly, Jane and Heidi wrapped in the comfortable silence of longtime friends. I tried to imagine life with a manic child. I remembered my first impression of Jane. Today quick is what we do, and we do not always do it well.

Here's something you should know about Anacapa's humble deer mice. They don't need your scraps or your water. A specialized kidney allows them to extract all the water they need from the island's plants. Once the water jugs are empty, you'll wish you were them.

Jane was as hardy as the deer mice. On two counts, I stood corrected.

The Saturday afternoon boat brought four more campers. When I woke on Sunday morning, two of them were sleeping in the site next to mine. They hadn't been there when I crawled into my tent. They had set up camp in the dark, but it probably hadn't taken long. Their only visible supplies—two bottles—sat on the picnic table. The water bottle was still full, but the Jack Daniel's was almost empty. The two men snored in sleeping bags laid out on the dirt.

Brian was from Pasadena. I never got the name of his companion. Brian told me he had been out on Anacapa with his daughters earlier that summer, at the same time the western gulls descended on the island to nest. I already knew how the gulls commandeered the island, occupying every inch of ground. They take their own small square of land for their nest and then squawk madly at anything that comes close. But Brian gave the scene a darker tint.

"There were broken eggs and dead seagulls everywhere, dude. I saw this calico bass come up and gulp down this half-dead seagull that was floating on the surface. If you got too close, the gulls would dive-bomb you. The place scared the shit out of my kids. Like *The Birds*."

No bluebird of happiness, the western gull, but nature's rhythms bear little resemblance to a Disney storyboard. I recalled a story of a local whale-watching boat that came across two orcas in the Channel. The killer whales were tossing an object back and forth like a beach ball. When the orcas tired of the game, one crunched down on the ball, spraying the water with blood and sea-lion innards.

Nature requires supreme fortitude from its denizens, and that's just to survive among their own.

I walked to a bench that looked down on a spot called Cathedral Cove. A small cusp of bay, the cove gets its name from the sea caves that peer darkly from the base of the cliffs. Dozens of pelicans fluffed their wings on a rock outcrop in the middle of the cove. Across the bay, the cliff on the far side was smothered with pelicans too. From where I sat, they looked like chicken bones. The water in the cove was clear. Beneath, the surface kelp strained in the direction of the passing swells.

With the addition of four more campers, Anacapa had reached saturation.

I heard a polite cough.

"Sorry to interrupt your tranquillity." The interloper extended a hand. "Chris."

Chris bore a striking resemblance to Brian, only he was older and less rumpled, possibly because he had slept without the aid of Jack Daniel's. Chris and Brian, it turned out, were cousins. They both lived in Pasadena, but for years their families had shared a beach house almost directly across the Channel from where we now stood.

"It's been in the family for a couple generations," Chris said. "The moms and the kids would spend the summers at the beach while the dads worked in L.A. They were great summers."

One summer, when he was fifteen, Chris had worked on a sport fishing boat out of Oxnard Harbor.

"I was the pinhead, basically the low man on the totem pole. I was scrubbing the decks, cleaning the toilets, mopping up after all the fishermen who got sick."

It surprised me that men who spent a lot of time on the water would get seasick and I said so.

"Well, they might not have gotten sick if they hadn't been drinking beer in the parking lot in the dark before we even left the dock." Chris shook his head. "Fishermen are kind of crazy. All the solitude."

Chris watched the waving kelp far below. One summer of mopping up vomit had been enough, but he still liked to fish out at the islands, though fishing had changed dramatically.

"The fishing's way off now, not like it used to be," he said. "We've fished things out."

"They've got marine reserves now off some of these islands," I said.

Over 120 acres of water off Anacapa alone are stringently protected; no fishing, no taking any creature of any kind. The theory behind these marine-protected areas—MPAs in the parlance—is simple: leave the sea life alone, and it will come back.

"The reserves don't do much good," Chris said.

A line of pelicans flew past. Chris looked at me a tad hopefully. "Didn't the pelicans come back from the DDT?" he asked.

Yes, I said. And the bald eagles on the islands, also nearly wiped out by DDT—the infamous pesticide that turned their eggshells so brittle that nesting birds would crush them—had made a comeback too. In the last two years, six chicks had hatched naturally on Santa Cruz and Santa Catalina Island—the first time in more than fifty years—part of a nationwide bald eagle recovery that at least one environmentalist had dubbed "astounding."

"I heard sea otters are coming back too," Chris said, sounding only mildly buoyed.

This is true. For years sea otters had taken a beating in local waters, drowning in gill nets, and otherwise being bludgeoned by oil spills, pollution, and, as one scientific paper phrased it, "persecution"; namely, fishermen, angered by the otters' tendency to gobble from their nets, putting bullets through the creatures' heads. It is as easy to distance ourselves from such sad falloffs as it is to lament the abominable actions of the fishermen. Interesting note, many sea otters were also killed by a protozoan parasite called *Toxoplasma gondii*, the same parasite cats shed in their feces. The parasite doesn't kill the otters, but the encephalitis it encourages does the job horribly enough. The scientific conclusion? *T. gondii* enters the ocean after people flush Felix's cat litter down the toilet. Out of sight, out of mind.

Primarily due to a ban on gill-net fishing in shallow coastal waters, the sea otters are seeing a slow recovery.

We quietly considered these success stories, but they didn't cheer either one of us up much.

"Nature can be pretty resilient," I said, mostly to buoy myself.

"The fishing is still lousy," Chris said.

For some inexplicable reason I felt the need to defend optimism. Maybe it was the gloomy fog-shrouded morning.

"Some species rebound faster than others. Maybe it's just a matter of time for the fish."

"Maybe."

I don't know why, but I tried again.

"It seems like different species have different lines we can push to."

Chris suddenly looked as hung over as his cousin.

"We seem to push everything to the edge," he said.

The Sunday afternoon boat left at three. The day had gone even gloomier. The mainland had already disappeared behind a wall of fog.

I walked down the stairs to the landing dock to say goodbye to Heidi and Jane. Heidi had been at the dock ninety minutes early, standing right at the edge of the last set of steps leading down to the boarding ladder.

Jane said, "I might bring my mom out here."

From our dinner conversation I knew that Jane's seventy-three-year-old mother had once been a supremely capable out-doorswoman, schooling her children in the joys of nature, and practicalities like properly sawing up firewood. But time clamps down on us all. She had suffered a heart attack and three strokes, rendering her feeble. She lived with Jane too.

A flood of pelicans lifted off from the cove's eastern wall. Their beating wings caught the afternoon sunlight and made a sound like wet sheets flapping in the wind.

Jane smiled.

"I think she'd really love it out here. Bring enough meds. Sort of a last hurrah."

At the top of the stairs I passed Brian on his way down.

He pumped my hand and grinned.

"The island's yours, man."

I walked back to camp. The foghorn moaned. Gulls cried. The pelicans made no sound at all, riding on the thickening blanket of gray. By the time I reached the campsite, empty but for my tent, the world had disappeared in fog.

I opened my food storage box, hoping to fill the emptiness I felt with food. There were bags I did not recognize, packets of soup and hot chocolate, and individually wrapped cups of mandarin oranges, and M&M's I had admired the night before at dinner.

I sat at the picnic table eating M&M's in the fog. I barely felt the chill press. In my mind I saw Jane patiently escorting her mother up each one of the 154 stairs. I had no doubt she would succeed.

I woke before dawn to a starry sky and an oddly enervating thought. I could watch the dawn naked if I chose. It was true, Yancey was cozily ensconced in the ranger's house, but otherwise Brian was right. Anacapa was mine. In the end a Puritan nature and an overactive imagination quashed the act. I imagined Yancey, beset by insomnia, walking the trail, coming upon me, standing with only a flashlight in my hand. Thomas Edison Man. It would make for a long and awkward week.

Foggy gloom and loneliness had sent me crawling into my sleeping bag the previous evening at the embarrassing hour of five thirty. Since I am no longer five years old, I was wide awake again two hours before dawn.

I dressed somewhat reluctantly and walked to the northern ridge of the island, training my flashlight on the trail. I made for another of the island's contemplative benches and sat near the edge of a cliff. When I flicked off the flashlight, night flooded back; darkness is never more than a technological snafu away. Dawn was a long way off; the Big Dipper's ladle rested just above the lighthouse, the light making its unhurried swing.

Across the Channel only a handful of lights glimmered. The world was sleeping, my family included.

The night had been breezy, but now the wind had stopped. Except for the sonorous blare of the foghorn—the note of B flat, a music professor and day-tripper had told me—it was very, very quiet, the kind of vacuum silence that causes the skin to prickle, as if something might be sneaking up behind you. I sat listening. After a time a bird called, the faintest whisper of a whistle. From far below rose an equally faint *ker-plock,* like a pebble tossed into a still pond. This was immediately followed by a short chuff, a sea lion breaking the surface. More coffin silence, followed by a brief, savage shriek of triumph. I had glimpsed the owl my first night, a fast-moving shadow that blotted out a surprising number of stars. At least one deer mouse would not greet the dawn. Slowly the noises gathered momentum; rustlings in the scrub nearby, blurts and croaks from the Pacific below. Tiny bird shadows rose and fell back into the brush.

Nature can alter its countenance with terrifying swiftness—in two weeks, more than 500,000 acres of California would be consumed by raging wildfires—but more often it moves at the leisurely pace of Sunday-afternoon lovers. First light arrived in the east with equal languor. A pencil slash of deep blue sky against the black, it edged the ridgelines of the Santa Monica Mountains. Dawn waited upon the ridgeline for a very long time. Then the insects began to hum, and day came to the sky.

I have admired dawns before. Each time I do, I am struck with a mild pain, not wrought entirely by dawn's promise and beauty. Always I am plagued by a nagging thought. The dawns I have seen are greatly outnumbered by the dawns I have missed.

After breakfast I considered my options. Even as I had admired the sun rise, part of my mind had turned to planning my day, as if I were a CEO typing out the day's responsibilities on my Blackberry, though truth is I don't own, or know how to use, one. *Let's see, a breakfast meeting with no one, followed by a walk. Allot time to observing pelicans fly; note how they settle on the cliff edges as delicately as tissue paper. Watch breezes ruffle the water like schools of fish. Read the names on passing freighters. When the sun rises high enough to throw its full weight into the frigid waters of the landing cove, take a brisk swim, followed by another walk. That might take me to noon.*

As I sat at the picnic table, the realization descended like an anvil: the day ahead appeared interminably long. This produced a prickling fear. By God, I needed to do things. I confess I fairly leaped up and ran from the campsite.

I started by climbing the slight rise to the lighthouse, but advanced no farther than the sign warning me that advancing farther might render me deaf. To be deafened by solitude didn't seem right.

I walked back down and stepped inside the small visitor center, where I browsed through the suggestion book. This was enlightening. If I was to draw a conclusion from my reading, it was that America's greatest concern regarding its national parks are its toilets. *Toilet was gross!* one visitor wrote. *Empty the john!* scrawled another. A German visitor was Teutonically concise: *Better toilets.*

It seemed as if the majority of visitors had spent most of their time on the island peering down into Anacapa's four pit toilets. There were exceptions: *Clean the Friggin' Bird Poop*, though this seemed a Sisyphean task, and *Keep the Humans Away*, though again this might have been related to the toilets. It was true that here and there a visitor had dispensed with suggestion and simply noted Anacapa's beauty—*Very unique and beautiful.* And John Gomez had grasped the island's potential—*Develop the area/Homes.* The very last entry, penned the day of my arrival, lamented the lack of lighthouse magnets. I left the visitor center sorely concerned for the absence of my countrymen's breadth of vision.

While I was sitting at my picnic table, eating a nine-thirty lunch, Yancey stopped by. He was accompanied by his girlfriend, Krisy Simpson, who was staying with him on the island. Krisy was a seasonal ranger too. She had just finished a summer stint at Kings Canyon. I had seen her earlier, a tall, long-legged blonde, jouncing along the island's paths. Yancey ran too, but he was not as enamored of the exercise as Krisy. I had already noticed that Krisy usually ran a loop or two before Yancey joined in.

Now they were just walking, and they stopped at my campsite.

"How are you findin' it out here?" Yancey asked. "Bit different, huh?"

"I like it quiet," I lied.

Yancey looked at me more closely than I would have liked.

"It's like backcountry camping," he said agreeably. "For the most part, it's pretty remote. You can feel pretty secluded. There's times, when the coast is fogged in, you could be in the middle of the Pacific. Some people have a hard time with it."

All three of us considered this remote possibility.

"Did you see the owl?" Yancey asked.

"Just for a second, a night or two back. I think I heard it take a deer mouse this morning."

"We get barnyard owls out here now and again. If you can, watch the moon come up. It's real pretty beside the lighthouse."

Krisy looked at Yancey and smiled a white-toothed smile.

"Yancey likes the quiet life. I don't think I could do it."

Yancey smiled back but said nothing.

"How do you like it out here?" I asked.

"Well, the head ranger told me Anacapa was a small island, that I could get stuck out here if the weather went bad, and that visitation could be low," Yancey said. "All of which was pretty much fine with me. There are times when you think, 'What am I going to do today?' but at the same time there's nobody around tellin' you what to do. That's one of the things that attracted me about the job. For the most part, I've had a lot of luck with that."

Yancey's time on Anacapa was drawing to a close. By the end of the month he would be unemployed. He had arrived on Anacapa in early June. He had spent the summer alternating between eight-day stints on the island and six days off on the mainland.

Yancey didn't volunteer a great deal, but I asked a lot of questions that he politely answered. Slowly I learned that he'd been born and raised in rural North Carolina. Growing up, he'd had a creek running through his backyard. Yancey had spent large chunks of time catching snakes and frogs, a skill that served him well during a seasonal ranger stint in the Everglades.

"They have these Burmese pythons down there. They're people's pets and they escape into the Everglades. They're breeding now. They've found nests full of babies. They're not supposed to be there, and they pretty much eat everything, so we were killing them. Well, actually I'd catch them, but I'd make the other rangers kill them."

It occurred to me that snatching up a Burmese python might differ slightly from scooping up a garter snake.

Yancey gave a small nod.

"They're a little nasty-tempered, but I didn't have trouble. Just kind of pin it down, grab it behind the head, and put it in the sack. I kind of enjoyed it."

There were things Yancey didn't like. He'd gone to L.A. once during his time off. It was his only visit.

"Visiting L.A. is just crazy, like a beehive. I kind of like detective stories, Raymond Chandler, *L.A. Confidential,* that kind of stuff, so I wanted to look around. But now that I've seen the place, it's kind of a turnoff."

The three of us sat silent for a moment. Whitecaps dotted the Channel.

To my surprise Yancey volunteered something without being asked.

"There's something about this. It's hard to articulate what it is." I watched him, a quiet man, struggling calmly. Finally he said, "It's that not-livin'-in-the-city feelin'. Cities have movies and bookstores and those kinds of things, but they kind of get old before too long."

He and Krisy got up.

"Listen, it's supposed to get pretty windy tonight," he said. "If you need to, you can sleep in the visitor center."

Yancey said it wasn't national-park policy to offer up a visitor center to campers, but Anacapa wasn't the South Rim of the Grand Canyon.

"I can't have a whole campground in there, but you're the only one out here. You may have to share it with a few mice."

The wind did pick up. Blowing from the north, it gained steam, transforming the whitecaps into impressive swells, kicking malignantly at my tent, and blowing my carefully ladled scoops of powdered lemonade off in the direction of Antarctica.

I walked down to the landing-cove dock to hide from its incessant beating. Inside the cove, the wind only swirled slightly and the sun was warm, but beyond the cove's mouth large waves boomed against Mr. Cabrillo's arch, and on the open sea the wind slashed off the tops of the waves. When the sunlight caught the mists just so, they formed brief, tiny rainbows, like shy fairyland creatures ducking in and out of the air. I noticed that the pelicans had vacated the ledges and crannies on the opposite cliff, which faced the full brunt of the wind. My side of the cliff was now jammed with ass-to-beak pelicans, most of them sleeping soundly with their beaked heads folded beneath their wings. It was obvious they were riding out the wind, an inaction that made complete sense. I felt I should crawl into my tent and do the same, but twenty-first-century man's instinct is less hardwired for waiting than it once was. I watched the pelicans. They ignored me. The wind whopped in my ears. I decided to walk across the island to Inspiration Point.

I only made it as far as the campground, because when I got there, I saw my tent bucking like a tortured animal. Once, on a beach in Mexico, I had watched some idiot's dome tent bound down the beach like some misshapen beach ball, until I finally recognized the tent and gave chase. Having learned my lesson, here on Anacapa I had already used every stake I had, driving them so deep into the hard dirt that I was fairly certain I would have to borrow a jackhammer to retrieve them. Now, with a sudden rise in heart rate, I saw that two stakes had pulled free from the ground, and my leaping tent was striving valiantly to yank out more.

I crawled into the tent, lending my weight to the battle. Deprived of the opportunity to send my tent into space, the gusts now turned their vindictive selves to flushing me from the tent, hoping to accomplish this by malevolently mashing the roof of the tent flush against my face. The waiting was like

Chinese water torture. Lying atop my sleeping bag, I could hear the bigger gusts coming, the wind rising to a distasteful self-congratulatory howl. In the next instant the gust would stomp the tent roof down against my face, allowing me to ponder the irony of being smothered by breathable fabric.

Outside, the sun was setting. Inside the tent, my behavior turned unseemly; I shouted stupidly at the wind, and once I gave the tent a petulant kick of my own. Defeated, I took the tent down and headed for the visitor center. As I walked, I saw a red-tailed hawk balanced perfectly still in the sky.

Yancey and Krisy left the island on the park service boat the following afternoon.

The incoming ranger was Josh Knotts. I met him an hour later down at the landing dock, where I fled again to escape the wind. Unlike Yancey, Josh was a permanent ranger. He, too, spent eight days on the island and six days off, but, for now at least, Anacapa was his year-round beat.

When I asked him how he found life on the island, he admitted to mixed feelings.

"It's a funny setup. When you first get out here, it's way too quiet. Then just as you're getting used to it, thinking this ain't so bad, then you're jerked back to the mainland."

At twenty-eight, Josh was three years younger than Yancey, and three centuries younger than me.

He rubbed his goatee.

"Maybe I have a harder time adjusting to life out here because I'm younger. It's possible I'm a little bit more suited to the fast-paced life than I am to island time. I like to get out at night."

With few happy-hour options, that evening I once again walked up to Inspiration Point to watch the sunset. Low to the horizon, the sun ladled its soft light across the water. The cold wind raked the light into a vast field of golden shards. From the rocks below, the sea lions marked the end of day in their particular fashion, doglike barks punctuated here and there by higher, sharper cries, infinitely more wild.

I should have been depressed—the wind remained unrelenting, and along with kicking mercilessly at all my belongings, it had wedged some object, perhaps a ball of grit or maybe some unfortunate insect, deep into my right ear, rendering me half-deaf, so that I wandered about the island pinching my nose and blowing cautiously, this would be a bad place to have an aneurysm—but instead, as I was standing at Inspiration Point, a feeling of immense satisfaction slowly washed over me. A half mile away I had watched the sun rise that morning, the first light of day gradually rendering the revolving light obsolete. Now, behind me to the east, bathed in evening's gold light, the lighthouse stood rigid, a soldier awaiting duty. I had followed the sun through the entire course of its day. The thought filled me with a deep-seated contentment. By society's measure I had accomplished nothing—not one dish washed, not one bill paid, not a single word written—but I felt I had accomplished something far greater, though precisely what it was I couldn't yet surmise. With equal surprise I realized the constriction in my chest—the clenching that had disembarked with me on the landing dock, the clenching that had followed the departure of my campmates—was gone. Suddenly I realized what had made me afraid. I had feared what I didn't know. How to be alone.

In the end, the human mind is unfathomable. I was so overwhelmed by the joy of solitude that I called home.

My thirteen-year-old son, Graham, answered the phone, his voice clear as a bell.

"Hi, Dad. What did you do out on the island today?"

"Ruminated," I said giddily. "Do you know what that is?"

"No."

"It's when you think a lot."

He thought about this.

"Mom says she doesn't have time to think," he said.

A little of the gold went out of the evening.

"Is Mom home yet?"

"No."

"When you see her, will you tell her I love her?"

"OK."

"I'm watching the sunset," I said.

"That's nice."

In the background I heard music and canned laughter and a faint clicking. My fifteen-year-old son, Cullen, was on his laptop, no doubt downloading podcasts while listening to music and instant messaging friends. They were both watching television. Normally I would be there too, talking at them from the kitchen, asking them about their day at school, one more noise they would adroitly process. Their world was about so many things at once. I wondered if one day they would be able to sit still in a place like this.

I heard a light clattering, like fingers running over an abacus. The opening of a row of plantation shutters.

"Dad? I can see the sunset too."

Now that I was paying attention, I noted my own evolution. When I first arrived on the island, I had hiked about like some manic drill sergeant, moving from overlook to overlook, inspecting each seascape snappily and then moving on. Almost always I looked toward the mainland; for some reason the thin slice of coast with its backdrop of hazy blue mountains was utterly fascinating to me. Sitting in camp, marching around the island, standing on various bluffs, I scanned the coast, trying to decipher my home of twenty-two years. Several familiar landmarks were visible to the naked eye. Using them as benchmarks, I inched up and down the coast, placing things—my hometown of Ventura, the neighboring sprawl of the Oxnard plain—where I knew they should be. When I was confident I had everything in its place, I allowed myself to peer through the telescope at the top of the landing-cove stairs. Civilization flooded the eyepiece. Twelve inches off my nose I saw clearly a

beachfront hotel I knew, a familiar rise of freeway overpass arc-
ing over train tracks and the mall three blocks from our home;
even the letters—M-a-c-y-s—atop the largest store. Nothing
was where I had thought it should be; I had gotten it all wrong.
It was a mildly insane game and I had emerged a big loser; both
facts I kept to myself.

As the week progressed, I stopped returning to the telescope.
Now I climbed to the northern edge of the island and looked
out to sea. There was nothing on this horizon except clouds,
but the view was soothing. In my mind I visited people and
places I had known beyond this white cauliflower curtain.

A pair of red-tailed hawks had made Anacapa their temporary home. That they were a pair was clear. The female redtail is
larger; plus this one was clearly calling the shots, either running
the male off or turning abruptly and streaking madly for some
distant point, as if Macy's had just announced a storewide half-
price sale. Each time, the male would bank dutifully and follow.

I became fascinated by the hawks, possibly a trifle obsessed.
Watching them proved easy on a small island bereft of cover,
and it was made easier still by the fact they often seemed to follow me. At first I made light of this. I imagined them, lofting
easily, having a hearty chuckle as my dinner was blown off the
picnic table or I stumbled from the pit toilet, pants around my
knees, clawing at the remnants of spider web clinging to my
face. But after a time their graceful soaring brought me an easy
peace; it didn't seem they were mocking me at all, but rather
watching over me. I recalled a friend who remains convinced
that her departed brother has taken the form of a redtail that
frequently hovers over their home. When she is outside gardening, she often speaks to him by name. I half wondered,
should a nighttime gust send my tent over the cliff, which ancient relation would swoop down and save me from an unseemly splattering.

Wandering the island, I found myself considering memories
I hadn't visited in years, and at night my dreams were startlingly

vivid, as if my subconscious had thrown some long-mothballed switch in an effort to entertain me.

One evening, an hour before sunset, I made my way toward Inspiration Point, passing through the small coreopsis forest that runs along an upsweep of the island's ridge. I had just suffered a depressing dinner, and the oncoming night didn't look so hot either. At dinner the wind kept blowing the tuna right off my fork, and already my tent was performing push-ups. The wind continued to gather steam even now, though it had been whopping without surcease in my working ear since dawn, perhaps hoping to complete its task of rendering me as wild-haired and deaf as Beethoven.

In short I was feeling sorry for myself, and at first glance the half-dead coreopsis didn't do much to lift my spirits. But I found if I hunched low, the waist-high plants afforded some small windbreak, so I stopped amid the forest, motionless and half-bowed like some paralyzed monk.

A strange thing happened. With nothing else to do, I observed the coreopsis closely. It was true, they reeked of death. Their stalks were mottled as old hands and their ends held not flowers but drooping strands, thin and withered as a skeleton's final hairs. Within this relatively quiet glen there was a familiar sound I couldn't quite place. Closing my eyes, I listened until it came to me, the hiss of sand running through fingers. The wind spat salt spray; I felt it against my cheeks. Salt is something few life-forms relish, but upon the coreopsis stalks, life flourished in the form of dozens of tiny lichens. Reaching out, I gently ran my fingers along the plant's drooping strands; surprisingly, they possessed the moist suppleness of hope.

I had forgotten my appointment with the setting sun. Nearly on the horizon, it now bathed the entire miniaturized mossy forest in gauzy gold. The coreopsis bobbed agreeably. I realized that I had been standing stock-still for nearly an hour. From where I stood, I could see the trails I had fairly sprinted over in my need to master all my surroundings. Why is it that we want so much when so very little will do?

Coreopsis lie dormant for nine months, erupting with brilliant yellow flowers come winter's rains. I gazed again at the mottled patches, and smiled. They did not remind me of death. In my mind I saw again the hands of my ninety-year-old grandmother clasping—nay, fairly crushing—the arm of the frightened five-year-old great-grandson she had just met, holding this new life as if it were a treasure not to be believed, a bridge to renewed hope and possibility.

Like Yancey and Krisy, Josh proved good, and kind, company. He too stopped by the campground to chat. Several times he found me down at the landing cove, hunched pelican-like to avoid the wind. One night he invited me to dinner, a somewhat embarrassing affair that saw me wander about his quarters like some idiot castaway, staring stupidly at tidy spice racks and comfortable couches as if I'd never seen them before.

Like Yancey, Josh's primary job was enforcement, but with all the pit-toilet haters gone from the island there was little to enforce.

"I would like to be around people a little bit more," he told me one afternoon. "It gets pretty lonely out here. Did you bring your laptop?"

"No."

"You're not up there writing?"

I shook my head

"What are you doing?"

"Thinking," I said. It sounded self-inflated. So that we both might understand, I added, "I'm trying to take a look at the world we live in from a quiet place."

"Well, you picked the right spot." Yancey shook his head. "I couldn't do what you're doing, camping out here for a week. I'd go nuts. I need TV. Or something."

Having grasped my purpose, Josh had some fun. When we crossed paths one morning, he said, "What do you have planned for today?"

This stumped me for a moment.

"A little hiking."

He looked at me with concern.

"Got a compass?"

Josh readily admitted to being bored. Anacapa gave him time around the ocean he loved, but he allowed that his four-month stint of field training on the South Rim of the Grand Canyon had been far more entertaining.

"That was fun. We were cops. Tons of drugs, tons of drunk driving. I was putting people in cuffs every other day. You get a different crowd there. You get a lot of transient people in the Grand Canyon, people running away from things, on their way West." He paused for a moment, his gaze running over a large part of the island. "Out here we don't get people just passing through, looking for a better life."

Maybe they should, I thought. Maybe they should all pass through here, the confused, the lost, the overwhelmed and the addled, looking for answers.

But odds are they'll be in too much of a hurry to find them.

When the Island Packers boat arrived on Friday, a dozen day-trippers trooped off. I looked at them with their white-bright socks and their crisp new Lands' End jackets, tilting back their shiny Diet Cokes. They looked at me with my scrubby gray beard and week's coating of dust and windblown food bits.

I joined them as their naturalist took them on their guided hike. My gear already rested, packed up and ready, down at the landing cove.

A woman sidled up beside me.

"Do you live here?"

"No. I was just camping."

"For how long?"

"A week."

"Really? Why?"

I chose the easiest answer.

"To see what it was like."

"And what was it like?"

I smelled perfume.

"Quiet. And in the beginning, kind of lonely."

We hiked past the empty campground. The two wooden johns stood still and regal as royal palace guards.

"I didn't realize it was going to be so deserted," she said.

"What did you think it would be like?"

"I thought there would be houses out here. I read something in the literature about not disturbing the residents. This is like a Robinson Crusoe island."

We had reached my coreopsis forest. I stopped to say a silent goodbye.

The woman turned back to me.

"What are you doing?"

"Just taking in the scenery."

She shook her head.

"Everything's dead and brown," she said, before continuing on.

A Sequoia in the Desert

▪ ▪ ▪ ▪ ▪ ▪ ▪

THERE IS A SEQUOIA in the desert. It should not be there, but, contrary to the opinion of many, there it is, nearly seventy feet high. It is a fine tree, reaching strong and straight into the sky.

The man responsible for this tree is ninety-eight years old. He does not see or hear well. Most of his teeth are gone. But these are not requirements for living. Recently he published his third book of philosophy. He and the tree have watched each other grow old, though in the end the tree will keep a longer watch.

The tree and the man, Father Eleutherius, live at Saint Andrew's Abbey, a Roman Catholic Benedictine monastery just outside Valyermo, a tiny smudge of town in the Mojave Desert some sixty miles northeast of Los Angeles. More and more people are going to such places to temporarily escape the world's din, and, in silence, sort things out, whether religion plays a role or not. Some visitors are not religious at all. They do not believe in God, but they place hope in the restorative powers of contemplative silence; the sadly rare opportunity to just plain think. An empty island serves the same aim.

Neither Father Eleutherius nor his tree cared which path a visitor walked, they merely engaged them, each in their own charming fashion.

When I met Father Eleutherius, he was sitting on the walker-cum-seat that he pushes before him, beside the gravel drive that wends through Saint Andrews Abbey. He was sitting in the sun because it was February in the high desert, and where there was no sun, the cold remained sharp. He wore a dark puffy down jacket and a black knit cap so that he resembled a mix of the French Connection and the Michelin Man. When you are ninety-eight, it is not so easy to slough off the cold. There is indoor heat, of course, but Father Eleutherius prefers the charms of the out-doors. Whenever possible, he finds a place in the sun.

I had just arrived at the Abbey for a three-day visit. Father Eleutherius was not visiting. He was here for the duration. He had wanted to be a priest ever since he was six years old. He entered the monastery of Saint André, in his native Belgium, in 1927 (at the age of eighteen). He arrived at Saint Andrews in 1961, which is also when he planted his sequoia sapling.

I could have walked past Father Eleutherius with just a nod, but beside a quiet road with no one else in sight this is impo-lite. I try not to be rude to anyone, especially not a Benedictine monk who I am likely to run into numerous times over the next few days. Saint Andrews is very small place. If you don't linger, you can walk from one end to the other in ten minutes; but you should linger because that is the point. So I stopped beside the pile of down, and when I did, the head perched atop the down gave me a sparse-toothed grin as if it had known I would stop all along.

"The heat here is free," Father Eleutherius said.

The nearby San Gabriel Mountains were draped in snow. When the wind descended from their summits, you knew winter was not done.

I said, "The best things in life are free."

As I came to see, if you said something that pleased Father

Eleutherius, he would either lean forward and stab a finger in your direction or he would stick out his tongue. In both cases, he would smile widely. His smile was like a broken shutter, but broken shutters let the sun in.

"*Exactement!*" he said, and stuck out his tongue.

My French is not very good. Fortunately he continued in English. "I am nearly blind," he said. "I cannot walk well. The only thing that works is my tongue."

Somehow he managed to stick it out farther. He looked like a wrinkled old truant with the teacher's back turned. After a beat, he drew it back into his mouth.

"It is a fine thing to walk," he said. "I have never had a car."

And so our acquaintance began, and my education received a sizable boost. I had come to Saint Andrew's to experience a place where people sought solitude, and perhaps the very lucky found a degree of transformation, not just monks but people like me, confused people, people hoping for meaningful answers beyond today's headlines and to-do lists, people who might not think it sane to spend a week alone on a windy island, people who wouldn't know Saint Benedict if he took a prayer book and whopped them over the head. Not all who came to Saint Andrews were pious, which suited Father Eleutherius just fine.

He grinned again.

"If people don't believe in God, they just come here to see the crazy people like me," he said.

During my time at Saint Andrews my conversations with Father Eleutherius always took circuitous routes. Sometimes they hopped from subject to subject like a happy frog. Other times they meandered easily like a slow-running summer stream. Topics arose and disappeared, and then resurfaced again. To the listener accustomed to hurried conversation sometimes the dialogue appeared to wander far off track, but I came to see that Father Eleutherius never lost his point; he merely wove it with an intricacy rarely seen in today's rushed world.

During our first conversation we discussed, among other

topics, his garden and the beauty of winding roads. Father Eleutherius admired winding roads. He knew the town I lived in. He remembered visiting there, arriving by a winding road. I knew the road. It is one of my favorites. In a world of freeways bordered by Subway sandwich shops and Wal-Marts, this road makes its ambling way past farm stands and orange groves. If you drive along it early on a spring morning, a gauzy mist hangs above the soldierly rows of trees.

Sadly, though, we have removed the kinks from many roads.

"The old cities in Europe, they were made for horse carts," Father Eleutherius said. "They had, what do you call it, character? The streets, they used to be windy and now they are straight. The city is no longer agreeable. It is practical."

Nor was Father Eleutherius a fan of the automobiles that rushed along them. If I gathered correctly, he had never driven a car. Friends drove him, or better still he traveled by public transport; this allowed him to meet many different people, something he thoroughly enjoyed. Of course not everyone was comfortable sitting beside a Catholic priest on the bus, but many found it a rare and pleasant opportunity.

"Priests are intimidating when we are in the church," Father Eleutherius. "Less so on a bus. Because I do not drive alone in a car, I have heard confessions everywhere."

Father Eleutherius told me he visited with old people and with juvenile delinquents. "I speak with crazy people too," he said. "You accept them as they are."

He informed me that his name, Eleutherius, was Greek. "It means 'free.' It means 'giving.' Those who know Greek say it is a beautiful name." He gave me a sly puckered grin. "Those who don't know Greek, they don't know."

We talked for a long time, the two of us warmed by our puddle of sun. I do not know how long we talked; to me it seemed counterproductive to bring a watch to a place that was the antithesis of rushing. At one point another monk walked past with a friendly nod. After a few moments he returned with a chair for me. This is the way things are at Saint Andrews.

Regarding the garden, I learned that Father Eleutherius had planted, and tended, all the trees himself, not just the sequoia but the tidy rows of Lombardi poplars—"pop-a-lars," he pronounced them in his Belgian accent—from Italy too, all saplings in the beginning.

He held up a mittened finger. The mitten had a hole in it.

"The sequoia sapling, the trunk was no thicker than this. You know what is interesting? To see things grow in life. First, the family: the children, the grandchildren, the great-grandchildren. And the garden. According to my ninety-eight-year-old mind, the greatest gift of God is family. Do you have a family?"

"Yes."

"Do you have a wife?"

"Yes."

"Love her."

Enter Saint Andrews Abbey from the side entrance, and there is a beaten yellow sign that says Slow. Then there is dust and birdsong and yucca, and tidy, low-slung buildings clustered together in a narrow fold between the scrubby desert hills. There is also a small pond with real and rubber ducks—just for fun; the monks have a fine sense of humor—and a cemetery on a hill just above the monastery, and, of course, Father Eleutherius's garden. There is a cloister for the monks and separate lodging for visitors; clean, comfortable, spare, and bereft of telephones, wireless access, and in-room movies. Visitors pay a modest sum for lodging and meals: breakfast, lunch, and dinner shared with the monks.

The monks at Saint Andrews adhere to a rigid schedule of prayer and reading and other pious things. From eight thirty in the evening until after breakfast, the monastery, acceding to one of the many rules of Saint Benedict, observes a Grand

Silence, which forbids speech. Many people find this silence pleasing and beneficial, but it puts some people off too.

"It's not infrequent that people get freaked out," said Abbot Francis agreeably when we met for the first time in his small office just off the kitchen. "We've had people who've said, 'What? No television?' And we say, 'Of course not. This is a retreat center; it's not about television and Jacuzzis.' Still some people come expecting this to be some sort of spiritual resort."

Abbot Francis Benedict (no relation) is in charge of Saint Andrews. Keeping it short, he makes many of the decisions and manages everything but the money, ensuring that people beat a path to his office like techno-geeks seeking the latest version of the iPhone. His own phone rang constantly—parole officers, men whose mothers are dying, a recovering addict shopping at Wal-Mart—and his printer clacked and labored like R2D2. One monk informed me that Abbot Francis mediated disputes between the monks too, though such conflicts were hard to envision: *Abbot Francis, Father Luke superglued my robe to the pew*, or maybe *Father Matthew spoke rudely to me in Latin*.

Abbot Francis was also Saint Andrews' primary conduit to the outside world, as at least some of the monks prefer to be left alone to do what monks do. As he diplomatically phrased it, "Many of the monks don't have the capacity for people that I have. That's nothing against them. It's just my calling." He was a bear of a man, possessed of the warm, wise manner you would expect of a priest. He was erudite, versed in scripture and Latin, but he was not removed from this world. He had spent time in the shantytowns of South Africa. Over the years he had counseled all manner of humanity, including murderers, crack addicts, and assorted other con folk. Consequently he was adept at recognizing a tall tale.

"If someone's bullshitting me, I can smell that real quick," he said when we first met. "I'll tell those people, 'I love you, but you're full of shit.'"

I found such openness refreshing and, as you might imagine,

mildly surprising. A finely tuned bullshit-o-meter was also a bit unnerving. It was true I had immediately and clearly told him I was writing a book examining our times. I told him I was spending time alone on the Channel Islands, juxtaposing those bouts of nature and solitude with the louder life most of us know. But I had pitched this to Abbot Francis as a dispassionate examination of all the other pathetic slobs struggling for meaning while pinwheeling through chaotic days like mindless gerbils and sinning profoundly.

I had also neglected to come fully clean. This particular matter was not so much a lie as a matter of believing that it really didn't matter. Nearly a decade earlier I had come to Saint Andrews to write a magazine article about the latest trend of people fleeing to monasteries for temporary respite and escape. Magazine editors very much love to announce trends; it is their version of catnip. Hoping to eat, the intrepid freelancer finds trends everywhere.

I remembered Abbot Francis vividly from that visit. He had made me feel welcome, answering all my inane trend-oriented questions like a patient and kindly uncle. Now I had returned, hoping for his kind help again. Though it is the way of much of the world, I doubted monks turned crotchety and closed-minded with age.

I was sure Abbot Francis wouldn't remember me, and I saw no point in bringing my previous visit to light.

Now one eyebrow went up.

"Have we met before?"

I heard the bullshit-o-meter humming.

"Yes."

My mouth rushed through a bumbling explanation while my mind screamed, *Priest means full disclosure.* Growing up, I had many friends who had attended Catholic school; now I recalled their stories of the priests' and nuns' finely tuned powers of observation.

But Abbot Francis did not produce a wooden paddle and

smack my backside. He did not care about my harmless omission at all. Sitting in the soft lamplight of his office, I knew something else too. He knew that my book and I were one.

Folding his meaty hands beneath his chin, he said, "So. Tell me what I can do for you."

Many believe solitude and silence are where true transformation takes place. For centuries various seekers, addled by the noise of the world, have disappeared into hellish, desolate places for Rip Van Winkle time frames, returning compassionate and at peace.

But not everyone I talked to found silence golden. When I told my mother-in-law that I was going to a monastery, she said, "Don't decide to stay."

I was surprised to learn that she, too, had gone to a monastery, with a girlfriend many years before.

"I wouldn't do it again," she said. "We couldn't talk at all. It was so strange. I mean, to go eat and not talk to anybody? You should be able to talk when you eat."

Cullen weighed in too.

"You'll come back with ADD," he said. He did not look up from his typing. His foot tapped to the beat of whatever music was pouring from his laptop. These were just the visible signs of what he was up to. "When you get back, you'll just want to talk all the time."

I did not miss the irony of my son lecturing me on the dangers of attention deficit disorder. But I quickly learned that, in one sense, he was right. Unless you actually *are* a monk, ours is a world of noise and incessant activity, and such a world does not easily bid adieu. Even when you are alone, it is very, very hard to stop yourself from yakking. Hence there is anxious silence and there is peaceful silence, and it is no easy feat to move from one to the other.

Before I came to Saint Andrews, my mind had turned increasingly uneasy. I am not Catholic. I had not been to any church in years. I could not remember the last time I prayed. More honestly, praying has always made me uncomfortable. Having a one-sided conversation with someone who may or may not be listening makes me feel self-conscious and silly. If they are capable of listening, they don't need to hear my bumbling prayer to decipher the riot of sin and shortcomings beneath it. If they aren't listening, I'm talking to myself.

There was also the matter of religious customs, which, regarding arcane detail and indecipherability, take a backseat only to any government form. I conjured up all manner of horrible gaffes. Trying to fit in, I would mumble some Latin vow inadvertently committing myself to a lifetime of monastic devotion and, worse still, lying to my mother-in-law. My car alarm would go off during the Grand Silence. An Internet search would reveal that I had once kept *Playboy* magazines under my bed.

Obsess on something ridiculous long enough and you'll see it to fruition. On the morning of my arrival, a monk approached my cabin. I had done my best to convince myself not to be intimidated by the monks. Though I knew Abbot Francis to be kindly, I also knew he was the Abbey's official mouthpiece; the other monks would be austere and dark-cloaked, as approachable as the Queen's Guard at Buckingham Palace. Well, what of it? Why should I be intimidated by men who selflessly dedicated their lives to something I could barely grasp? What if they *were* living life on a completely different and higher level than me?

So when Father Philip spoke to me I heard what most of us hear when we are self-conscious and intimidated, namely, the panicked chattering of my inner voice. Through this din I could barely make out his words, or my rushed replies. He asked if I was Ken, and I think I at least identified my name correctly. Then he said something about Abbot Francis meeting me that evening, and I mumbled something in return. Even in my own ears it sounded as garbled as pig Latin.

Father Philip's gray pointy beard lent him a wizened,

gnomelike quality. He cocked his head and gave me a slightly bemused smile.

"I think he intends you to find *him,* not him to find you," he said, already turning to go.

What had I done? I fairly shouted after him.

"Will you thank Abbot Francis for the lovely quarters?"

It was true, the Abbot had arranged for me to bunk in a private cabin and not a shared room. But my words still rang in the desert silence like a pathetic yelp for forgiveness.

Father Philip shrugged. He still wore his bemused smile.

"If you think it's necessary," he said.

Arsenius, a Roman imperial tutor who fled to the desert to find transformation (he is one of the most revered of the early Christian monastics known as the Desert Fathers), once said, "I have often repented of having spoken, but never of having remained silent."

I watched Father Philip go, his robe as dark as my heart. I envisioned him reporting to Abbot Francis.

He expected you to meet him.

Any minute now he'll be ordering room service.

I'll see to his turn-down service.

Monks like to have fun.

On that first evening, before dinner and my initial meeting with Abbot Francis, I hiked up to the cemetery above Valyermo. The cemetery sat atop a hill. It was already getting dark. In the distance the Mojave Desert wavered behind a gray curtain of dust stirred by the wind.

The cemetery was divided into two sections: one for oblates (laypeople who lived as much like Benedictine monks as possible but did not take monks' vows) and one for the monks. Oblate or monk, the graves were plain. The gray stone crosses of the monks, eleven in all, faced west in a precise row: Vincent Martin, Gaetan P. Loriers, Felix L. Tang, Wilfred Weitz—men whose labors in this world had ceased.

Looking to the east, I saw that the distant desert now twinkled with the lights of a small town. As darkness fell over the dead, the lights of the living spread and brightened. The wind was raw. I had intended on contemplating alone, but the lights were distracting. They reminded me of my beautiful wife and my sons. At this very moment, the warm lights of my own home were no doubt flicking on. Suddenly I wanted to be neither contemplative nor monastic. I wanted to go home. In the monastery below, a bell chimed signaling dinner.

We ate in the dining hall, the monks and some half-dozen retreatants seated at long tables that formed a U. There were a few paintings of desert scenes on the walls, but nothing more. Think the Great Hall at Hogwarts, robbed blind. The food was hot and homestyle—fried chicken, macaroni, cooked carrots and broccoli—and we helped ourselves from the steaming trays. I was famished, but I scooped dainty servings. After my gaffe with Father Philip, I didn't want to add the sin of gluttony to hubris.

The monks ate wordlessly in a small knot. We retreatants huddled together too. Talking was allowed, the Grand Silence was still two hours away, but no one said anything beyond a brief murmuring. Later I would read that, though not demanded, the preferred mode for dinner was also silence. A monk sat alone at a table by the door, reading scripture aloud. This, I would discover, was part of the meal ritual, except for during the silent breakfast.

The particular evening's reading dealt with the gift of love, the continued presence of sin and certain other deeply spiritual matters, but I couldn't concentrate on them. The man seated across from me wore an Oakland Raiders knit cap and a two-day stubble. More entrancing, he ate with his mouth open, affording me a clear view of a great bolus of noodles and carrots rolling about like clothes in a slimy dryer. Each bolus was short-lived. Apparently he had not eaten for several months, and prior to that he had taken his meals in a cave with the cast from *The Night of the Living Dead*. I tried to banish these unkind thoughts, but he continued eating with a great smacking, and once he belched, ejecting some small food item onto his front. Eventually he noticed me. He lifted his coffee cup and leaned forward.

"The best coffee is in the other room," he whispered. "This isn't very hot."

The other retreatants ate in self-conscious silence, slowly raising and lowering their forks as if utensil and affixed appendage were being drawn up by some sleepy puppeteer. Eating felt painful and uncomfortable. We shot one another surreptitious glances, and if we happened to glance at the same time, we made polite nice-to-meet-you-sorry-to-intrude-on-your-private-space faces. Across the way the monks ate in self-absorbed rapture, as if they did this all the time, which, of course, they did. Abbot Francis sat at the center of the head table, leading this exercise in culinary contentment.

Here to plumb deep matters, I made a mental note to myself. An hour later, sitting with Abbot Francis in his office, I unashamedly sacrificed my mother-in-law as an example.

Abbot Francis nodded thoughtfully.

"It's true, a lot of people have a hard time eating in silence," he said. "Your mother-in-law is probably a social animal, an interpersonal person, so she can't imagine another form of communication besides conversation. But there are many forms of communication. I forget the exact percentage, but some people say that eighty percent of our communication is body language."

He moved tactfully, and rightfully, into the third person.

"A lot of times you communicate with people so that they'll communicate back, so that you'll feel important, when really you're important to begin with. A lot of people don't know that. There is also this constant need to be doing something. These days it's almost an addiction. People seem to feel that nothing is happening unless they're doing something. Sometimes people forget the being part of life, and that's what monastic life is about, our spirituality. It's not unique to us as monks. This is true of anyone who is on a spiritual journey. You focus on *who* you are not *what* you, or other people, are doing."

My unseemly dinner thoughts shouted in my ear.

"What goes through your mind while you're eating?" I asked.

"Oh, I just look at people, and I'm kind of observing them and loving them and praying for them. I don't need to be talking to everybody, you know? It's not necessary."

He paused. A clock ticked. By some miracle, I knew to stay silent.

"It's really important for people to develop the skill of silence, and the skill of contemplation, and the skill of attentive listening and observing what's around you."

He must have observed my discomfort.

"You know, we're very deeply Christian here," he continued, "but we're not hard-sell. We're not trying to add evangelical notches to our belt. We realize people come here for many different reasons. And the numbers are increasing. People are longing for some anchoring, for something that will enhance the meaning of their life."

He smiled warmly.

"Of course, we can't promise miracles, but solitude does seem to have a wonderful effect. It's hard to say what heals. Sometimes people are healed by the simple act of hospitality. Sometimes the prayers of the community are healing. Sometimes the environment itself heals people. The ancients, the ancient monks in particular, a lot of their spiritual teaching was observing nature and then giving examples from nature. I often recommend that to people. If they're going through trials or struggles and they can't pray, just go out and look at the beauty in nature."

Slowly I relaxed. Abbot Francis's office was pleasant and cozy. It also felt a bit like home. He was messy like me. His desk was buried in paper and books. There were letters, requisition forms, Rosary note cards, and books titled *Essential Monastic Wisdom* and *Sex, Ecology, Spirituality*—an interesting mix if ever there was one. The whole lot looked as if it had been delivered to his desktop by shovel. There wasn't a spare inch of empty space on the bookshelves either; books jutted off the edge like Father Eleutherius's tongue. Little magnetic signs were stuck to the filing cabinets. My personal favorite proclaimed, *Jesus Is Coming. Look Busy.*

The messy office and Abbot Francis's easy manner—he sat slouched in a big stuffed chair, as if we were old friends sharing intimacies after supper—made me feel at home.

Before I could stop it, my tongue betrayed me again.

"I'm surprised," I said.

"By what?"

Not by my lack of self-control.

"That monks can be so . . ."

"Human?"

Hoping to change the subject, I told him about my afternoon with Father Eleutherius.

"He was the best philosophy teacher I ever had. Did he tell you he goes out to the old folks' home?"

"Yes."

Abbot Francis chuckled.

"Most of them are twenty years younger than him. You know, the older fathers here, they're very industrious guys and very happy people. They don't have excessive luxuries, they're just very engaged in life. They read, and they think, and they converse, and they pray, and they're silent. They have an inner life too. It's an inner life of 'I have meaning and purpose in my life just because I am.'"

This was precisely what Father Eleutherius had told me that afternoon, though he had framed it differently. He had said he simply tried to be the best teacher and priest he could possibly be, and he was happy.

"So the secret to happiness is to do your best?" I had asked Father Eleutherius, possibly stating the obvious.

My question had produced a fevered fit of finger poking, *and* he had stuck out his tongue. Then he had quieted.

"I could be very miserable," he had said. "I cannot see. I cannot walk. We see often the whole aspect of our life. We miss the gifts. I am blind. Wrong. I cannot walk. Wrong. But I am still alive. Right. I can still preach. I can still hear confession. I can still teach."

Abbot Francis said, "Did he tell you about his garden?"

"Yes."

"Have you seen it?"

"Not yet."

"You should go see it."

I walked back to my cabin in the dark, along the edge of the pond. Below, through the chapel windows, I saw several monks praying in the chapel, but I barely glanced at them. I preferred to look at the moonlight, dappling the dark water.

The following morning I attended the 7:30 A.M. service in the chapel. The monks were there, and about two dozen parishioners, who had appeared possibly from nearby Pearblossom and Valyermo. There was chanting and silent prayer. Now and again a monk blew his nose boisterously, the sound like a goose honking. Someone read some scripture. But mostly I enjoyed how the birdsong fell into the silences.

After the service I caught up with Father Eleutherius as he and his walker made their methodical way up the drive to breakfast.

Abbot Francis was there too. He smiled at me. I smiled back, but said nothing. The Grand Silence was still in effect.

Abbot Francis said, "Father, you are like those powerful Belgian horses."

Apparently Saint Benedict's rules could be mildly bent.

Father Eleutherius looked up from his labors.

"Do you know what they did? They pulled the beer!"

He paused, tottering slightly. The drive was steep. For a

moment I thought he might fall backward. I took his arm. At least I think I did; it was hard to tell with all the down.

Abbot Francis said, "You should keep walking, Father. It's steep here."

Father Eleutherius lowered his head to his walker, but not before smiling.

"Always it is 'Come on, come on.' I move slowly, but I move. It is what I do to survive."

He made his way into the dining hall. Taking my own seat, I watched him. Bathed in soft morning light, he ate his porridge alone with his memories. During the course of the silent breakfast I discovered one irrefutable truth: monks make terrific porridge.

After breakfast I walked to Father Eleutherius's garden. Here, skeletal and white, were the Lombardi poplars. They, too, rose high into the sky; even in their leafless and emaciated state they gathered protectively about the sequoia at their center. A smaller pine huddled against the sequoia.

Already the desert's harsh light bathed the Abbey, but it did not reach the shade beneath the pines. Winter's rains had left the grass lush and soft, so I did what any contemplative seeker should. I stretched out in the grass and stared up into the pine-smothered boughs of the sequoia. They ascended like stairs. I remembered a pine tree in my grandmother's backyard. When the wind moved through its boughs, it made the same soothing distant sea sound, but I was a small boy then and so cared less for the tree's soothing song than for its obvious gift. The perfectly spaced limbs allowed me to climb up, up, up until I balanced on the uppermost limb, the one that barely took my weight, so high that I looked down on the neighboring rooftops far below. As the years passed, I was unable to ascend to those heights; strangely the uppermost limbs no longer supported my weight. I imagined Father Eleutherius, young and strong-limbed, striding across the grass, the finger-thin sapling in his hand. What a trick life plays on us, turning us old.

When I caught up with Father Eleutherius, walking to lunch, I fairly jerked him around.

"I saw your tree, Father!"

He regarded me just as I had hoped he would.

"Ah! You saw the sequoia! The big tree! I plant it small. I told you."

"What is the other tree, Father?"

"An incense cedar. I plant a pine tree there too, but the pine tree died while I was gone. People did not pay attention."

Tree lovers both, this turned us momentarily sad.

"I hope they will continue to water the sequoia," Father Eleutherius said after a few beats. "It will be an even bigger sequoia. People will be amazed. They will say, 'How is it here?'"

He and his walker began to clack forward again.

"I am glad you love the tree," he said.

I found myself drawn to both the cemetery and Father Eleutherius's tree glen. Over the next few days I traveled back and forth between them. In these two places you might see metaphor—death and life—but I must confess my visits were not entirely about contemplation. I was still driven by the worldly urge to be doing something, and hiking filled that need.

Plus it was beautiful out in the desert. One evening I hiked up to the cemetery. Instead of stopping I continued down a dirt road that pushed on through the rock and shrubs. Eventually I was stopped by a wire fence, so I turned and walked along it. The fence separated me from private property; down the sloping hill I could see a house fronted by tilled, empty fields.

The sun was setting, the sky already purpling. This last light touched the snow on the mountains, ladling soft pinks alongside the mild purples. The blanket of delicate colors did not strike me as an ending. It was more like a bridge, a very private bridge, for tomorrow these silent hills would again be privy to another quiet sunset. To the east, a dirt road rose into the foothills, a winding road that would have pleased Father Eleutherius very much.

I watched the road dissolve into darkness. The fields followed. The mountains went last, the snow returning the last of the day's light. I felt the wind absently, tugging at me gently with small child fingers. I stood for a long time. A bell from the monastery chimed. Only then did I realize I was praying.

My contact with my fellow retreatants was spare, but interesting. One morning, during the silent breakfast, I watched the woman beside me fold the paper napkin in her lap into a very small square. She had long, lovely fingers, and she folded the napkin very, very tightly. At lunch, bolus man told me he wanted to become a monk. I had no answer for this, though I did wonder what the upper age limit was for Cotillion. Another day at lunch, the woman beside me said, "There's so much change in this world. I feel so insecure."

These encounters were brief. But one morning, after the Grand Silence ended, I visited with Anne and Marilyn in the guest lounge. Both women were grandmothers; both were experienced retreatants and keen observers of life. The only difference was that Anne seemed more certain of herself, at least in the environs of the Abbey, perhaps because she had served as an oblate at Saint Andrews for twenty-four years. I had noticed her immediately at my first meal, eating as comfortably as the monks.

When I said I still found silence strange and a trifle unsettling, Anne declared, "My husband decided that silence was possibly the wisest thing human beings could do. Good way to save a marriage. You get used to it if you come here enough."

Marilyn was a longtime seeker of solitude.

"When all of our kids were little, sometimes I'd lock myself in the bathroom just to get some peace and quiet. It didn't bother them much. They'd just line up and wait outside."

I gave a commiserating nod. Any parent knows that you can love someone with all your heart, and want them to shut up just as much.

Now that I had divulged one weakness, it was easier to confess others. The night before in my cabin I had tried to ponder deeply, and my mind popped up in more places than Elvis.

"Does anyone else have a hard time focusing?" I asked.

Anne gave me a knowing look.

"I think we spend our lives with the struggle. It's part of who we are."

I waited—maybe there was some oblate secret—but no additional help was forthcoming. I complimented Anne on her unself-conscious table manners.

"I just like to eat," she said. "How long are you staying?"

I had planned that out.

"I'm leaving so I can be home on Valentine's Day."

Anne's face tightened.

"I don't celebrate Valentine's Day anymore," she said. "My husband was an oblate. He's buried here."

How often do our words do others any good?

Sometimes words are good. Solitude, I was coming to see, is only one tool in the path to discovery, albeit an important one. I was also thoroughly enjoying my conversations with Father Eleutherius and Abbot Francis. Sitting still and just listening was a surprising salve.

When I said this to Abbot Francis, he smiled.

"To have and to take time to talk with people is very important," he said. "A really deep conversation is like a sacrament, as far as I'm concerned."

At times, Abbot Francis and I talked for several hours. I doubt this was life-changing stuff for Abbot Francis; there was little I could tell him. But I noticed how he spoke openly of hurdles in his own life—at one point he had had serious misgivings about not having children. "Every once in a while I still have a little twinge of pain about it, but the older you get, the more you accept what you have and what you don't have." After a time he affectionately dubbed me "the man with all the questions."

The conversations, both with Abbot Francis and Father Eleutherius, provided me with comfort, but they also caused me pain. I realized that in twenty years of marriage I had never had a conversation like this with the woman I love. That life conspires against us is the feeblest excuse.

Father Eleutherius's voice chimed in my head.

Love her.

I had done that, but now there were things I meant to change.

"The great problem now," said Father Eleutherius one afternoon, "is technology."

We sat again in the sun. Now several days into my stay, I had learned to keep quiet, though it still took considerable restraint. I knew I would learn nothing from my own voice, but I also knew that the proper rejoinder would earn me a finger-poking or a tongue-jutting that would warm me for the rest of the day.

He continued on.

"We discover the marvel of atomic energy and we create Hiroshima and the problem of the disposal of nuclear waste. And that is humanity. It means we destroy ourselves. And now the sun."

By this I assumed he meant global warming, but I did not have time to ask.

He shook his head, and for once he did not smile.

"We are no longer the master of events," he said. "Events are mastering us. I am glad to be my age now, but I fear for my great-grandnephews. What will the world be fifty years from now? We do not look ahead."

I remembered a book I had seen on Abbot Francis's jumbled shelves. The book was separate from the others. It lay on its side, its title clear on its spine: *Journey of Faith*.

It was, no doubt, a religious tome, but faith takes many forms and we choose the one that concerns us. It may be something as small as a sequoia sapling; it may be something as grand as the world not coming to an end. Whatever it is, sometimes you just have to convince yourself to believe, and then labor to make it true.

The morning I left the monastery, Father Eleutherius was nowhere to be found. So I did the next best thing. I walked up to the garden and said goodbye to his tree.

The desert wind was blowing again. The boughs tossed themselves in a showy fashion that made me smile as Father Eleutherius had smiled, with a touch of happy madness.

When I am gone, people will come and say, "What is a sequoia doing in the desert?" And someone will say, "Oh, it was planted by a crazy man who did not know."

San Miguel Island

· · · ■ ■ · ·

ON MY TRIP OUT to San Miguel Island, seventy miles from Ventura Harbor by boat, a park service employee noted my camping gear and gave a knowing smile.

"San Miguel is the island that makes all the wind for the other islands," he said.

He didn't know I had already camped on Santa Rosa and Anacapa. On Santa Rosa the wind had sculpted my hair so that it pronged straight out, like Jack Nicholson's in *The Shining*. On Anacapa the wind had simply stomped the roof of my tent flat against my face.

"Yep." He nodded. "Should be a pleasant escape."

A few notes about San Miguel Island. It is the westernmost of all the Channel Islands. Look at a map of the Channel Islands and you will see that San Miguel rests alone beyond the protective lee of Point Conception, the crook of mainland that acts to protect, to a degree, the other Channel Islands from the full brunt of riotous seas and chill winds from the north. No such buffer for fourteen-square-mile San Miguel. The prevailing northwest wind blows steadily and it comes from far, far away.

As Ian Williams, the island ranger, pointed out, "The next piece of land to the north is the Kenai Peninsula in Alaska."

This is a daunting fetch. Even Jabba the Hutt could reach terminal velocity over such a distance. These northwesterly winds blow across cold water. One April a weather station on San Miguel registered a 17-degree windchill. Ian was uncertain as to the veracity of this reading, but he had used it in arguing for double-paned windows in the ranger station.

San Miguel Island is home to the earliest-known coastal site inhabited by humans in North America; archaeologists, carbon-dating remains from a camp on San Miguel, found it to be roughly 11,600 years old. Since then the Chumash Indians dwelled on the island. Sheep ranchers denuded it. The navy bombed it, honing their weaponry. Mariners soiled their pants as they tried, sometimes vainly, to avoid hitting it. Still it sits, Buddha-stoic, wind-raked, current-swept and fogbound, waiting for whatever comes next.

In short it was the perfect place for solitude, though few indulge in the opportunity.

"The reality is that most people will never see San Miguel," Ian told me the day I arrived. "We get maybe a hundred campers a year. It's just too much work to get here."

The island rangers and assorted other official personnel— this week's stint included Ian and two researchers—fly out to San Miguel in a six-seat Cessna aircraft, landing on a dirt airstrip fronting the ranger station. Nonofficial folks are consigned to boats, and it can be a long and heaving ride. And even for the park service folks, gazing down on green-faced boaters from on high, there is no guarantee; on plenty of occasions, inclement weather has made landing on San Miguel impossible. The public comes ashore in skiffs at Cuyler Harbor, the beach just down from the campground, though there is nothing resembling a harbor, not a pier, not a buoy, not a schlocky gift shop named Barnacle Bob's.

As Ian put it, "The Channel Islands aren't officially designated a wilderness area, but in many ways they're more of a wilderness area than designated wilderness areas. Even the almighty federal government can't come and go as it pleases."

I knew from the way Ian said it that he preferred it that way, and for this I liked him instantly. Like the other island rangers, Ian alternated a week on San Miguel with a week on the mainland. It did not take me long to figure out which stint he preferred. Nor was it hard to pinpoint his priorities. Many of his fellows spent a few years as island rangers, then used the job as a stepping-stone to promotions on the mainland. Ian was serving his sixteenth year as San Miguel's ranger, and he planned to step nowhere else.

Ian wasn't greatly seduced by civilization's enticements.

"The joy of being on an island is what it's about," he said. He gave a diffident shrug. "Besides, after a while you just sort of become fundamentally unemployable. Where else am I going to get a job working with sea lions and feeding foxes?"

Even for the rangers, with their planes and their gas ranges and their double-paned windows, life had not always been easy. It was true that Ian now resided in spiffy new quarters with all the amenities of home, but for twelve years he and the other rangers had lived in what amounted to a shipping crate.

Ian smiled.

"Fifty-dollar housing with a million-dollar view. Kind of cold and damp, but boy, when you woke up in the morning and looked outside, you felt like a frog on a pond."

Ian walked with me to the campsite, nine empty windbreaks, each fronted with a weathered picnic table. Ian, I would find, was not the sort to offer unsolicited advice, but he offered some now.

"If you've got a little extra rope, you can tie your tent down," he said. "We've had tents blow away, but we've never lost a picnic table."

The two of us stood quietly, looking across the Pacific

toward the distant hazy blue mountains of the mainland. The sky was overcast, the afternoon uncharacteristically still.

A sparrow's song rang harp-clear.

Ian said, "You don't have to go far to go far away."

No matter how many escapes I made to the islands, the psychology remained the same. As the trip approached, I grew excited. Then, as I gathered my supplies, I grew worried. How was I going to schlep all my gear to the campground, which, inevitably, was located at the end of a long, hernia-inducing climb? What if I forgot something? When he required supplies, Thoreau walked into Concord, or borrowed them from his mother, but if I forgot my sleeping bag, I would have to kill an animal, gut it, and crawl inside; this would prove a tight squeeze on San Miguel, where the largest animal is the housecat-size island fox. The night before my departures I was tormented by dreams in which I slept naked in rainstorms or watched as the Island Packers boat pulled away, the crew dancing about with my bags of marshmallows over their heads. Whatever the island, by the time I set foot on it, I was already lonely, mildly depressed, and clinging to my dignity by a tenuous thread. It took considerable willpower to not follow the rangers back to their cozy stations, tugging on their green sleeves. *Hey, you've got a spare couch, right? Can I stay with you? Huh? Huh?*

Fortunately, Ian preserved my dignity by leaving the campground quickly. I unpacked my gear. The sweetly singing sparrow departed. Two ink-black ravens alighted on the windbreak. They watched me silently with midnight eyes, now and again making odd cracking noises with their necks, a sound that brought to mind cattle rustlers or pirates testing the carrying capacity of a noose. Ravens are among the smartest of all birds. Researchers have shown that members of the genus *Corvus,* which includes both ravens and crows, can count and use rudimentary tools, placing them one evolutionary rung above entertainment reporters and contestants on *American Idol.* In one interesting study Japanese researchers observed city crows dropping nuts on city streets, where they were promptly cracked open by passing cars. The crows swooped down to pick up the meaty innards when the cars were stopped by a red light.

Cynics might see holes in this study—what Japanese car weighs enough to crack a nut?—but I only knew what I saw. The two ravens perched on my windbreak obviously knew how to fend for themselves; they were each the size of a dwarf.

Ian had warned me that the San Miguel ravens knew how to work a zipper. My new companions eyed my freeze-dried dinners as if deciding between vegetable lasagna and beef stroganoff.

I put everything in the campground food box. I tied down my tent so that the windbreak, the picnic table, and six inches of sod would have to peel away before it went airborne.

Having finished setting up camp, I stood listening. The silence made an actual humming, as if some great generator labored far beneath the earth's surface. The gray cloud ceiling sank lower. The wind started to blow. I looked at my watch. Six o'clock. I crawled into my sleeping bag and went to sleep, accompanied by the muted barking of distant sea lions.

The beauty of morning is you wake to a new day, and this one was bewitching. On Anacapa Island I had been entranced by the coreopsis. That was October, and the plants had been dormant. More to the point, they looked gray and dead, though, running my fingers along their thick stalklike boughs, I had felt the faint beat of life in their underlying suppleness.

Now it was March. Winter's rains had come. San Miguel's campground sits amid one of the largest stands of coreopsis on the Channel Islands. With the rain, the coreopsis had bloomed. I had inadvertently staked down my tent so that the open flap faced east. When I lifted my head, the sun was just rising into a clear sky. Not yet fully awake itself, it ladled sleepy, tender light on the coreopsis field, which smiled back a thousandfold, a sea of brilliant yellow flowers that blazed without any help from the sun. The coreopsis rose upon their same, strange Seuss-like foundation, only now, instead of withered strands, their stalks thrust forth pom-poms, thick and vivid green, each pom-pom bursting with flowers. En masse they swept eastward, a chest-high forest. It was the sort of scene a child would paint, and it was mine alone.

I had noted the coreopsis the day before, but if you are sufficiently depressed, Angelina Jolie looks like the cleaning lady. Now, quick as the sunrise, I dissolved into the next phase of my solitude evolution. There was nowhere else I wanted to be. The sun rose. Birds sang. My raven pair arrived for breakfast, the sun striking their glossy feathers so that they fairly glowed. I was in such good spirits that I considered setting a place at the picnic table for them, but on further consideration I deemed this unwise. I had already noted the mischievous cant of their heads. If they learned to use a spoon, they might scrape the dirt away from my tent stakes and so enjoy a great cackling guffaw as my tent soared over the coreopsis.

On the other Channel Islands you are free to wander off on your own, but San Miguel is different. Except for a few trails near the campground, you cannot hike anywhere without a ranger. These restrictions are the result of an agreement between the navy—which still holds title to the island—and the park service, which is agreeable in the matter. The park service, for its part, does not want the natural glories of San Miguel disturbed. The navy, from what I could surmise, does not want hikers vaporized. The navy, I read in one official account, "will not guarantee that there are no pieces of live ordnance still lying around the island."

So each day I set off with Ian to explore a different part of the island. San Miguel is not small. As I mentioned, it comprises fourteen square miles. The hike from the campground to Point Bennett, San Miguel's westernmost point, is fourteen miles roundtrip. Even short hikes on Miguel can be daunting.

The evening before, Ian had suggested we spend my first day hiking to Cardwell Point. I had already utilized the campground's sole pit toilet, and so noted the map posted there. Cardwell Point was only three miles from camp. At home in Ventura I had also perused the topographic map I had intended to bring; though standing outside the pit toilet, I saw the map in my mind's eye, still resting on my desk. No matter. A quick scan of the map had, in professional outdoorsman terms, revealed a blessed paucity of those tight-knit squiggly lines that indicate sheer climbs and, worse still in my mind, the potential for terrifying falls. The hike to Cardwell Point promised no more than a tepid decline to the water, and an equally comfortable incline on the way back.

Ian was taking me to see the elephant seals. Though it is impossible to measure such things—among other things, San Miguel has seen a remarkable comeback for the resident island fox—the island's greatest boon may be its role as a pinniped sanctuary, a haven for honking hordes of northern elephant seals, California sea lions, harbor seals, and northern fur seals, who arrive on San Miguel at various times of the year to scarf down fish and squid and bark, blare, breed, birth, belch, and bark some more. Nowhere in the world will you find more pinnipeds. Their gathering on San Miguel represents one of the largest congregations of wildlife in the world, and certainly one of the most vocal. The previous night, answering nature's call in the aptly named wee hours, I had heard their cries drifting up from the beach at Cuyler Harbor. From a distance the cacophony sounded like some insanely fun fraternity party to which I wasn't invited. During my time on the island, their noise waxed and waned, but, midday or midnight, it never ceased. It was as if they had discovered the party-goers' version of Viagra.

As we hiked toward Cardwell Point, Ian told me that the height of elephant seal breeding season had just passed. It had peaked, coincidentally, around Valentine's Day, and, as with any species, competition for mates had been heated.

"It gets pretty loud," said Ian, who was also distinguishing himself as a master of understatement. "There's a lot of vocalization, posturing, and bluff charging, but there's not a lot of actual fighting. A lot of it is settled at lower levels of force. Every once in a while the bulls will latch on to each other and give each other a few swats, but that's about it. It's so much saner than what humans do. We go straight for the trigger."

The hike to Cardwell Point was uneventful, but the beach was not. The cries of the elephant seals and sea lions reached us long before we reached the point, and when we topped a small rise and the beach came into view, it was immediately apparent that most everyone was exhausted from the Valentine's festivities.

The sandy beach formed an arrowhead whose blunted tip disappeared beneath emerald-green inshore waters that leaped and frothed in a dance of wave and wind. An inconceivable tonnage of blubber lay scattered across the beach, bratwurstlike forms that, for the most part, lay stone still, like a narcoleptic Sumo wrestling convention. Many of the blubbery forms were small, at least by elephant seal standards. The pups, for the most part, lay alone in the sand. Most of the females had already left the island. Now and again a pup lifted its head and issued a plaintive cry.

"Most of these elephant seal pups were born this winter," said Ian. "Some of the pups get kind of whiny when Mom leaves. They're kind of wondering where their free meal went. But by the time their mothers leave, they don't need the mother's milk anymore. They'll spend about two months just living off their own fat."

The mature males were easy to pick out. Their great noses wobbled like some grotesque blend of elephant trunk and turkey neck, while the rest of their bodies were roughly the size of a barn. For the most part the males also lay still, though now and again one lifted its head as if suddenly goosed and made a basso, throaty plocking noise not unlike a clogged sink finally draining. Certain males found additional energy reserves. Rising slightly, they inchwormed forward, their great bodies exhibiting a Jell-O–like rippling, as if their back ends, forced to wait for a beat to pursue forward momentum, were hurrying along to catch up. These bursts were short-lived. Like a plane nosing into a runway, the elephant seals abruptly followed their dangling proboscises back into the sand.

I watched a large male emerge from the water. Actually he let the waves push him. When the waves weren't pushing, he simply lay flat, surrounded by soupy froth. Elephant seals, like the males of other species, dispense their energy wisely. Lest you think them lazy, consider that a single alpha male may mate with fifty or more females, an enticing prospect turned exhausting.

Ian and I sat atop a bluff, eating lunch in a submissive hunch. If the males on the beach saw us, they might consider themselves challenged. Except for the sea lions and elephant seals the windswept beach was lonely, and sorely alluring.

"Big as they are, they're surprisingly quick," Ian said, munching on his sandwich.

Between bites he casually informed me that, though most of the females were gone, many of the males remained randy. Now and again the randiest attempted to mate with a pup, a sometimes deadly pairing.

Ian said nothing more, but I did not miss the implication. If the males didn't regard me as a threat, they might regard me as a beau.

We looked across a deep blue expanse toward the emptiness of Santa Rosa Island.

Ian spoke quietly.

"It's hard to believe that all this happens so close to civilization."

The wind shoved at me, its cold biting my cheeks. Down on the beach the elephant seals lay as if sunbathing at Saint-Tropez. Crouched on the bluff, my skinny, goose-pimply frame encased in long underwear and down, it occurred to me yet again how our achievements, while impressive, blind us to the fact we remain feebly adapted to the rawer world. The elephant seals and sea lions on the beach below us came and went as they pleased. Humans arrived only when the weather gods smiled. The current population dichotomy of San Miguel highlighted this. Pinnipeds, in the thousands; humankind, Ian, two field researchers, and me.

Some might call Cardwell Point a lonely beach, but it wasn't lonely at all. It was a springboard for a new generation.

The wind bit even colder when we turned for home. At first I noted this absently. In short order, I realized the wind was blowing directly in our faces. I leaned forward slightly, assuming a more aerodynamic bent, but now again a gust stood me upright, and once my baseball cap flew off my head, whirly-gigging twenty yards before falling into the shin-high grass, which, in turn, ran in a visible river back toward Cardwell Point.

I tried to adopt a cheery attitude—the sky was a lovely blue, outdone only by the purple-flowered lupine on the gently rolling hillsides—but the incessant wind turned me peevish. How far *was* it back to the campsite? It felt like we had already been hiking for an hour. Was Ian lost? How the hell could *that* happen? The man had been stationed on the island for *sixteen* years, for chrissakes; it was like forgetting your way to the bathroom in your own home. The thick grass along the hillsides continued to ripple as if the earth itself had turned liquid, and alongside the trail, shrubby bushes jerked about madly, as if each experiencing their own joyous orgasm.

Though forty-seven and sporting a reddish beard lightly touched by gray, Ian still reminded me of a small boy. Maybe it was his reddish hair, but he bore a vague resemblance to Opie, or, if you've never seen *The Andy Griffith Show,* then Ron Howard with hair. At Cardwell Point he had even unwrapped a white-bread sandwich.

As we hiked, he seemed to grow younger and younger. He walked much faster than a forty-seven-year-old should, and since he was behind me, I had to do the same to keep him from hiking right up and over my back. I walked faster. He walked faster. I had the distinct impression he was herding me back to camp. He probably had filet mignon defrosting on the counter. Despite the wind, I began sweating profusely. I wanted to kick the orgiastic bushes and Ian too.

At one point the trail dipped mercifully into a small ravine. It was as if someone had suddenly thrown a switch. Ian used the blessed respite from whopping to speak.

"Like they say," he opined cheerily, "it's three miles down to Cardwell Point and thirty miles back."

I tried not to bare my teeth.

"Is this wind normal?"

"This is par for the course."

Ian was already lifting one foot and then the other, the universal hiking signal for moving on. Unfortunately I was still standing in front of him, and the ravine was too narrow to step aside and allow him the lead. He was clever as a sheep dog too.

That evening I ate lasagna from a bag and watched the world go dark. The gloaming came on as discreetly as dawn had arrived. Nature feels no need to beat her chest. Twilight deepened, but a spectral glow remained. The sea of yellow coreopsis flowers seemed to throw back the light of the departed sun, but the bushes still stood silently before the falling night, like a respectful crowd. As it grew darker, the world lost the sharp edges of reality. In the distance the peaks of Santa Rosa Island flattened; close at hand the coreopsis dissolved so that lollipop bushes heavy with lemon drops could indeed exist. In the darkness, lovers become who you want them to be. At the very last the blackest sky bent down and kissed the earth.

How often do we stand outside and watch darkness fall? Not often enough.

Across the black water, the lights of Santa Barbara glowed feebly. I thought of something Ian had said about the elephant seals. When I mentioned how I liked that their battles rarely ended fatally, Ian had said that the strategy made sense. If the alpha males killed each other off, the gene pool would be left to the weak.

Standing beneath the stars, I thought of the crosses on the beach in Santa Barbara, the young and the virile killed before they could advance the cause of our species, leaving behind the old and the infirm. War is a subjective argument, a matter of outlook, and politics and strident speeches for and against. But humming beneath the clamor is an unassailable fact that cares nothing for debate. Pinnipeds understand natural selection, even if we don't.

Should you be lucky enough to visit San Miguel—along with the elephant seals and sea lions and beating winds and ocean vistas—you will see the last remnants of a life once shared by Herbert and Elizabeth Lester, also known as the king and queen of San Miguel. The Lesters, and their two young daughters, Marianne and Betsy, lived on San Miguel from 1930 until 1942, and theirs is as sweet a love song as you'll hear.

The remains of the sheep ranch they operated sit just up the hill from the campground. They rest at the edge of a rise that faces toward the mainland, a view, to borrow Ian's poetic phrase, which surely pleased all the frogs at the pond. All that's left of the ranch building is a jumbled pile of bricks that was once a chimney, two basement-looking structures that likely served as rainwater cisterns, and several rust-encrusted sinks the Lesters pulled from the staterooms of a wrecked ship. On an island, this is known as hardware from heaven.

From 1930 until 1942, through the Great Depression and on, the Lesters ran a sheep operation, shipping wool and mutton to the mainland. What they did is less important than who they were. If you read *The Legendary King of San Miguel*, it won't take you long to discern the kind of folks the Lesters were. The book is written by Elizabeth Lester—Elise to her friends—and you need read no more than a page to discover that Elise Lester is a wonderful writer with a keen sense of humor, and that the husband she depicts—honestly and forthrightly, in all his glory and warts—was the love of her life.

Herbert Lester was an adventurer, a Hemingway character brought to life, a collector of rare guns, a compulsive recorder of everything and anything, a lover of béarnaise sauce, a man who brought home and tended sick and abandoned field mice. As Elise writes, he was "as delighted when his pet field mouse had babies out in the shed . . . as when he learned we were to have our first child."

The book is filled with wonderful stories of island life, and I read them on the island, sometimes sitting near the remains of the chimney so that, now and then, I might glance up and enjoy the Lesters' view. The Lesters became quite famous, their lives glamorized in magazine and newspaper articles of the time, though Herbie, as he was better known, garnered most of the reporters' ink, leading Elise to write, "Apparently there was not going to be enough room on the tiny isle of San Miguel for a Queen, much less progeny." The Lesters received fan mail and requests for grains of sand. Once, they received a letter from an elderly pensioner in the Midwest, who asked if he might come live with their family so that he would not die lonely and alone.

Island life was hard—though there was love, often there wasn't much else—but it was the life both the Lesters wanted, a life far outside the mainstream. According to Elise, her husband told her he came to San Miguel to escape "from the shallowness of civilization and its incessant and inconsequential demands—particularly the horrors of the drug store lunch."

Thoreau said basically the same thing, though, as always, he phrased it in more flowery terms.

"How watchful we must be to keep the crystal well that we are made of, clear!—that it be not made turbid by our contact with the world," he wrote in an October 1853 journal entry.

I read *The Legendary King of San Miguel* in bits and snatches, up on the ridge beside the last of their ranch house, at the campground picnic table, the ravens reading over my shoulder, in the grass among the coreopsis. As I read, I came to like Elise and Herbie Lester very much. Herbie rescued the very birds that ravaged their vegetable garden. Presented with the gift of a new rifle, he slept with it, permanently staining the bedsheets with lubricating oil. He performed primitive surgery on a friend's nasty wound, applying a woolsack sewing needle to the patient and a fair share of liquor to the patient and himself. Elise recorded it all with humorous, hard-bitten honesty.

One afternoon Ian and I hiked to Harris Point on San Miguel's north side. I had not finished the book yet, but Elise had already provided intimations of its end. On a flat rise on the way to Harris Point we passed a scattering of shells, their bleached insides gleaming ivory white.

"A group from the University of Oregon ran a date on a mussel shell from that camp and it dated about seven thousand one hundred years old," Ian said.

Ian did not dwell in the past, but he understood it.

He smiled.

"Minus the windbreak, this was a campsite like yours once upon a time. This is the same breeze that they felt, the same smells, the same sounds. You don't have to imagine much to share the same touchstones that they did. Archaeologists figured this island supported a population of about one hundred back in prehistoric times. Which is about the number of campers we get today."

This side of the island seemed wilder and more elemental; the wind beat, the waves beat, a peregrine falcon circled overhead. Nearing Harris Point, Ian pointed out Castle Rock, an offshore hummock around which the sea fairly boiled. The tiny island is a favored haul-out for northern fur seals. Apparently this species of pinniped usurped the aggressive gene. On Castle Rock pinniped researchers move about the beach in what amounts to an enclosed box on wheels so that the fur seals won't chew their legs off.

On the final stretch to Harris Point, Simonton Cove swung into view. I have spent a lifetime exploring beaches, from Alaska to Australia, and I have seen some beauties. Simonton Cove took a backseat to none of them. Far below us, the broad beach ran in a great and empty scimitar arc. Off the beach enormous breakers curled over casually, detonating, at this distance, without a sound. The beach was backed by sandstone and shale cliffs, not sheer, but eroded by time and gradually sloped, and great rivers of white sand, driven toward the island's interior by prevailing onshore winds, ran up every gully and ravine, probing inland like skeletal fingers.

Loveliest of all, the breaking waves threw up a gauzy mist. The winds swept this mist over the beach and up along the ridgelines, blurring everything slightly so that the whole scene assumed an ethereal air, something not quite of this world.

It was stunning. I wanted to sit and stare down at it, but Ian had something else to show me.

We hiked another half mile. At the last we climbed a steep slope of loose rock. The wind held its breath. When we reached the summit, it blasted us with Kenai Peninsula cold.

Ian sat down. We couldn't go any farther. Just off our toes the cliffs fell straight down to a seething cove far below. Large waves swept into the cove, and the wind that didn't blast directly into our faces ran up the cliff face before doing so.

Ian smiled contentedly.

"This is the way all trails should end," he said. "You're sitting on Lester Point. This was Herbert Lester's favorite spot on the island. It's also where he killed himself."

That night I would finish Elise's book.

Ian nodded toward a sloping hillside about a half mile behind us.

"He was buried back there in 1942. Elizabeth is buried there too. Their daughter, Marianne, was buried there just a few years ago. The headstones have just melded into the coreopsis."

Actually, if you knew where to look, Marianne's headstone was clearly visible, a thumbnail of white amid the coreopsis.

Ian said, "*A place where I can lay my head, and rest and think and dream and love. No other place is there like this, in other lands or up above.*"

He looked at me.

"It's on Marianne's headstone. She wrote it when she was thirteen. She was a wonderful poet."

I knew this already, just as I knew that Herbert Lester shot himself because he feared that his failing health would make him a burden to his family. His wife had recounted his end in the same straightforward yet poetic manner she had recounted everything else. The date was June 18, the year 1942. Elise was busy ushering the two Lester girls through their last day of school. Her husband appeared and asked for some paper to write a note. Distracted, Elise handed him a piece of paper and he disappeared. He returned and kissed his wife and daughters. "I'll be going out to gather wood," he'd said. "Don't worry if I'm late for dinner." Like any wife, Elise Lester lent her husband half an ear.

They found him in his favorite spot, a grassy swale where he often went to sit and meditate harking to the sound of the wind.

Elise wrote this long after her husband was gone. Immediately after he shot himself, she was occupied with packing up a life and moving herself and her daughters to the mainland. She never remarried.

On paper their love story ended badly, but in truth it did not end, for the truest love stories never really do. On December 4, 1981, a helicopter flew a thirty-pound sack of concrete, water, buckets, flowers, a marble headstone, and the cremated remains of Elizabeth Sherman Lester to San Miguel so that Elise could again rest beside her husband.

Ian looked up toward the visible headstone. The wind beat past us.

"It's not really a place we hike to," he said.

I said, "It's OK. I'd prefer to leave them in peace."

Ian nodded.

"If you can't be alone out here, where can you be alone?" he said.

After a moment, he added, "It's really an enchantingly beautiful place. I can see why he would have liked it out here."

The two of us were silent for a time.

Ian turned to me.

"Have you ever been to Walden Pond?"

"No," I said.

"I worked in Boston for a while. I went to see it. It wasn't really what I expected. You could hear traffic."

Ian looked down into the cove.

"This is where he should have come," he said.

That night I lay in my sleeping bag, listening. The wind carried the sounds of the sea lions on the beach at Cuyler Harbor. There were barks and cries, and gibbonlike whoops.

Quiet allows memories to flood in. I once had an uncle, Dwight McCain. Uncle Dwight is long dead, but when he was alive he had a magical touch with animals and children—so you know what kind of man he was. I was one of those children, and I loved visiting him at his apple orchard in the Maryland countryside.

He also ran a boarding kennel; maybe apple orchards weren't profitable enough—as a ten-year-old you don't concern yourself with such tangents. One of my most vivid memories was rising before dawn to feed the dogs. Uncle Dwight had great bins filled with dried dog food, and we'd scoop it out and mix it with water in buckets in his kitchen, and when we finally pushed the screen door open, the dogs heard the creak a half mile away. They sent up a raucous barking that filled the night.

Lying in my sleeping bag, my memory seamlessly melded a gap of forty years: I walked again in the dark beside my stooped and kindly uncle, carrying smelly buckets of dog food while the dogs yipped and howled. It's wrong to ascribe our emotions to animals, but I don't care. Those dogs sounded as if they were stupid-silly with the sheer joy of simply being alive. Here on San Miguel, listening to whatever member of pinniped was yelping and yowling, I was convinced they coursed with the very same thrill. And, tucked warmly and mildly malodorously in my sleeping bag (there is no running water on San Miguel, at least not for campers), I felt my own rising joy. It was the barking of Uncle Dwight's dogs, it was the frog chorus in the stream beside the campground on Santa Rosa, it was the whooping hoots of the gibbons we visited regularly when Cullen and Graham were little, Kathy and I trotting after our small sons as they fairly sprinted through our local zoo. It was—unapologetic anthropomorphism here—the joy of life. *This is my time, my brief minute to shine, and I am going to fill it with sixty seconds of self-absorbed noise.*

In the dark tent, thoughts bouncing between past and present, I felt awash in delight, and when I stepped outside the tent, a shooting star flared across the sky, winking out so quickly that beginning and end nearly joined, tidily underscoring the beauty and brevity of our song.

Solitude is hard on some and easy on others. Ian had lots of stories. One of my favorites involved a cherubic gray-haired Russian émigré who showed up unannounced at the ranger station early one Sunday morning in his socks. *Is this the mainland?*

Peter Ivanov could be forgiven his confusion. He, and his twenty-four-foot sailboat *The Makai,* struck the east side of Harris Point in pitch darkness. With no idea where he was, Peter somehow nimbly leaped to shore and trudged through the dark, turning here and there on the trail as if he had been leading guided hikes on San Miguel all his life. And so he arrived at the ranger station.

As Ian would slowly learn, Peter was a novice sailor. Somebody had given him the boat. He had borrowed money from a brother with which he bought a new Honda outboard motor and a generator, but felt he did not have enough leftover cash for a GPS or a nautical chart. Sailing from San Francisco to San Diego, he simply kept the mainland to his left. But on the return trip, keeping the mainland on his right did not erase other hazards, such as a fourteen-square-mile rock.

I admired Peter's can-do spirit. I wouldn't have hired him to pilot a water taxi, but I would have picked him to be beside me in a life-threatening jam. Ian was astounded by the man's luck. Alone, without help or a clue, he had taken just the right steps to see himself to the station and safety.

"He should have gone back to the mainland and bought a lottery ticket," Ian said.

Being alone on an island was not easy for others. The San Miguel ranger station houses a series of log books dating back to 1977. Paging through one of the earliest log books, I found an entry written by a volunteer who had come out to the island for a week to perform some service for the park. What service she performed was not clear. What was clear was that her imagination had run away with her. Her logbook entry began with a detailed account of how she had placed the key to her crude accommodations on a pole. (Perhaps a flagpole? Again, she wasn't clear.) But when she returned at the end of the day, the key was gone. She managed to wedge her way inside, and so was spared nights of being raked by wind and cold, but she lay awake anyway, imagining everyone from Freddy Krueger to pasty-faced Avon ladies rattling outside the door.

How can you enjoy the peace and quiet when weird things happen, she wrote. *I should never have watched all those stupid horror movies when I was a kid—you know the type, about ghosts and goblins and crazy, lunatic, homicidal maniacs?*

It didn't take much reading between the lines to realize it had been a long week. I imagined the ravens watching her stagger away on the day she left, waiting as if for a traffic light, before letting themselves in with the key.

The woman's fears, of course, were, well, lunatic. Freddy Krueger doesn't know how to sail. It's true, Avon ladies are both indefatigable and industrious; they might have constructed a boat out of lipstick and rouge. But really, the woman had simply been the victim of an undisciplined mind. Life is full of unexpected surprises, and there is a psychological term for people who are unable to adjust: silly scaredy-cats.

That night, eating dinner at camp, I sat so that the windbreak was against my back. When I stepped outside in the middle of the night, I took only a few steps from the tent. Why should I go farther? The whole campground was my own private loo. When the entire horizon lit up in a sudden flashbulb *pop,* I confess I don't recall if I pushed aside the tent flap or plunged through the side of the tent. I lay inside the tent, pitch-black now; no doubt the drooling aliens were ably utilizing the cover of darkness to sneak up on me. For some reason I had to pee again; for an equally inexplicable reason my body refused to allow my bladder to go outside.

The next day when I casually mentioned the light to Ian, he said, "Probably a squid boat down in Cuyler Harbor. They use really bright lights to attract the squid."

Life is full of surprises.

During my stay on the island I saw other wild glories. Ian led me out to Point Bennett, a desolate outcropping of white beach and dark rock, where we knelt behind a rise in the dunes and snooped on yet another sprawling pinniped gathering, and also glimpsed the spouts of gray whales.

It was a beautiful day, bright sun and blessedly little wind, the sandy beach yet another haven of reprieve and contentment.

Like Cardwell Point, the beach at Point Bennett was also populated with a mix of sea lions and elephant seals, and far up in the dry sand, Ian pointed out some northern fur seals too.

Most of the elephant seals and sea lions were down near the water's edge, and the longer I watched them, the more they assumed human characteristics. The male elephant seals made their slow, rippling way through the crowd like distinguished gendarmes. The juvenile sea lions swaggered along the water's edge like strutting teens. And—my personal favorite—out in the waves the dark forms of small pups played as if no one was watching. For a time I amused myself by watching a female elephant seal rebuff the advances of a mildly amorous male. Inch-worming close, he would drape an enormous proprietary flipper over her. In response she would use her own flippers to douse him with sand before moving away. This repeated itself at least a half-dozen times. Oddly, it brought to mind several of my own early courtships.

It was a beach scene reminiscent of the Jersey Shore or Coney Island, a mass of life swaying to nature's urges. Of course pinnipeds are nothing like us, but the thought was entertaining, and I am easily amused.

All that life sprawled on the beach was encouraging too, and truth be told, these blubbery forms littering the water's edge were only the tip of the iceberg. Point Bennnet, like Cardwell Point, had already largely emptied. Some twenty-five thousand sea lion pups had been born on San Miguel during the summer just past, Ian said. Performing simple extrapolation, pinniped researchers figured on twenty-five thousand moms, and at least twenty-five thousand males and juveniles during the breeding season. Seventy-five thousand sea lions, in rough sum; never mind the other three species of pinnipeds.

"It's wonderful to think of so much life in one place," I said, and I meant it with all my heart.

"Yep," said Ian. "It's a population that would seed some California cities."

It was immensely reassuring to see that such places still exist, though mildly disconcerting to think that one day, quite possibly, they may be all that survives. Back at home newspapers were stacking up in our living room, their headlines trumpeting diminishing fossil fuels, thickening ozone layers, and psychopathic despots wielding nuclear arms.

Several days earlier I had asked Ian how the island was recovering after a long history of assault by man. San Miguel, Ian told me, was very gradually returning to itself.

The thought made him smile.

"Like they say, nature bats last," he said

Looking out on the beach at Point Bennett, awash in wilderness, I thought of the bushes and vines smothering Herbert

Lester's ruins. It is quite possible that one day great hordes of sea lions may loll on the beach at Coney Island, watching with liquid-eyed disinterest as ravens poke curiously at the skeletal remnants of amusement rides.

Of course mankind, ever adaptable, may survive for millennia. But whatever time we have left, we should spend it well, which is why, on a sun-kissed morning, I found my way to the small, birdshit-stained cross that honors the Spanish explorer Juan Cabrillo, who may or may not be buried on San Miguel Island.

If you follow such things, Cabrillo has more final resting places than Jimmy Hoffa, and historians debate this ad nauseum. Frankly I didn't care if Cabrillo was buried under my tent. I was just grateful that his monument on San Miguel forced the park service to maintain a small clearing among the coreopsis, a clearing big enough to comfortably accommodate anyone who chooses to stretch out in the grass and stare up at the sky.

I had a friend once, an older woman recently claimed by cancer, who owned a large parcel of land adjacent to her home. A conga line of developers had offered her astronomical sums for the land, but always she refused to sell. I don't know what she told them, but I know what she told me. She kept the land so that children had a place to lie on their backs and look up at the sky.

Indeed, and why not adults as well? Why is it so hard for us to simply stop for a moment? We are not so important— the world will continue grinding on—but I guarantee you, the seemingly idle moments you steal will be immeasurably gratifying. Still on the fence? Let me tell you this. Lying in the grass is sinfully pleasant, as pleasurable as, well, other sins you'll have to imagine.

When I stretched out under the sun, the world returned to me. The sky looks bigger when you're on your back, and bluer too, and since it was spring and the winter rains had been heavy, the cool, spongy ground pushed against me with a hint of fecund promise. Turning my head to the side, I saw tiny purple flowers, still as paintings, just off my nose. Towering above these flowers, tawny blades of grass, nudged by the faint breeze, bobbed about like a fickle crowd. Closing my eyes, I heard the beat of a raven's wings like book pages turning, the zipper-quick whine of a passing bee, the shy skirt-rustle of wind through the coreopsis, and the muted roar of the sea. Doing nothing is accomplishing much.

I might have dozed, I don't know, but when I opened my eyes, the ravens still circled overhead, soaring upon the breeze with the same effort I had expended in opening my eyes.

Watching the ravens, I recalled a poem I had once read. The poem was written by Robert Penn Warren. One of America's greatest writers and poets, Warren was something of a naturalist too. As a boy he had wandered through the woods of Tennessee and Kentucky, catching snakes, listening to geese honk northward, and, I have no doubt, lying on his back too. He might not have known it, but he was also cultivating the skills that would make him a great poet.

I wish I could tell you I remembered Warren's poem verbatim, but my memory does not stretch much farther than a four-item grocery list. But I know how to look things up, and when I returned to the mainland two days later, I did precisely that.

The poem is called "Mortal Limit." It begins with Warren watching a hawk. *It rose from coniferous darkness, past gray jags / Of mercilessness, past whiteness, into the gloaming* . . .

How the poem continues matters greatly, but not to my point: Robert Penn Warren lived, as much as possible, like a man lying on his back in the grass. Warren had a gift for poetry; poetry, in turn, bestowed a gift on Warren. For a moment he saw the world clearly, as it was meant to be seen. Poetry, Warren once said, was "a way of existing meaningfully as much of your time as possible. And that's never much."

Thoreau understood this, and I'm betting Herbert and Elizabeth Lester did too. Sitting at my desk, writing this, I see in my mind the stand of coreopsis that hides their graves. I see, too, the cliffs sloping down to Simonton Cove, the great waves throwing up their mist, the wind palming that mist and ushering it inland, up and along the dune ridgelines in a foggy skein, causing the sandy spines to waver miragelike, as if the island itself is lifting away into the sky.

Life lifts away too, sometimes, as in Herbert Lester's case, quickly. Making it all the more important to see things clearly, and, like the pinnipeds of San Miguel, make hay while the sun and moon shine.

Almost Famous

. . ■ ■ . .

THERE IS NO SILENCE on Hollywood Boulevard. The clumps of twenty-something girls in tight miniskirts; the purple-haired skateboarders; the "Goths," dressed in black, faces powdered pale as vampires; the rappers hawking their soon-to-be-famous CDs; the break-dancers throwing elbows, knees, and, now and again, punches; the gaudy marquee lights of the El Capitan Theatre blazing in midday—being noticed here is about brazen clamor.

Outside Grauman's Chinese Theatre, and along the sidewalk that passes in front of the shopping-dining-and-entertainment complex known as the Hollywood & Highland Center (home to the Kodak Theatre, which is, in turn, home to the Academy Awards), standing literally atop the stars who have already made it—Kevin Costner, Harrison Ford, Britney Spears, Johnny Depp—a small legion of street characters work the tourists. Elmo, Sponge Bob, Darth Vader, Marilyn Monroe, Freddy Krueger, the Tin Man, Dorothy, Batman, and a host of other imitators and crusaders vie for attention and dollars. The characters pose for a picture with you or your loved ones. If you wish, you tip them. The commerce is straightforward. Still, many of the tourists don't get it, or they pretend not to.

Here you have street hustle at its finest. It has to be.

And so, standing upon the sidewalk spot for which he has fought, James Hill is as audacious as the character he plays: the eye-shadowed, goateed, hip-swaying, dreadlock-dangling charismatic and cocksure Captain Jack Sparrow, of the comedy-adventure films *Pirates of the Caribbean* (masterfully embodied in the films by actor Johnny Depp).

"Hey!" calls James. "You need my picture! I need your money! Savvy?"

A girl walks up. Girls are good. At twenty-six years old, James doesn't fail to noticed that she has blue eyes and curves a pirate could swim in.

"Johnny Depp?" she asks.

"Yes, my love?"

"Can you move? I'm trying to get a picture of Harrison Ford's star."

There are many things to admire about James Hill. Perhaps foremost, like the hero of *Pirates of the Caribbean*, he is indefatigably undaunted in his quest.

The girl still stands in front of him, snapping Harrison Ford's star on the Hollywood Walk of Fame, but she has already vanished from James's world. A boy of five has stopped, wrought bug-eyed by Captain Jack, bandanna'd, bejeweled, and dark-booted, armed with cutlass and flintlock pistol and the unmistakable air of a man willing to shoulder both reward and risk.

"You, sir! You need my picture! I need your father's wallet!"

Like the rest of his body, James Hill's hands are always working, beckoning, pointing, brandishing a flintlock pistol. In one motion the hands remove a small pump, fill a red balloon, and with a rapid-fire series of squeaks transform said balloon into a sausagelike sword, extended to the boy.

The boy takes the sword, and the father is hooked. Captain

Jack and the boy pose together, Captain Jack swashbuckling and flamboyant, the boy holding the sausage sword limply, still mildly stunned.

Dad takes the pictures with his cell phone and reaches for his wallet.

"How much?"

"Fifty dollars."

The man smiles wearily.

"Twenty?" says James. "Ten?"

The man opens his wallet, fingers through bills. James cranes forward.

"I'll take the five."

The man's fingers pause.

Captain Jack smiles down at the mute boy.

"I think he's going to do it."

The man hands over the five.

For a brief instant, Captain Jack falls away. James thrusts both arms overhead. Even here, amid the din of traffic and commerce, his shout turns heads.

"Yeessssss!"

The bill is added to the already fist-size roll, mostly ones, tidily smoothed first, for James is fastidious, and then stashed in the leather pouch dangling at Captain Jack's side.

James turns to me and raises one dark eyebrow.

"Everything's not all about money. But everything's about money."

The real truth, as explained by James Hill in a quieter moment, is slightly more involved but equally clear-cut. It's not so much the money that interests him, it's what money brings. Money brings power and recognition (power alone, says James, is useless if no one knows who you are), and power and recognition allow for unfettered creativity; the films, the scripts, the acting that, in the end—and James must believe in this end with all his heart—will bring James full circle to the comforts that plenty of money brings. No more living in the street, no more standing on your feet for twelve hours plus, no more gnawing worry, no more people stiffing you or giving you the finger, no more combat, mental and sometimes physical, with the other hustlers, no more snipers (tourists who take pictures from a distance and slink away), no more games.

Well, maybe more games, but that's fine because James Hill can play games with the best of them.

The sun beats down. The sidewalk in front of the Hollywood & Highland Center is dark charcoal terrazzo. By mid-afternoon the heat wafts up like baked desert.

James scans the passing flood of humanity. The boy and his father, not yet ten yards down-current, are forgotten now too. In pursuit of a dream there is no coming about.

James calls out to no one and everyone. "Come here! You need my picture! I need your money!"

Bring me that horizon. So said Captain Jack Sparrow.

People *are* discovered here in Hollywood, but many of them pay some dues first. Not far from Hollywood & Highland, Brad Pitt danced in front of a fast-food joint in a chicken suit. He also delivered refrigerators and chauffeured strippers in limos, but when the Hollywood tour guides tell Pitt's story, it's the dancing chicken they mention because this makes the tourists laugh.

James knows the chicken story. It doesn't make him laugh.

"He did the same thing I'm doing," says James. "Sleeping on couches, broke-ass poor. All the money went to film."

All the money goes to film. This is James's mantra, though what exactly he means by it and his actual plan for breaking into the acting business are not perfectly clear. Nevertheless, he follows this philosophy very nearly to the last worn bill. In pursuit of his dreams James is taking a substantial risk. James doesn't sleep on couches. He sleeps on the street. The money he makes each day, with the exception of a few dollars for food, balloons, and other small sundries, does all go "to film." Specifically, it all goes to a man named Ash Tray who, in James's mind, is the one who will soon remove them both from the street. Ash Tray, when he isn't acting, plays buckets in the Metro subway station just down the block from where James hustles. You can see the big M, marking the station's entrance, from James's spot on the sidewalk.

It gets a little strange and, I'll be honest, at times a little hard to believe. But in the time I spent with James Hill, he was, if anything, utterly forthright. When I first took a deep breath and stepped out of the crowd to ask him if I might spend time with him, he looked at me for a long moment and then asked me for money. Because I understand dreams as well as any of us do, I eventually gave it to him.

I also confess that I came to admire and like James. People have coveted fame—and the power, riches, glamour, and as-sorted other puff that accompanies near-universal recognition—since humankind's first self-aware and acquisitive heartbeat. In our current times it seems we have reached near madness in our obsession with fame, with questionable journalism ("TOM CRUISE BUILDING BACKYARD SPACESHIPS TO ESCAPE EARTH!") and questionable photojournalism ("LINDSAY LOHAN GOES BRALESS!") ruling the day. But the foundation of such things has been with us since gossip, and the whisper of entrancing possibility—why can't that be us walking down the red carpet?—were relayed via papyrus and singing minstrels.

Fame and fortune are beguiling sirens. Who doesn't want a taste? You can see it in the way Grauman's Chinese Theatre, the Hollywood Walk of Fame, and the Kodak Theatre draw the tour-ists like some black whirlpool. You hear it clearly in the words of the street characters, telling you about their upcoming audition or the screenplay they wrote that "just missed"; and you hear it in the voices of the tour guides, saying they're working on a movie score and that this is only a temporary job.

It whispers more subtly in the way the young girls pose on the staircase rising up to the Kodak Theatre, their arms thrown wide while their friends snap pictures and laugh. And more subtly still, in the way many go briefly quiet, smiles and facades for a moment falling as they bend to look at the bronze sidewalk stars, which, if the sun hits them just right, shine gold light back into their downturned faces. *What if?*

Much of the world hungers for fame. Here's the difference between much of the world and James. He is willing to work for it.

Don't let the frozen smiles and the incessant glad-handing of Elmo and Sponge Bob fool you: the sidewalk in front of the Hollywood & Highland Center is tough enough to set Cookie Monster bawling. The meek and the quiet are summarily eaten. There are only so many tourists and so many dollars, and you are up against not one but three Batmans, the stiletto-heeled Catwoman, the bantering Joker, and Marilyn Monroe's feminine charms. The tourists must thread a gauntlet of superheroes, cartoon characters, mock movie stars, and costumed characters of unknown but attention-getting pedigree. There's a muscled man clad only in a loin cloth, a leggy policewoman with handcuffs at the ready. Distinguish yourself or perish.

It is a world of Darwinian one-upmanship, not unlike the elephant seals' mating wars on San Miguel, only instead of the hostile charges being bluffs, here they are real. Weeks before I visited Hollywood & Highland, I read in the newspaper that Chewbacca had head-butted a tour guide. The tour guide, who claimed he was attacked while coming to the aid of tourists whom Chewbacca was harassing for money, told the reporter he merely asked Chewbacca to leave the tourists alone. Miraculously, after years of guttural grumblings and growls, Chewbacca found his tongue. Shouting "Nobody tells *this* Wookiee what to do," he took off his mask and applied his forehead to the tour guide's. Since this was Hollywood, Superman promptly called producers from *Jimmy Kimmel Live,* which was taping just across the street. A cameraman got footage of Chewbacca being led away by police officers. In an unrelated altercation, Batman was also led away in cuffs, but this didn't stop him from kicking out the window of a patrol car. *Biff! Bang! **%%$#! Ka-Pow!*

The passersby aren't all finishing-school graduates either. The street characters are stiffed, shoved, cursed, groped, and propositioned. Apparently there are those who find the temptation of a one-night stand with Supergirl or Mr. Incredible titillating. One afternoon I hear shouting. Turning, I see a man on the sidewalk, darting back and forth, waving his hands in front of Anakin Skywalker's face (Anakin is the central character of the *Star Wars* franchise). I had noticed Anakin earlier, standing alone near the curb in a hooded brown cloak, looking young and shy and out of place.

Now Anakin looks frightened. The man keeps jumping at him, making strange karate motions and shouting obscenities. People have gathered quickly, as people do. Some of the other street characters group themselves about Anakin. When push comes to shove, they look out for their own, but only the rashest are willing to actually tangle with the public and risk fines and possible prison time. Plus, the recent actions of Chewbacca and Batman have put all the street characters at risk. It is always possible the city will legislate them off the sidewalk. For many of the street characters this would be worse than a ban on Lycra.

The man jumps back and forth, cursing in Anakin's face.

"Please," says Anakin.

I want to take Anakin's lightsaber and run the man through myself.

Finally the man storms off. Anakin puts up his hood, and the world moves on.

The bold and the brash suffer too. James was kicked in the stomach by a break-dancer for protesting about the dancers setting up in front of him. You don't make money when people don't see you. James did not strike back.

"I just wanted them to talk to me," James explains. "I wanted to tell them that they couldn't just come in and push me out. I don't like fighting." Lest you think him noble, in the next breath he says, "This has happened like seven times. The first time one of the dancers accidentally kicked me. I know it was an accident, but I kicked him back. One of the last times they tried to set up in front of me, I broke a bottle on the sidewalk."

James turns and spits into the street. He is forthright in his disdain too.

"When the break-dancers came, all these other characters left. They were chickenshit. I was the only one who stayed and fought for this space. It's mine now. I don't like fighting, but I'll do it, mental or physical, if I have to."

But it isn't the potential for violence that makes this sidewalk tough. Most of the street characters and the tourists are well behaved, the commerce of the sidewalk carried out with smiles and polite thank-yous. The hardest part is less visible. But find your way to the hidden corners of the Hollywood & Highland Center, away from the crowded courtyards and the shiny eateries, and you'll see Spiderman step from a service elevator, his mask off, face sagging beneath a shock of rumpled gray hair. You'll see Supergirl—pretty, blond, and beaming on the sidewalk—slumped in a chair outside a pizzeria without a smile for anyone. Look closely at Elmo's hands and you will see that the bedraggled fur is threadbare.

The other street characters come and go. Barring the unforeseen, James Hill is on the sidewalk seven days a week, ten, twelve, and fourteen hours a day.

"Lady! You need my picture! I need your money!"

James Hill is unrelenting on many fronts.

During my visits I often saw the other street characters talking together, three Batmen hobnobbing with the Joker, Catwoman in rapt discussion with Elmo, Freddy Krueger (the undead serial killer from *Nightmare on Elm Street*) discussing the day's tips with *Halloween*'s butcher-knife-wielding Michael Myers. Mostly, James keeps his distance. You don't make money if you're talking. There are other reasons James usually stands alone. He was friends with some of the other characters, but the friendships soured. Some of the characters think he's crass, always shouting about money. Many think he's a fool, giving almost all his money to a man he hardly knows. James doesn't like negativity. Now he stands on his patch of sidewalk mostly alone.

He's not hiding anything.

"Talk to the other characters," he advises. "See what they say. 'This guy's trouble.' 'He's on drugs.' 'He drinks a lot.' 'He's crazy.' 'He's homeless.'" He gives a winsome smile. "Now, that last part is true."

James will talk, but he never stops watching. Now he watches a family walking down the sidewalk, a boy and a girl, maybe six and eight, trailing mom and dad by a step. James already has two balloon swords at the ready, tucked inside a waist sash against his back. He pulls out the swords and a rascal's smile.

"Here, children. You need swords. Without swords you might get held up by pirates!"

Children are without guile or wallets. They smile brightly and take the swords and scamper after mom and dad, who studiously ignore the exchange.

James growls after them, "Arrrrrrrr," which is his standard response when folks pass without stopping.

His mind, like his hands, is always working. He picks up his last thought.

"I couldn't be out here ten to fourteen hours a day doing speed," he says. He gives a scofflaw's grin that would make Johnny Depp proud. "It's true, sometimes I smoke a little weed or take a little drink, but what's the harm in that?"

James's story as he relayed it to me between hustles is but one of the innumerable variations on a very old theme. He came to California from Colorado when he was eighteen. His mother attempted suicide and, for reasons unexplained to me, this allowed him to leave. He lived for a time in nearby Santa Monica with an actual roof over his head and then gave up roofs altogether. He traveled homeless around Europe seeing the sights and then returned to Hollywood. He enrolled for a time at the Musicians Institute in Hollywood, taking guitar and voice lessons, but soon realized he was too far behind the curve to be Eric Clapton. Two and half years ago he arrived on the sidewalk in front of Hollywood & Highland. He played Chewbacca for a time ("Not the head-butting one"), and then assumed the role of Jack Sparrow.

"It couldn't be any other character," he states.

For a moment I think this is a soulful thing, the words of an actor consumed by his role.

"Playing him, I can live homeless. I can be dirty. In fact, that's what gives me an edge. Makes me look like a real pirate."

A juggernaut of Japanese girls moves giggling along the sidewalk. Sponge Bob squeaks something, but the girls ignore him. Darth Vader says goofily, "Feelin' good in Hollywood!" and they avoid him too. Now the skittish girls are picking up the pace, throwing glances at nefarious Captain Jack.

"Ladies!" says Captain Jack jauntily. "I need your money."

James turns his palms up. Jutting from torn gloves, his fingers beckon with a slow, spiderlike come-hither. The girls veer away. An eyebrow cocks up. James struts toward them with a perfectly executed effeminate swagger. He returns to his spot on the sidewalk, giggling girls in tow. They are already reaching for their purses. It is joy to watch anything done well.

Unlike some of his colleagues, James takes money from anybody.

"Some of these guys get mad at me," he says. "I'll take money from kids, the disabled, the elderly. If you're on your deathbed, give me money. Why not? It doesn't hurt to ask."

In the days I observe him, James does take money from everybody.

One afternoon Freddy Krueger, standing nearby atop a small bucket and sweeping his trademark metal-clawed hand at the passing tourists, drops a dollar. He steps down to pick it up.

I've been watching Freddy, and he's been having a bad day.

For several hours now people have been walking past him as if he's the Invisible Man. At one point he shouts out, "Next! Next in line! Don't rush!" Here again no one pays him any mind.

As he bends for the errant bill, the wind scoops it up and blows it toward James. Freddy takes several quick steps and snatches it up. There is anger in the movement.

"I'll take that dollar," James says with a smile.

"Fuck you," mutters Freddy, and thrusts it at him.

James takes it.

When he poses for pictures with the tourists, James is quick. Some of the other street characters talk to the tourists after the pictures. James charms them while the pictures are taken, but then he moves them along, often without subtlety.

"Arrrrrrrr. Go on, get out of here. You smell like dead fish!"

He pretends to be egalitarian in his merciless pursuit of cash, but watch carefully and you'll see exceptions. Two forty-something women, possibly sisters, take turns posing for pictures with James. They pay him. The sister in the wheelchair starts to leave, but James grabs the chair.

"Maybe I'll keep the pretty lady," he says with a salacious leer.

The woman flushes, and suddenly she is indeed pretty.

"I'm pushy with the money," he says after the women go. "But I still want them to leave happy."

James accepts quarters, dimes, nickels, and pennies, but he doesn't keep the coins. They go into a separate pouch. Sometimes he gives them to the panhandlers. Sometimes he just leaves them where he sleeps.

"Karma," he says, "comes back."

Other times he neglects karma. As soon as the sisters leave, he bestows balloon swords upon two small boys and engages them in swordplay. The parents watch, but I can see them already backing away. James trades a few whacks with the boys, then says, "Look! Kevin Costner!" The boys turn, and James stabs them both in the back. One boy is not mortally wounded. Spinning about, he gives James a resounding whack.

James scowls.

"Give me the sword, you brat."

To the uninitiated James is angry, but it's a better guess he is just moving a fruitless opportunity along. Either way, the boys and their parents depart quickly.

In the time I spend with him, not once do I see him lose his composure. When he is ignored, he merely growls "Arrrrrrrrr" and moves on. When he is stiffed, he does the same. Hour after hour he beams, beckons, cajoles, and cries out dandily. He hates this sidewalk.

"Originally I wanted to be an actor because I couldn't stand the thought of being in the same place every day," he says. Amusement briefly lights his face, then quickly fades. "I really can't stand being here every day, but it's getting me where I want to go."

His belief in Ash Tray is unshakable. This man Ash Tray must be something.

"My plan before I started hanging out with Ash Tray was the same as everyone else's: get a home, a cell phone, a car, and then start acting," James says. "Then I met Ash Tray and he said, 'You know what? Do the acting and live in the street.' Most people are just worried about making their rent. I don't worry about that anymore."

James sees this single-minded approach, and Ash Tray, as his way out.

"I don't want to be stuck here. Opportunities come once in a lifetime, maybe twice. This is my opportunity to get out of here and do something real."

Most of the time James seems to have absolute confidence in his chosen path.

"I have faith that the money I'm giving Ash Tray is going to a good thing, so eventually it will come back to me. My time will come. When all this is good and done and all the smoke has cleared, I'll be the one telling these people 'I told you so.'"

These people are not all convinced. A girl works a nearby

sunglasses kiosk. James knows her. She keeps his only bag of possessions while he works. They appear to be friends, though it is hard to tell. When James fails to charm yet another passing beauty—"Come here, love. You're going to want me once you have me."—she watches with amusement.

"They don't want you," Sunglasses Girl says.

Earlier James had told me exactly that. A homeless street hustler is not viewed as a prize mate, even in the short term.

"One day they'll all want me," he crows now.

"Or there'll be a day when you're totally wrong and you get hit by a bus," says Sunglasses Girl.

James gives this a moment's thoughtful consideration and then produces a flawless ruffian's grin. "That could happen too."

There's no telling what's over the horizon for any of us.

And, of course, it can be done. Proof pulses all about James, the Hollywood Walk of Fame stars at his feet, the celebrity handprints and footprints in front of Grauman's Theatre, the names of famous actors on the El Capitan Theatre marquee at his back, the two-story profiles of Russell Crowe and Leonardo DiCaprio on a billboard across the street.

One evening there is a movie premiere at Grauman's Theatre. The sidewalk in front of Grauman's is cordoned off. People press against the barricades. Gaudy lights go up. Red carpet is unfurled. Security guards in dark suits and sunglasses are everywhere, standing around looking beefy and threatening. It looks like an audition for undertakers. One dark-suited man struts about issuing overly loud directions into a headset.

From behind a barricade I watch this security guard. Beside me a girl holds up her cell phone. The man straightens as she takes his picture.

The scene reminds me of Antoine de Saint-Exupéry's philosophical book *The Little Prince*. At one point in the story the Little Prince visits a planet whose single inhabitant is a conceited man. The conceited man recognizes the Little Prince as, of course, an admirer. The first thing he does is teach the

Little Prince the one skill he needs to know: *clap your hands, one against the other.*

I walk back to where James stands and ask him about the premiere. Will the stars show up?

"Probably."

I tell James that the movie stars Mark Wahlberg.

"Matt Wahlberg will probably be here," he says.

"It's *Mark* Wahlberg."

"Oh."

"Do you see many movies?"

"I don't see any movies. I'm always here."

For two days James has answered nearly all my questions with monkish patience. Now he is unmistakably curt.

One day would he like to be the centerpiece of a premiere? He barely heeds the question.

"When it comes my time."

It takes me a moment to realize what has happened. The barricades are blocking off the sidewalk. The premiere is interfering with business. To reach the horizon, one must constantly stay the course.

If Mark Wahlberg does arrive, he will no doubt do so by limo. His feet will touch down on the sidewalk for a few minutes and then he will disappear inside.

James has been standing here for nine hours.

"Would you like something to eat?"

"I'd rather have the money."

A man as focused as James suffers no peace offering.

"You're amazing," I say. "I'm worn out."

James just looks at me.

I keep struggling to figure out James's specific goal, because each time I ask him, I get a different answer. He talks about writing scripts, he talks about making films, he talks about putting on street shows and working on comedy skits, he talks about acting, all of it between hailing pocketbooks and wallets.

Hoping to get things clear in my own mind, I am forced, once again, to adopt that most honorable of interviewing techniques, repeating oneself idiot-savant style.

"So do you hope to be an actor?" I blurt one afternoon.

James regards me as though I am missing the savant part. His face is hard.

"I don't hope to be, I'm going to be."

"I'm sorry I keep asking the same things," I say. "I'm just trying to figure things out."

His face softens. "I'm just trying to figure things out too." Speaking slowly, perhaps for my benefit but perhaps not, he adds, "This is what I have to do to make money. Then I pay that money for my own career."

As far as I can divine, there is very little career at the moment. There is Ash Tray, whose real name, James will tell me, is Ben Cherry, a real actor who, according to James, is about to take the world by storm, debuting two weeks from this October afternoon as the lead in a film called *Buckets*. James tells me he has a part in the film. Again he is honest.

"I play a tree. I covered myself with pine needles and leaves. It's just a snippet, but I need it for SAG. You have to get three parts, above work as an extra, to get a SAG card."

SAG is the Screen Actors Guild. James tells me you can also just pay up front for a SAG card, but I now know this is not James's style. *All the money goes to film.*

James tells me that Captain Jack's clothes are the only clothes he owns. Eighteenth-century pirate garb is not always conducive to twenty-first century life.

"What do you do if you go somewhere?" I ask.

He says it very slowly so I will get it. "I don't go anywhere. All I have is this."

James sleeps nearby, but not to shave time off his morning commute.

"I need to be ready when Ash Tray calls me with work."

On this sidewalk many wait to be discovered. James tells me

that most of the street characters are aspiring actors. Some, he says, like Superman, have gotten acting parts, though he doesn't see Superman becoming Brad Pitt any time soon.

"He has stuff going on but I don't really think he'll make it. He's not that great an actor."

The sidewalk is home to others hoping to make themselves known outside of film. A man wanders about, holding out headphones attached to a CD player. He approaches a man walking by.

"Listen to this."

"Bother someone else."

"I'll be famous!"

On the sidewalk I meet a poet and short-story writer/song-writer (many here seem to have more than one calling card) named Funwi Numfor. We meet when he also holds something out. It is a small white book, a collection of short stories, poems, and songs called *The Difference Is Me*.

"Please," he says. "Just read one. Only thirty seconds."

I read a poem carefully. It takes more than thirty seconds, but I know it took him more than thirty seconds to write. I buy Funwi's book for five dollars.

"It cost me two dollars to make it," he says apologetically.

Of course most people brush past when he holds out his book, but some do stop.

"I met Amy Winehouse's manager—you know, Winehouse, the singer. He read through some of my writing and said it was good. He gave me a number to call. Some of my poems could be songs."

No one stands still on this sidewalk for long. Funwi is no exception. He is already moving away, a new book in hand. I don't ask him if he called the number. I'm not even sure he wants to be a songwriter.

"I went to school for sound engineering," he says before he turns away. "I would like to get into movies."

Maybe everybody is just keeping several doors open.

■ ■   ■   ■   ■

A flood of tours depart from the Hollywood & Highland Center and one morning I take one, signing up for a tour of the stars' homes. Perhaps I'll get a glimpse of the life of fame, wealth, and power that James and many of his colleagues are doggedly pursuing.

To get the most out of this tour, I bring along Martin Turnbull, who is something of an expert on the matter of celebrity. Martin is Australian, but he knows Hollywood's history intimately enough to conduct historical walking tours for the respected Los Angeles Conservancy. He also does celebrity tours of his own, and he worked for a time as a tour guide at Universal Studios, watching people lose every shred of dignity at the mere sight of Jennifer Aniston and other actors from the TV show *Friends* eating lunch on the back lot.

This tour hits the ground running. In the first ten minutes we see the comedy club where Michael Richards (*Seinfeld*'s Kramer) was videotaped shouting expletives; Hyde Lounge, where Britney Spears was photographed without underwear; the restaurant where Marilyn Monroe and Joe DiMaggio had their first date; and, much to my joy, the actual chicken joint where Brad Pitt danced. It looks like a movie prop itself, grubby and sad. A street-scuffed man sits outside holding a cardboard sign. People carrying out greasy bags ignore him. It is not hard to imagine what kept Brad Pitt going. It is also not hard to imagine James giving the man the contents of his coin pouch.

After a time the tour bus turns off the main streets and begins winding through the perfectly coiffed environs of Beverly Hills and Bel Air. The sky is china blue. Grass, flowers, precisely culled shrubbery—it all fairly gleams in the sun. The landscaping reminds me of my father's dress shoes after he polished them on Saturday afternoons. The neighborhoods are manicured by Hispanic men in sun-bleached ball caps and rusted pickup trucks. They come, they buff, and they go.

Our tour guide is Christian Davis—he's already sold one

movie musical score—and he keeps up a constant banter. We pass Ringo Starr's house, where a friend of Christian's once saw a mattress being delivered; and Elvis's former home (or maybe he still lives there), where people still stop to scratch "I love you" on the wrought-iron gate. We pass the home of international soccer star David Beckham and his pop-music-star wife Victoria (aka Posh Spice), who, Christian informs us, recently received a Napa Valley winery for her birthday.

Martin is intrigued.

"How do you wrap that?"

Christian nods. "We've got to get to know these people," he says. "For my birthday, I just got a watch."

Enormous hedges proliferate in Beverly Hills and Bel Air. It's as if the Jolly Green Giant spilled Miracle-Gro. We pass Robin Williams's hedge, the hedge belonging to Tom Cruise and Katie Holmes, and the hedge Lindsay Lohan ran into while allegedly driving drunk, and perhaps even braless. Not infrequently we pass groups of people taking pictures of these hedges, for you cannot see the homes. More often we pass people clasping star maps and standing befuddled, looking a bit like Red Riding Hood lost in the woods, a fairly accurate metaphor if you think about it.

As we tour, my fellow passengers discuss the stars as if they know them, for in this cyber age the stars have few secrets.

That's Jennifer Aniston's house. She's building a tennis court for John Mayer.

Didn't they just break up?

Really? Gee, Jennifer just can't seem to keep a man.

There are star homes that aren't hidden behind hedges. Many of them look cold and empty, like mausoleums with pulled blinds.

The mansions and the manicured neighborhoods are seductive: no one here is worried about rent, but money and hedges and gift-wrapped wineries don't alter the workings of the human heart.

Martin tells me about a friend, Bob Molinari, who owns a Disney memorabilia store in Hollywood called Fantasies Come True. Michael Jackson used to come into the store, often after closing time. Bob and Michael would sit alone, talking quietly about Disney and Peter Pan. Michael, as you likely know, is big on Peter Pan. Bob treated Michael like just any other customer. Michael responded in kind.

"He would ask Bob for a discount," Martin tells me. "At first I'm thinking, *Why on earth would he ask for a special deal? He's got to be one of the richest men in the world.* Then I realized what was happening. Normal people ask for discounts and want a good deal. He was trying to be normal."

I wonder if Michael Jackson might also enjoy being hustled by James Hill, beckoned from the faceless sea of purses and wallets, relieved of a few dollars and discarded without thought. I wonder if James Hill will ever wish he was standing on this sidewalk again, tourists walking past as if he didn't exist.

Here is a snippet of what I read when I opened the sidewalk-poet's book:

> Those who have plenty, those who have nothing
> keep searching alike.

Likely there is no stopping the yearning, whatever the circumstances.

We are not alone in our dreams, and no path to a dream is more clogged than the path to fame on stage and screen. Diligence and hard work may be enough if you aspire to be a chemical engineer, but they guarantee nothing if you want to be an actor. Even talent is no guarantee, for there is enough of that waiting tables and dancing in chicken costumes. There are myriad intangibles.

One morning I visit a writer who has spent a lifetime writing biographies of Hollywood stars. He talks about various paths to fame, actors and actresses on the verge of desperation who, at the last, got their break. Several times he raises a cautionary finger and smiles. "You can't mention this, but [pick a famous actor/actress we all know] got their break because they slept with the director."

Here on the sidewalk radiating heat, James Hill's career isn't the only one hanging in the balance. He's not even the only Captain Jack Sparrow. At times as many as nine Jacks have clogged the sidewalk, sashaying about with their swaggers and their savvy. Sometimes it's *Pirates of the Caribbean* in a hall of mirrors.

James isn't even the best Captain Jack Sparrow. That honor, at least in my mind, goes to Jim Weringo. Jim dresses and plays the part of Captain Jack Sparrow so impeccably—right down to the sashes, rings, and play of the wrist just so—that there are times I am certain I am standing beside Johnny Depp. More than a few passersby stop to look: not the children, the adults. Now and again Jim addresses these gawkers by jerking his head back slightly, canting his head off to the side, and fixing them with a skeptical narrowing of his own shadowed eyes. It is frightening.

But Jim Weringo ("That's my stage name") is not Johnny Depp. Jim is thirty-nine. He has an apartment he pays for with several jobs. He works as a pirate impersonator, hired for office parties, birthday parties, street fairs, and pretty much anything where a pirate comes in handy. He also makes lavishly beautiful and properly authentic pirate outfits, which he stitches himself, largely by hand. He recently completed the sweeping seventeenth-century gown worn in *Pirates of the Caribbean* by the lovely Elizabeth Swann (portrayed in the films by actress Keira Knightley). Jim is a disciple of detail. It was a painstaking endeavor.

"I think I have an ulcer from making that thing," Jim tells me.

Jim comes to the sidewalk maybe a few times a month and for reasons that are different from James's.

"I have a little nobility out here," he says. "It's about the glamour and myth of Hollywood. I'm just doing my little bit to make Hollywood an exciting place. Really, there's nothing else to downtown Hollywood but this right here. The rest of the place is a dump."

Some of the tourists do not speak English; others, their English is broken. But popular culture is a powerful common denominator and most know Captain Jack Sparrow. An elderly man approaches Jim, smiling and making slight bows as he deferentially advances.

Jim bows grandly back.

"Good sir. Where are you from?"

The man processes this.

"China."

Jim produces a gold-toothed smile.

"Welcome to the end of the map in Hollywood."

Jim accepts tips readily enough—the money helps pay for the costumes and probably a little goes to rent—but he does not pursue the dollar with James's mercenary myopia.

"I always say, how would Johnny act? He wouldn't be asking for money."

On the day I am lucky enough to see him, Jim is inordinately kind and gracious to everyone, which, ironically or otherwise, actually sees him haul in the dollars as ably as James.

Unlike the other Captain Jack Sparrows, whom he spurns, James Hill makes space in his sidewalk square for Jim. Sometimes Jim wanders off, but for large blocks of time they stand together. It is a curious relationship. I never ask James why he lets Jim stand in his space, but, given James's primary aim, I suspect it does not hurt to have such an eye-catching Jack Sparrow immediately at hand. Jim, in turn, appears to tolerate James the way he would a younger brother. He quickly lets me know he has little respect for the way James conducts business.

Jim is indeed an ambassador. He engages the tourists in conversation. He often strikes numerous poses, allowing for three or four pictures to James's standard one or two. When the posing is complete, Jim tells the tourists to check their pictures and make sure they turned out. If not, he promises to pose again, no charge. All this palaver takes time. I see James chafing at the bit.

After a series of poses a man rummages through his wallet.

"Have you got change?" the man asks James.

"Change?" crows James with incredulity. "Just give me the hundred."

"I've got change," Jim says quietly.

After the man leaves, James leans toward me. With Jim but a stride away, he confides, "I don't know if you noticed, but Jim's a little bit more of a perfectionist. I'm not, but the way I reckon it, a real pirate wouldn't be posing for pictures at all."

A minute later Jim leans toward me and nods to James, who remains but a few feet away. "This guy's a little uncouth."

A boy comes up to Jim. He poses with Jim alone. James returns to lean into the last picture, leering and pointing his pistol at the boy's temple. The mother hands a dollar to Jim and holds out a dollar to James.

James points his pistol at Jim. "Give it to him. I came in late."

Jim dreams too, though I am not so sure if Jim's dreams have been nearly battered into surrender. Jim actually attended film school at the University of Texas in Austin. He has made films and written scripts. He has had close calls.

"I wrote a Batman script in '99. I really had people interested in it. That was my big hope. I've still got my underground stuff, but I've been sewing every day, making costumes. It's tough. I should be producing movies for HBO. I should have three hundred thousand dollars in the bank, a house, a girlfriend, Thanksgiving and Christmas. I don't have that."

James stands beside him. He calls out, "You, sir! You need my picture! I need your money! I'll also take those gold teeth!"

"I don't want to come out here and do the tip thing," Jim

continues. "I need to pay attention to the script thing. The dream is to be producing movies. When I was in Texas, people said, 'Dude, you're the next George Lucas.' And then you move out here and all you do is pay the damn landlord and keep the wolves from the door."

He smiles Jack Sparrow's sad and knowing smile.

"There's a joke. Someone said I'm the guy Hollywood doesn't want."

Jim has had his share of obstacles: sickness without insurance, a stolen car, his father's death.

"It's hard to keep ahead of the disasters," he says.

He shrugs.

"So you know what? I do things on my own. That's my spirit. But I'm stuck in the trenches. Sometimes you just can't win in this world. But I'm still here."

Sometimes the horizon stays where it is.

Eventually Jim leaves. The other characters also come and go, as if rising and sinking into the sidewalk. Now and again I slip into the cool innards of the Hollywood & Highland Center to escape the sun and the sameness. I see other characters inside, eating or just sitting at the tables outside the fast-food restaurants staring straight ahead, perhaps looking to a place beyond this. James stays out on the sidewalk, spiderlike fingers beckoning, drawing the world and its cash in.

One afternoon James does break for lunch, maybe because I'm buying. He orders a three-dollar Caribbean taco from Baja Hollywood Mexican Grill inside Hollywood & Highland. I have to press him to buy a drink. Caribbean tacos are not on Baja's menu. James is already famous. The guys behind the counter named the taco after him. He orders it almost every day.

James gets the taco to go. If he eats at the restaurant, people come up to him. We eat in a back stairwell on rust-brown metal steps, the unfinished cement like mold overhead. Before eating, James lies on his back and brings his knees to his chest.

"This is good for lower-back pain," he says.

James eats and talks at the same time, his words echoing. As soon as he finishes eating, he counts his money, pulling the roll from the pouch at his side. He is never shy about this. He displays the wad of cash freely on the sidewalk too.

I regard people's money as their own personal business, but in James's case I have to ask.

"How much do you make?"

"As much as I can," he says deftly. "But every day while I'm making what I'm making, the powerful people are making a whole lot more. They don't need my money. They don't need me. I don't have a special talent that they need. Yet."

Thumbing the last bill flat, he puts the roll in his pocket and stands.

"I'd better get going, sir," he says.

He has been calling me "sir" since we met. I know he forgot my name immediately. It's not important to him, and whether he knows my name is not important to me.

I leave with the first cool of evening, a smoggy yellow full moon climbing into the sky. It takes an hour to drive from Hollywood to Ventura. I eat dinner with my family. After dinner Cullen, Graham, and Kathy do their schoolwork. I do the dishes and catch up on the myriad things that always require catching up on. Kathy and I kiss the boys goodnight. I step outside to consult the stars. Eventually I crawl into bed, exhausted. In the darkness the digital clock glows ten thirty. James may still be on the sidewalk.

Closing my eyes, I hear the sound, the softest shuffling, like tissue-paper cards, James counting his money in the silent stairwell.

James is there each time I come, but Ash Tray is not. I never see him. Perhaps he is consumed with the movie business. I really hope so, because I want James, a man who works so hard, to have at least a whiff of a chance. On a half dozen different occasions I walk to the end of the block and down the stairs into the bowels of the train station where I hope Ash Tray sometimes plays his buckets. One afternoon as I walk down the steps, an odd wind, warm and robust, blows up from the bowels of the station. I want it to ferry the scent of hope, but it just carries trash and the faint sour smell of too many bodies.

It worries me that James is putting all his eggs in one basket. This worry is not alleviated by the one moment when I see him let down his guard. It is late in the afternoon. Maybe James is tired. Maybe a day's worth of questions has worn him down. Uncharacteristically his eyes hold mine.

"If I don't make it with my friend, I don't have a career," he says softly. There is no raffish smile. It occurs to me, not for the first time, that James may be the perfect actor. "If I can't make it with the most real person I ever met, how can I make it with anyone else?"

Before I leave, I ask him if he will be on the sidewalk tomorrow. He finishes transforming a balloon.

"Unless I get a call for a film."

James may not be popular with the other street characters, because he speaks his mind. Late one afternoon Marilyn Monroe appears on the sidewalk wearing a backless white evening dress. She is accompanied by a young girl, also dressed as Marilyn Monroe in a backless white evening dress. The girl looks about twelve, but it's hard to tell exactly, with all the makeup and the curly blond wig. The older Marilyn reviews several Marilynisms. Together they bend slightly, put their knees together, and pout, but the girl still has matchstick legs and big puppy feet in slippers.

James says loudly, "That's not a good choice for a little girl."

The girl looks stung.

"You should be Shirley Temple. Marilyn Monroe is not your character."

The older Marilyn starts to lead her charge away.

"Do you know who Marilyn Monroe was?" James shouts after them. "She was a drunk and a druggie. Not a good choice!"

"Mind your own business," says the elder Marilyn.

Everyone minded Marilyn's business, which is one of the undersides of fame. The real star-crossed Marilyn Monroe is buried not far from the Hollywood & Highland Center. I know this because Martin Turnbull took me to her grave. She is buried at Westwood Village Memorial Park. Westwood Village is a small cemetery, a postage-stamp oasis of quiet green tucked between L.A. high-rises and traffic-choked Wilshire Boulevard. George C. Scott is buried here alongside Burt Lancaster, Eve Arden, and Eva Gabor. Some stars are buried in the grass; others take their final rest among the walls of the crypts that border the north and east side of the cemetery.

Quiet places tell you something about fame too. Marilyn Monroe is buried in one of the walls; her crypt rests at chest height, just a small square inscribed "Marilyn Monroe 1926–1962." Martin and I stood before her grave. Coins lined the protruding edge of Marilyn's square, a mystical tribute of some kind left by fans. There were lipstick marks on the marble too. Above Marilyn, Richard F. Poncher rests. Richard's inscription reads, "To the man who gave us everything and more. You're one in a million, Freddie."

A professor specializing in culture and mass media recently opined, "We live in a culture where if it's not documented, it doesn't exist. And if you don't have people asking who you are, you're nobody."

So I asked Martin who Richard was, even though I knew he wouldn't know, and then we left.

I returned to Westwood Village Memorial Park another afternoon. The stars rested quietly. I made my way to Marilyn Monroe. Rummaging in my pocket, I found a coin and placed it on Richard Poncher's grave. On Wilshire Boulevard I drove beneath billboards spread with beautiful people advertising beautiful things. Their beauty made me happy.

Even in this age of clamor not everyone wants to be seen; some of the most beautiful things will forever remain a secret.

Some will frown on James Hill's aims. They will argue that if he applied his work ethic to some other enterprise, he would likely have a life of considerable comfort. But comfort comes in many forms, and if James Hill's aim is to be noticed beyond the sidewalk at Hollywood & Highland, to become moneyed, famous, and powerful by means and medium yet to be wholly determined, and possibly not even determined by him, who are we to label him foolish? Why not audacious? What, asks James, is wrong with a leap of faith?

And borrowing from the forthright pirate code of James Hill, the truth is that all of us desire at least a piece of James's dream. We all crave reassurance, the knowledge that a scrap of us will last beyond the flare of our life. For many, this assurance is called children. But there are certainly other means of reaching for a gossamer scrap of immortality. Perhaps this is why Michael Jackson forfeits the chance to ever have his bargaining taken seriously, why Father Eleutherius plants a tree, why James Hill embraces grinding monotony, why some put their thoughts to paper. It is a deep-seated fear, to be forgotten, and neither celebrities, nor monks, nor captains of their fate, nor writers are beyond it.

But we should also ask ourselves the question the Little Prince poses to the conceited man when the clapping is done: "I admire you, but what is there in that to interest you so much?"

Santa Barbara Island

. . ▪ ▪ . .

It is a difficult practice to master, but why dwell in the past or the future when dawn's tawny light touches butterflies chasing one another above the grass like children?

Thoreau watched the world from his cabin on Walden Pond. On Santa Barbara Island I had the researchers' bunkhouse on a cliff edge facing east, so each morning I stepped into darkness to sit on the patio and watch dawn's unfolding. I enjoyed the changing colors—the blast-furnace oranges and smoky reds upon the sky, the shy pinks ladled softly on the ocean—and the way shadows remained, as they do in life, so that the gliding pelicans resembled dark cutouts against the sun. There were sounds too, for it was often tomb-still at dawn, the subtlest hypnotic lullaby. Small waves swelled over rock outcroppings with a mother's whisper; the pelicans' measured wing beats made a rustle like a bag of sand lightly shaken. And when morning's light at last crawled over the edge of the sheer volcanic cliffs to spread over the island's thigh-high sea of brown grass, there were the butterflies, making hay while the wind held its breath.

Most of all I enjoyed what this dawn watch entailed: a languorous, patient exercise in detail, and a reminder of how life might be conducted—slowly, and with great focus, for there is no getting the moment back.

I found such languid observation easy on Santa Barbara Island, for there were no distractions. For most of my week I was completely alone, one square mile of volcanic rock and me. This solitude was a matter of geography and fortuitous circumstance. The southernmost island of Channel Islands National Park, Santa Barbara Island is largely absent from the world. It sits only thirty-eight miles off the coast of Los Angeles—draw a straight line from Long Beach—but it is little visited. Look to the east from the patio in front of the researchers' bunkhouse and, on a clear day, you can see Catalina Island twenty-four miles away; Catalina is where the mainland flocks, for it has time shares and golf courses and glass-bottom boats and expensive Italian restaurants where the waiters regard you with pity when you mispronounce *gnocchi*. By chamber-of-commerce standards, Santa Barbara Island offers nothing. When I arrived, it didn't even have much in the way of an arrival. Four months earlier, apartment-size waves had returned the park service's small landing dock to the sea. One could still come ashore by skiff, then make one's way gingerly across slick rocks, the process made the more interesting by the surrounding blurt and madcap shuffle of panicked sea lions tumbling into the water like teenagers still yanking up their pants. But this is not the sort of landing most visitors relish. Given these circumstances, the number of human visitors to Santa Barbara Island at this late-April juncture was expected to be: me. The park service saw no need for a ranger.

And so, for almost a week, I was in charge. The park service has a volunteer program in which those of able body and mind might lend a hand in a wide variety of duties. On the islands one might schlep supplies for a plant biologist, or notch gull counts for a seabird researcher, or simply walk the trails to keep them free of nesting birds. It is not wise to abandon an island entirely, a lesson the park service learned firsthand on Santa Barbara Island. Park facilities on Santa Barbara consist of a tiny enclave of buildings just up from the now-battered Landing Cove dock, a single low slash of building comprising the researchers' bunkhouse, which sleeps four, and the adjoining ranger's quarters, and just back from these living quarters, a small building that houses tools, equipment, and researchers' supplies. Down at the Landing Cove, another small structure holds additional gear. Once, after the passage of several months without human habitation, park service personnel returned to find pretty much everything—how to put this delicately?—covered in bird shit.

So the park service kindly saw to my transport to Santa Barbara Island via helicopter, where they picked up two seabird researchers who had spent the previous week on the island. Before they departed, Laurie Harvey, the senior researcher, shepherded me about the station, providing a whirlwind overview of important dos and don'ts: don't shower unless absolutely necessary, don't flush the toilet unless absolutely necessary (there is no natural water source on Santa Barbara Island; water is delivered in vast containers by park service boat), don't wait until you are bleeding to read the evacuation procedures posted on the bunkhouse wall, don't go into the ranger's quarters. Here is how the radio works, here is what you do if the solar-powered electrical system shuts down, here is how you assemble a Lamborghini from dental floss and a broken toothpick.

I put on my best intelligent-journalist face, pretending to absorb every detail.

Scientists are trained observers.

"It is a lot to remember," she said, fixing me with a keen look. "Just use your best judgment and be careful."

And with that they were gone, the helicopter rising in a swirl of grit and dust and banking away. For a few minutes the whopping of the blades hung in the air; the helicopter was absorbed by blue, and the cries of the birds returned.

Getting right to the point, Santa Barbara Island is the sea-bird island. Yes, there are house finches, horned larks, peregrine falcons, orange-crowned sparrows, barn owls, burrowing owls, and short-eared owls (the owls journey across from the main-land to dine upon the island's succulent deer mice). There are also the aforementioned deer mice, as well as sea lions, elephant seals, the island night lizard, native ground-dwelling beetles, and six endemic species of land snails.

But the seabirds reign. In various seasons the island's grassy uplands and plunging cliffs serve as nesting ground and haven for various species of seagull, California brown pelicans, black oystercatchers, ashy and black storm petrels, cormorants, and the largest known breeding colony of Xantus's murrelets in the world. Were it not for Santa Barbara and the rest of the Chan-nel Islands, there would be no seabirds in southern California.

We are not talking smatterings of birds. We are talking avian armies, Hunnish hordes of winged creatures that, in their sea-son, splatter the island with their presence and their latest meal. Alfred Hitchcock would have been set joyfully aquiver. I am not the first to make this connection. That evening, leafing through the park service logbook in the bunkhouse, I read the recently departed junior researcher's entry.

I had not missed how she had fairly clawed her way into the helicopter. Now I understood why.

It is my opinion that Hitchcock must have been present on Santa Barbara Island during gull nesting season when he was inspired to do The Birds—*obnoxious little buggers! Avoid at all costs!*

My own undergraduate degree in environmental science told me this was no coldly objective scientific notation. It of-fered no solution. It was more like the linchpin paragraph in a mystery novel. *They're outside the door. I have no time. The only way to avoid them is arrrrrgggggh . . . .*

I reached my own scientific conclusion that afternoon on my very first hike. The only way to avoid the gulls was to radio for the chopper. Santa Barbara Island has no trees. It is a fetching effect, for everywhere you look there is horizon. And from the nubs of my hiking boots to the edge of every horizon, I saw western gulls. They were everywhere, making their nesting preparations like overwrought and very, very loud nannies. The gulls abutting the trail fidgeted nervously as I approached, and then lifted off with raucous cries, milling over my head, throwing shadows and more concrete offerings on the grass about me.

There were great gatherings of California brown pelicans as well. I saw fledgling chicks too, white as snow; though not quite ready to fly, they beat their scrawny wings enthusiastically, rocking their puffball bodies about. The adults rocked over them, like the parents of most infants, sleeping on their feet.

Unlike the gulls, the pelicans exhibited a sort of Zen equanimity. Hiking about the island, I always did my best not to excite any of the resident birds, but gulls, I learned immediately, are followers. When a few rise and begin to shriek, the remainder in that particular ZIP code rise shrieking too, though it is my scientific surmise they have no clue why they have risen and joined in the squalling. In this they are not unlike many people. The pelicans, however, were far less excitable. Often I was able to walk quietly past their gathering spots without raising a single pelican into the sky. I also noticed that in many instances they nested away from the gulls. The pelicans had a habit of glancing toward the gull colonies and then raising their long beaks to the sky and clacking them pointedly, a posturing that resonated disdainful dismissal. *Good Lord, Muffy. Look at that absolute mess over there.*

But truth was I would become attached to the gulls, two gulls in particular, for Santa Barbara Island held beguiling memories for me. Kathy and I had celebrated our first wedding anniversary on the island, camping for two glorious nights. It was not paper products, but it was what we wanted, and now, back on the island, the memories enveloped me. Though it seemed impossible, twenty years had passed.

The island had not changed. It remained a single ridgeline

with rounded hills at either end (the island's high point, Signal Peak, reaches 635 feet) and grassy Serengeti-like slopes that swooped to the east and west. Everything was brown when I arrived. Spring's rains had come and gone; the grass crackled underfoot.

That first evening, I hiked to the ridgeline to watch the sun set. The sky was cloudless and vast as the sea. There is something instinctually soothing about being beneath a wide sky, as if this is where we were meant to be. Some skies also lift you off your feet, and this was one of them. On the other islands I had spent my first day wallowing in lonely self-pity. On Santa Barbara Island I was happy from the outset, content to be on my own.

But the world expects you to travel in twos. Perhaps with romance in mind, the park service had placed a wooden bench on the saddle of the ridge. I will not waste words. There is no better place to see a sunset. Following the serpentine trail to the ridge, I made my way to the bench, rousting two seagulls perched there. This pair rose silently, without any shrieking. For a moment I wondered if pelicans and gulls had found a way to crossbreed.

I sat on the bench. The wind had risen, as it would each evening. It blew hard and ragged, and, scraping along the steely scrim of the ocean's surface, it blew chill. But I had spent enough time on the islands now to know their moods. Though it was ostensibly spring, I wore long underwear, a down jacket, mittens, and a wool cap. Had some sturdy outdoorsman followed me up the path, no doubt he would have pinned me with a disdainful pelican glance. But the nearest human being was on Catalina Island. There was no one to impress.

Invariably sunsets bring to mind moments past, gold upon which you will never again lay a finger. As the sky turned dusky purple, I thought of my young bride. Love gone right bestows upon the graced recipient the deepest gratitude, for it is an immeasurable gift, and it elevates life to something beyond treasure. Sitting on the bench in the cold wind, I had only the vaguest inkling of where twenty years had gone, but I was certain that, for those twenty years, my wife had made life worth living.

The wind walloped. The sun sank into the sea. The world turned dark blue. I looked up. Overhead, the two gulls hovered, white undersides glowing in the twilight. They made no noise and their wingtips nearly touched.

Early each morning I was required to take a few simple weather readings—wind speed, the high and low temperature of the previous day, precipitation (pretty much zero), and the like. Then, at eight thirty sharp, the radio on the bunkhouse wall would crackle and the park service dispatcher would begin the process of checking in with each of the five islands: rangers on Anacapa, Santa Cruz, San Miguel, and Santa Rosa, and me.

Though the park service was very much interested in weather conditions, in my case in particular this early-morning transmission also assured the mainland that I had not fallen off a cliff or drowned in guano. No doubt they worry about all their volunteers, but I was certain they already had a special spot in their files for me. Having nearly deployed search and rescue on Santa Rosa Island, I suspected my propensity for wandering down the wrong path had not been forgotten. And even if you're the founder of Outward Bound, the park service takes safety very, very seriously. Back at park service headquarters in Ventura I had seen the sign taped to the wall of the dispatcher's office: "You may know where you are. And God may know where you are. But if Dispatch doesn't know where you are, you and God better be very good friends."

The other rangers were proven professionals. On the first morning, I recognized Josh's drawl from Anacapa, and Mark on Santa Rosa, and Ian on San Miguel. The familiar chime of their voices made me smile—I remembered Josh's kind dinner invitation, Mark's heartfelt "Thank God" crackling over the radio when I was finally located, and Ian saying softly with a smile, "Nature bats last"—but I was also mildly unnerved. It was like being asked to sing "Hey Jude" in front of the Beatles. And so each morning at eight twenty-five I began to pace back and forth in front of the radio, clearing my throat, sweating mildly, and wondering what embarrassing terms rhymed with *relative humidity*. Worse still, Santa Barbara gave the morning report first. I imagined the other rangers placing bets before my bleating voice washed over all the islands. *Yesterday's high was sixty-six, low was thirty-six, precipitation was zero, and I flushed the toilet twice in the ranger's quarters without thinking. Mother of God, just end it all now.*

On my first morning I gave a reasonable report. Then before I could stop myself, I blurted, "And it is a joy to be here."

There was a moment's silence. I imagined money changing hands. Then the dispatcher, a nice woman named Doretta, said, "I'm happy to hear that, Ken," and on Josh came, and the blows I imparted to my forehead were witnessed only by a fly crawling across the wall.

Along with monitoring the dawn and reporting the weather, each morning I also took it upon myself to water the small garden on the sloping cliff in front of the ranger's quarters. On paper it wasn't much of a garden, just a few dozen grayish plants, many of which looked as if they had been roundly stepped on. The plants were called silverlace and they were native to Santa Barbara Island, which meant that they huddled about the island in tiny pockets, fighting for their lives against a ruthless sea of nonnative invaders. Laurie had planted some silverlace on the sloping cliff. Between dos and don'ts, she had asked me to water them if I had the time.

I was drowning in time; besides, I liked the garden of silverlace as soon as I set eyes on it. I have always had a soft spot for the underdog. In my hikes about the island I had already seen tiny patches of silverlace here and there, cloistered like cowering villagers before a sea of advancing Huns. So, early each morning, in the soft smoky light of dawn, I secured a watering can from the equipment building and then made a dozen or so trips from the bunkhouse sink to the cliff face, where I walked from smushed plant to smushed plant, making my small contribution to island restoration. It felt good to see to the bedraggled, for they are the ones neglected in every society.

When I arrived to water the plants on the second morning, two gulls were perched on the cinderblock wall that protects the ranger's patio from the inquisitive, albeit rare, gaze of campers in the campsites a stone's heft away. Briefly I entertained the thought that these were the gulls from the previous evening's sunset come to visit, which of course was ridiculous, since the gull population of Santa Barbara Island numbered in the gazillions.

As I approached with my first watering can, one gull flew off. The second gull was larger, with a muscled chest The Rock would have envied. I had already noticed that most of the Santa Barbara gulls appeared to be in fighting trim, perhaps because they spent less time foraging in Kentucky Fried Chicken Dumpsters and more time plucking fish from the surrounding waters. Mr. Venice Beach lifted one leg like an Irish dancer readying to jig, but he did not fly off. As I passed, I spoke softly, commenting on the fine morning and assuring him he had nothing to fear. His dark beady eyes did not leave me, and he remained perched on one leg, but he stayed where he was.

The big gull watched each of my subsequent trips, his rotating head marking my passing, his raised leg marking his unease. By the sixth trip, the leg went down. On the ninth trip, his companion returned. They watched me together, heads turning in unison as if attending a tennis match.

I found their company pleasing and a tad flattering—was I truly so fascinating?—but for the most part I paid them little mind. I was focused on my watering and my surroundings. Let me be clear. I am no gardener. More to the point, I have always felt that an interest in gardening as an activity is a matter of timing, that time being right after you lose your teeth, and right before you lose your mind.

I know now I was wrong. Caring for the silverlace was immensely soothing, and it was made the more pleasurable by my breathtaking surroundings. The ocean sparkled with freshly risen sun. Flocks of gulls sat on the water like snowflakes refusing to melt. Pelicans soared. Far below, off a rocky outcropping, sea lions leaped from the water, their bodies curved in dark apostrophes. The cries and barks of their brethren, hauled out on the rocks of the Landing Cove, echoed in the air. And the garden faced east, toward the new day, as hopeful a positioning as any.

At first it was a patch of sagging silverlace, barely clinging to its rightful land. In a half-dozen trips to the sink, it became the loveliest garden in the world.

It is a fine thing to have a full day of nothing stretched before you. With that in mind, I took my time watering the garden, and so drew all the more pleasure from it.

It was also a fine thing to have the amenities of home at hand. I had enjoyed camping on the other islands, but let's be honest. If you could carry a refrigerator in a backpack, you would. On Santa Barbara it was wonderful to have a refrigerator, and a stove and a bed. It was comforting to know that I wouldn't return from a hike and find the whole lot blown into the sea. I remembered how, after a grit-blown week on Anacapa, I had wandered about Josh's quarters like a visitor from another planet, touching the soft couch, admiring the tidy line of spices in the space rack, and fairly kneeling before the glorious stillness produced when walls deflect a howling wind. Now I had a tile floor beneath my own feet, and a bunk bed on which to lay my sleeping bag, and a phone book I would never use. True, the ranger's quarters next door were a lot nicer, with an enormous TV and a cushy-looking couch—I wasn't allowed to go in, but no one said I couldn't peek through the window— but I was supremely content. There was even beer in the fridge, left there by a previous occupant. More than once I considered drinking it—it fairly called out to me—but I stayed my hand by conjuring up the vision of a drunken morning report in which I relayed not only the temperature but how it felt substantially cooler in the nude.

I also broke my rule about eschewing technology on the islands. On the other islands I had brought nothing; no computer, no iPod, no radio. But the Santa Barbara Island bunkhouse had wireless Internet, so I brought a laptop, mostly because I had been told that the Internet might provide the only reliable communication with the mainland. Before leaving, Laurie had advised that I also check in with someone at a prescribed time each night; for if I locked myself outside naked at eight thirty-two in the morning, it would be a long, cold twenty-four hours before anyone realized I was in need.

So each evening I sent an e-mail to Kathy, assuring her I was fine and omitting the part about how I had spent the better part of the afternoon lying in the grass observing how the wind blowing across its wheatlike tops made a hissing sound like the most delicate rain. A happy marriage is about communication, and not communicating too much. My wife's return e-mails went something like this: She had dropped off and picked up Cullen and Graham from surfing, skateboarding, soccer practice, friends' houses, and some half-dozen other locales. She had papers to mark, a test to take for her master's degree, and the dishes were piling up. There was no word from the plumber or Jimmy Hoffa. This was one day. When I had finished reading her e-mail, I thought, *That's where twenty years goes.*

I sat for a moment, hearing the clicking march of the second hand from the clock on the wall. I wrote back. I thanked her for all the things she did when I was home and when I was away. I told her how much I loved her, how the island brought back so many memories, how she walked beside me even when she wasn't beside me, and not just here on this island's trails. I told her she was allowed to resent me.

Fifteen minutes later I checked my e-mail again. Kathy had written back.

Are you warm? Do you have enough to eat?

I replied, *I have everything I need,* and then I walked outside to the patio.

The stars were out. As they had on every other island, they flooded the sky. To the south, Los Angeles produced a sooty glow.

I placed the computer on the picnic table. Technology serves its purpose. I found the song I wanted and clicked Play.

I don't like to dance in front of people. I possess the rhythm of a Hereford. I stood still for a moment, still pinioned by society's gaze, and then I smiled and slow-danced without a care, making small circles, though I wasn't alone.

Beneath the stars Nat King Cole sang "Unforgettable."

Of all the birds on Santa Barbara Island, the Xantus's murrelets are the most interesting (the strange name comes Xantus de Vesey, the Hungarian ornithologist who first identified them). I don't mean to offend the gulls and the pelicans, but we are familiar with their forms as well as their business. But the Xantus's murrelet, a tiny black and white bird belonging to the auk family, still presents the rarest of charms in this unearth-everything age. Two nights after their birth, the infant murrelets are called to the sea by their parents. Without hesitation or question they follow the call. Often this is no easy feat. On Santa Barbara Island many of the murrelets nest high up on the cliffs; waddling from the nest, the mini-murrelet plummets several hundred feet into the sea.

Later, this act was described to me by a biologist who had witnessed their leap of faith.

"They'll be hopping down the cliff and they'll be trying to follow their parents' calls," he said. "They've got great big feet, and they're like cotton balls, so they're not heavy, and their feet are kind of like parachutes. Sometimes they get stuck on a chollo (cactus), which is kind of sad, or a gull snatches them up, but most of them survive the fall just fine."

When they strike the water, they immediately know what to do; they dive and swim beneath the surface as well as any adult. After that, no one knows where they go or what they do. They simply disappear out to sea. Isn't that wonderful?

The murrelets were preparing their nests during my visit. At least that's what Laurie told me. She had pointed out several bushes, fast against the patio, that hid nests. More nests, she said, were coming.

"Make sure you close the bedroom blinds at night," Laurie said.

What? Were they going to going to line up outside the window and watch me change?

"They're attracted to light," said Laurie. "They'll fly into the glass."

So at night, not only did I pull the blind but I also left the light off in my room, and closed the bedroom door so that no light spilled into the room from the adjoining kitchen. Currently the Xantus's murrelet is officially classified as "vulnerable" by the International Union for the Conservation of Nature and Natural Resources, the global organization charged with classifying such things and producing oversize business cards. "Vulnerable" is not "endangered," but here is the asterisk: Xantus's murrelets were removed from the endangered list only because other auk species have become rarer. It would not do to wake in the morning and find a tiny pile of blunt-headed murrelets outside my window. I felt for them as I felt for the silverlace; a being small in this world, and woefully undernumbered.

As I hiked about the island, I searched for the murrelets in vain. It was true, I could have just nudged aside the bushes to look into the nests beside the patio, but this seemed invasive, not to mention heart-stopping to a bird the size of my palm. On many hikes I took binoculars. Finding a comfortable spot,

I sat and glassed the cliff faces for as long as an hour. I saw pelicans, and the sleek, oily black forms of cormorants, and several billion gulls, but I never spied the black-and-white form I sought. In the end, it seemed fitting.

As the days passed, I did observe something else. I sorely needed a shower. By my fourth day, hiking about the island had turned into sweaty work; the weather had turned unseasonably hot and the wind had gone still, so that the smell of perspiration and baking guano warred for control in my nostrils. I could now say that showering was absolutely necessary, but by my reckoning I had already dispersed several showers, and then some, upon my precious silverlace. I imagined the next group of park service employees checking on the water supplies and raising their eyebrows. I had an entire ocean at my disposal.

It is one thing to swim at a beach swarming with fellow bathers splashing and mentally undressing one another. It is another thing to swim alone, thirty-eight miles out at sea. Actually I wouldn't be alone, and it was my company who gave me pause.

On Santa Barbara Island there is one place to swim because, short of mimicking a murrelet, there is only one place where you can get to the water; a short, steep path that descends to the Landing Cove. And the Landing Cove, as I have said, is brimming with barking, honking sea lions.

I have made my life around the ocean, and, living in California, I have seen plenty of sea lions. In my home state their sausagelike forms are common; most often they are seen sprawled dozily atop one another along some shoreline, like orgy participants who have taken one too many Valium. Those sea lions that do move do so in a wobbly, ungainly fashion that is mildly amusing and endearing; it is not unlike watching someone who is fetchingly soused.

But in the water sea lions are another being entirely. I had observed this firsthand, in this very cove. Kathy and I had snorkeled with the sea lions. I had been mildly concerned then, for

I had not missed how the sea lions vectored through the water like amply fed darts, but I was Man, and Newly Married Man at that, and to remain onshore simpering was not possible. Plus on that particular afternoon there were other people in the water, and my hope was the same as everyone else's. If things went bad, they would go bad for someone else.

And so we had dipped our masks into the water. I watched as the first sea lion rushed at me, black eyes bulging. Even among the flood of bubbles created by my now-panicked exhalations, I could see his teeth bared. I was Unlucky Man.

Of course nothing happened. At the last second, my playmate veered off, and dozens of other sea lions took up the joyous game. Once I retrieved my heart from my mouth, I enjoyed it too. Finning down into the water, I spread my arms wide. Sea lions made for my outstretched palms; once or twice I felt whiskers brush past. Intoxicated, I had done twists—literally. I performed somersaults underwater and tight twirls like an ice-skater. In the green world about me the sea lions were driven to their own happy madness, making their own crazy loops. It remains one of the best days of my life.

But now it felt different. I put on my bathing suit and walked down the path to the cove, but I did not jump in. Instead I stood in the hot sun, uncomfortable imaginings playing out in my brain, imaginings aided by facts, that is, if anything on the Internet can be regarded as reliable fact.

The information age can be a curse. That morning, Googling *sea lion attacks,* I had garnered an unsettling amount of information. I read an Associated Press article reporting a spate of sea lion attacks on humans, including one particularly roguish San Francisco sea lion credited with biting fourteen swimmers and chasing another ten out of the water in a single month. Sure the article was nearly two years old, just enough time for this psychotic piece of blubber to make his way south. Giving weight to my theory, I read another article about a southern California lifeguard on a training swim who was bitten three times. Then, in Manhattan Beach, a beach stroller was bitten by a sea lion. Postbite, the sea lion, in the words of the reporter, "waddled into the water," an amusing description that made it seem as if the assault had been carried out by Charlie Chaplin. But I had already made a map in my mind, one tiny red dot vectoring straight down the coast.

Other creatures swim in the ocean too. Unlike the other islands that comprise Channel Islands National Park, Santa Barbara has only a brief history of human habitation. But one Buster Hyder was part of that habitation, dwelling on the island from 1914 until 1929. In a recounting of his life there, Buster told a writer that it was not unusual to see orcas swim right up onto the rocky shores in often-successful pursuit of sea lions. Buster was a man of simple words and pleasures. "I'd see them wallow right up on the beach and I'd watch the orcas eat them," he said. Buster himself claimed to have been the apple of not one, but two orcas' eyes, pursued as a small boy while a goggle-eyed uncle yanked frantically at the oars of their tiny skiff. No doubt coursing with adrenaline, the uncle rowed them right up onto the beach, where they both leaped from the skiff and ran. Young Buster, however, turned around for a gander. "Those orcas went halfway up that beach trying to get us . . . . There wasn't any seals or sea lions where we landed. They weren't after them."

All of which is to say my trepidation was not unfounded. But in the end my own smell, commingling with the appreciable scent of sea lion droppings, saw me jump. In midair I was already backstroking for shore. I plunged beneath the surface. For a moment I felt the exhilarating shock of the water, cold and pure; next my eyes opened to a bubbly bleary-green world filled with dark forms. It is tempting to say here that I cavorted once again in Poseidon-like fashion with the cove's residents—who would know, but me?—but the honest truth is that as quickly as I could turn around, I was freestyling across dry rock.

Clean but ashamed, I walked back up to the bunkhouse.

Standing on the patio, warm sun on my skin, I felt better. I turned to go inside to change, and then stopped. Let me just say that if you have not yet stood naked in the sunshine, do it as soon as possible. I strutted about for a few moments, issuing hoots of joy, and then I strutted about and shouted some more. I finally calmed, but emboldened by my newfound power, I did not go inside. Instead I sat at the picnic table in a state that would have seen me arrested in civilization's prudish environs, enjoying a most sensual balm. The sun poured itself like warm honey on parts that rarely saw the light of day, and the breeze, equally warm and gentle, traced its fingertips across my skin with sensitivity like lace. Slowly the breeze rose. It pushed against me with more pressure and insistence. It even seemed to blow in my ear.

It occurred to me that perhaps I was letting solitude get the best of me. It also occurred to me that sitting naked in the sun felt really good. Eventually I went back inside, but only when I felt like it. No one told me to.

That night I picked up a magazine in the bunkhouse and read an essay on socialization by Theodore Kaczynski, the infamous Unabomber. Kaczynski wrote surprisingly eloquently about how, from the earliest age, society tells us how to think and act, and, worse still, makes us feel ashamed if we behave contrary to its stringent expectations. Man, wrote Kaczynski, spends his life "running on rails that society has laid down for him."

I would never advocate following the example of the Unabomber, but after I finished the article, I sat quietly for a long time. The gulls rose in my mind. I saw again how they stood, stalwart and independent on their small patch of ground, but I saw too how their heads twitched constantly about, as if taking in the actions of their neighbors. Their behavior struck me as oddly human, for who has not peered out through the blinds at a passing walker, or conversely, shut those same blinds for fear that others might see whatever innocuous acts we are performing?

Why are we so obsessed with the opinions and doings of our fellows? And why do so many of us live out our only lifetime fettered by that obsession? How incomprehensibly sad to wake to this only at the last.

For four days I saw virtually no sign of my humankind. From my favored spots atop Signal Peak or along the ridgeline, most of the time I was afforded a 360-degree expanse of empty ocean. Now and then a smudge of boat passed at a comfortable distance. Even the skies seemed serenely empty, strange so close to Los Angeles; only now and again did I see a vapor trail.

Instead of walking the trails that traced the island's lowlands, more often than not I found myself hiking up to the ridgeline. I told myself I enjoyed the view, but I knew what I was doing, for each time I arrived at the ridge, I quickly peered down on the water, my heart stilled for an instant by mild trepidation until I saw that the waters remained empty. A mooring bobbed just off the Landing Cove. It was not visible from the bunkhouse until you walked toward the edge of the cliff. Each morning, when I stepped out to watch the dawn, my very first order of business was to creep to the edge and peer at the mooring. When I saw it bobbing empty, my heart gave a grateful hop.

In the mornings I enjoyed the sunrise and the silverlace. In the afternoons I walked until I found the proper vantage point, and then I simply sat and stared at whatever it was that had caught my attention; the sea running away into the distance, or a tiny hummingbird close at hand. In the evenings I hiked up to the ridge. In the last of the falling light, the gulls seemed to go quiet and the songs of the smaller birds rose. The small birds were both timid and bold; some whirred away over the tops of the grass as if shot from a crossbow, but some hopped along the trail, staying just an arm's length in front of me. These were lovely things to have to oneself.

One evening, walking back from the ridgeline, the insects just beginning to hum, I spoke out loud.

"This is a gift," I said, and the sound of my voice made me feel only mildly self-conscious.

Many evenings when I reached the ridge, I flushed the two gulls from my sunset seat. I was now convinced that the gulls were the same ones that monitored my morning watering, because I was now also convinced that I didn't give a damn if my fellow man judged me an imbecile. Each time I approached the bench, they rose without a word. Each time, I thanked them for giving up their seat. It was not the gulls who were obnoxious. I was the one who sent them shrieking into the sky.

The morning radio report also included information on comings and goings from various park islands. With summer approaching, business was picking up. I listened as the dispatcher reported Island Packer boats, swollen with customers, daytrippers mostly, heading for Anacapa and Santa Cruz—boats were even going out to distant Santa Rosa. I remembered the words of the perfumed woman on Anacapa: *I didn't realize it was going to be so deserted.*

But no boats were coming to Santa Barbara, and each time this was announced, I did a little jig.

And then one day the crackling voice said someone was coming, three someones to be exact, arriving to conduct repairs on the weather station. I knew the station. I had already hiked there many times. It sat near the island's northern tip, battered by wind and salt, a decrepit, rusted-out Mars probe.

Rocky Rudolph, Tyler Welbourn, and Andrew Reinhart arrived by boat on a hot, sunny morning and, deciding not to revert back to airs, I informed them almost immediately that I had gone swimming and then stood about naked. Tyler looked at me, raised his eyebrows, and said, "I'm surprised you weren't swimming nude," and with that we were friends.

They fixed the weather station, and then they went hiking and made their own discoveries.

"We got dive-bombed. Andrew got shat on," said Tyler triumphantly.

Tyler followed my gaze down to his own bare leg.

"Awww geeez," he said.

They brought beer, music, and taco fixings and they shared them all freely. They were in their twenties; Rocky was the same age I had been when I came to the island with my new wife. I must have seemed old and a trifle strange to them, out here writing about memories and seagulls, but they made me feel at home anyhow.

Tyler thought we should make the island our own country, maybe even return to simpler times.

"Sometimes I wish I could go back," he said, tipping back a beer. "The simplicity of a lot of stuff. You know. Go hunting. Build a house. Have the missus out. Grow a garden. But I'm sure back then you were thinking, 'Damn, I wish I had electricity, whatever that is.'"

There you have the tug-of-war that pulls the heartstrings of modern folk, at least in places where the Milky Way can no longer be seen.

Tyler was especially impressed by the night sky.

"Holy shit, it's dark," he said.

When he looked toward the sooty glow to the east, he stopped grinning.

"L.A." he said. "Smog and light pollution."

I turned the weather report over to Rocky, for he was actually a certified park employee, and I flushed the toilet a little more often, but I did not abandon certain parts of my routine. Each morning, over those last two days, I watered my silverlace and whispered greetings to my avian companions on the cinderblock wall. I continued hiking, though I did notice that, though I enjoyed Tyler, Andrew, and Rocky immensely, I still hiked alone, the act now leaning less toward introspection and more toward plain escape.

On my last afternoon I hiked for a time and then stretched out in the grass. The trail was one Kathy and I had walked often on our visit; it ran from the campground out toward a bluff that looked down a dark shoreline fairly cobbled with sea lions. Our fellow campers had not been hikers. Often we had stood on the bluff's edge, the barks and bleats and guttural coughs washing up over the cliff belonging to us alone.

Lying in the grass, I could hear the sea lions. Closing my eyes, I walked the trail with Kathy. The afternoon was warm and still. I fell asleep, and so was allowed to sleep again with my wife under the stars.

The next morning, before the helicopter arrived to pick us up, I watered the silverlace one last time. My two gulls stood on the cinderblock wall. Softly, I thanked them for keeping me company. Perhaps my voice startled them, but this time they both lifted away. They flew up and disappeared over the ridge-line. Mildly affronted, I finished my watering alone.

We lay claim to the things we come across in our lives, as if it is possible to own them, but you can no more own an island or a stoic gull than you can possess the fleeting moments that accumulate into a lifetime. It is good to recognize life's gifts, but foolish to hold them too tightly.

The gulls cared nothing for me or my memories. It was their island, not mine.

Lunch in Beverly Hills

· · ■ ■ · ·

THERE IS A CHURCH in Beverly Hills, on the corner of Cam-
den Drive and Santa Monica Boulevard. The denomination
doesn't really matter, it's the work they do there that counts,
but I will tell you that the church is All Saints' Episcopal Church.
You'll know it for the people who eat lunch there.

Lunch is served Mondays, from two until three thirty, though
if you can't get there in time (always a possibility when your
transportation is unpredictable), they'll set a plate aside. The
food is good—steaming meat loaf, turkey, fresh organic vegetables—served by volunteers who ladle generous portions, look
you in the eye, and ask, "How are you today, Ken?" They know
your name because everyone gets a name tag when they check
in with the volunteers outside the dining hall. It's also true that
some of the guests have been coming to All Saints' lunch for
as long as eighteen years. All Saints' feeds between 100 and 130
people at the Monday lunch.

Michael Deegan oversees the lunches. He has other duties.
His official title is coordinator of Mercy and Justice Outreach

Ministries, but he prefers to see himself as overseeing "the office of random," for if his job has taught him one thing, it's that he cannot control everything. *Management* is a loose term here. There is much letting go. Oddly, most of the time things work out. A truck pulls up offering fifty pounds of free coffee. A parishioner volunteers to pay for all the meats.

Michael is not a priest, though oddly he possesses a priest's unflappable mien. He is helpful to everyone, but he looks you directly in the eye, assessing your propensity for bullshit, of which he is a very keen detector. He is a former business executive, and you get the impression that as such he ran a tight ship. He is six foot five, with a big man's easy confidence. He is very protective of the guests he serves, but he does not coddle them. He requires but a few simple things. Wait your turn. Stay in your chair. Be reasonably quiet. Don't gang up on anyone. Don't harm anyone. There are adult spin-offs to these kindergarten rules: no drug use, no sex in the bathrooms.

"It's not that they have to have table manners," he explained. "They have to be courteous to each other. All you have to do is behave."

If you violate any of these rules, Michael will let you know, and if you continue to misbehave, he will ask you to leave. Then you will miss one of the best lunches in Los Angeles, which, if figures on such things can be assembled, is home to some 900,000 homeless, more homeless than anyplace in the world.

I came to All Saints' as a forty-eight-year-old homeless man in jeans, T-shirt, and old tennis shoes. Sometimes my clothes were spread with dust and perspiration; I made a point of not washing them after my time on the islands. Usually, I didn't shave. Michael knew who I was because I spoke with him on the phone before I came down, but I told no one else. Not everyone who attends All Saints' lunch is homeless, or even in need. People have parked brand-new cars up the street before coming to stand in line. Michael knows this, but everyone is welcome. No questions are asked.

"The idea is to offer hospitality, respect, and dignity," Michael said. "And then, once that's taken care of, there's the meal."

During my time at All Saints' I tried to blend in, but I wonder if even one of the guests was fooled. My time on the islands had browned my face, but my skin wasn't gnawed by wind, and rain, and cold—it can get very cold in Los Angeles—and my hands were soft, the nails smooth and unlaced with grime, and most of all I am a bad actor and an even worse liar, though I was never required to lie. In my lunch visits to All Saints', not one of the guests ever questioned me.

Homelessness has always been part of the world, but never more so than now. This is news to no one. You see it on your own street corners, people holding cardboard signs that say *God Bless* or, more to the point, *Hungry—Please Help*. A bit more out of sight, men roll sleeping bags out beneath freeway under-passes, and families stay in campgrounds or sleep in their cars. Or there is no campground or car. In my own town I have seen a mother and three small children disappear into the brush of a local river bottom. The homeless are everywhere, and they turn me equal parts sad, guilty, and uncomfortable, for the sight of them reminds me that I was born fortunate, while some jabber and gesture wildly to no one I can see.

One night, at a local gas station, a man asked me for change. Cullen, my fifteen-year-old, was sitting in the car. I want my sons to care. I gave the man two dollars, realizing that two dollars goes almost nowhere these days.

The man smiled through a bristly gray beard that jutted down to his chest. The hairs were like wire brush.

"Now I can get a hot dog," he said.

I pumped the gas. Two dollars ran past in about ten seconds.

The man came back. He pushed a rusted bike, but the bulging saddlebags looked new and the sleeping bag was in good condition.

"I want you to know I'm not going to buy beer," he said.

"Thank you," I said.

He touched the end of his beard.

"I look like this because it helps me make more money. Plus, then I don't have to shave. I've got an income of a hundred and eighteen dollars a month, and a place to live is a thousand dollars a month. The math just doesn't work."

"So where do you sleep?"

"In the bushes. It really isn't bad."

He saw me looking at the saddlebags.

"I've got a computer in there. I go to Barnes and Noble a lot, and get on the Internet."

I recalled the effusive claim of a technology writer: Google can find you anything you need in a flash. Maybe not.

People were waiting for the pump.

"God bless you," he said, and walked away.

Driving home, I asked Cullen if he had heard what the man had said. He repeated the man's words almost verbatim.

We drove in silence. Fifteen-year-olds comment only when they feel like it.

My son said, "He reminded me of Santa Claus. You know, when people have a beard they kind of look jollier."

In Britain they call them "rough sleepers." In the Netherlands, *zwerver* (wanderer) or *dakloze* (roofless). In Spanish they are *desamparado*, which—take your pick—translates to "abandoned," "deserted," "helpless," or "unprotected." At All Saints' they are called Susan, Gino, Stanley, Myron, Louis, Lloyd, Marilyn, and Larry, because those are their names.

Homelessness is too big to be tidily defined, but we try. There are forests of statistics and studies. We like to report things. Perhaps this helps us feel we have some control. I consulted several government studies. Among the sea of figures I learned that, in the United States, as many as 3.5 million people experience homelessness in a given year. Yes, 22 percent have serious mental problems and 54 percent were in prison at some point, but 40 percent were families with children; this last percentage was rising faster than any of the others. Some people were homeless for only a few weeks; some were homeless for years. One study drew its homeless numbers from telephone interviews, a sampling method with obvious limitations. There were also studies on public attitudes toward homelessness. One study concluded that familiarity breeds "compassion fatigue"; we are simply worn down and can do no more. Another concluded that familiarity bred sympathy.

I concluded that I wanted to see for myself. I knew that whatever I did would provide only the smallest picture. This did not matter. I only wanted something human. At All Saints' I received this in spades.

Initially I wanted to spend a few days around the clock with a homeless person, but when I broached the subject with people who knew better, including Michael Deegan, they politely told me this probably wouldn't work. Homeless encampments possess their share of the paranoid and criminal, not always people who respond well to a man taking notes. Even those with clear heads and records would probably not be amenable. Michael, I found, had a way of always adding an illuminating twist.

"It's like asking an executive," he told me. "You'll get the same resistance. I'm too busy. I don't have the time."

So I chose lunch at All Saints'. I chose Beverly Hills for two reasons. Los Angeles, or so one set of statistics claimed, has the country's largest homeless population; true, my involvement would brush just the tip of the iceberg, but it would take place in a legitimate arena.

I also chose Beverly Hills for the visions the name instantly conjures. One block from All Saints', on Rodeo Drive, you can purchase diamonds from De Beers, purses from Lana Marks, and Manolo Blahnik heels (the shoes worshipped on *Sex and the City*), within stores redolent of lavender and rosemary and discretion, and, should you not exhibit discretion, sunglassed security guards who dress like mafioso and look half as friendly. There are stores without a name; you're just supposed to know. The sidewalks are without stain or gum wrapper. Jay Leno shops here, as do former presidents Bill Clinton and George Bush (junior), Japan's emperor Akihito, and the rockers-turned-reality-TV-stars Ozzy and Sharon Osbourne. I know this because one shop window discreetly told me so; some of the names were hidden behind geraniums. Other store windows informed passersby that they might also shop for the same items in West Palm Beach and Dubai. I don't fault them. Who hasn't dropped a name?

Behind All Saints's, just back from the busyness of Santa Monica Boulevard, are the first of many hushed palm-, ficus-, and magnolia-lined residential streets. Drive these streets and, through *Lord of the Rings* wrought-iron gates, you will see ten Ferraris gleaming in the sun, or the upper reaches of the late Aaron Spelling's mansion, with a single room dedicated expressly to the wrapping of packages, or, in the case of Madonna's home, nothing, for it is fronted by a barricade of foliage. Had you wished to outdo even the stars, at the time of my visits, a few blocks from All Saints', you could have purchased a compound formerly owned by William Randolph Hearst and honeymooned in by Jacqueline and John F. Kennedy (in real estate too, name-dropping counts) for $165 million.

Not all of Beverly Hills is stereotypical excess and entitlement, but plenty of it is. Behind the homes are wide alleys and trash and recycle bins in which neither recycles nor trash stay very long. The bins are so big that the smaller women use long pieces of wire to reach down to pull things out.

The lunch line at All Saints' is an interesting place for many reasons.

On my first visit I waited in line behind a man pinching pimples on the halter-topped woman in front of him. In front of them a man's shaved head ably displayed a purplish scar the shape and size of a horseshoe. A woman walked past, conversing with herself in flawless French, *"Mon ami, mon ami. Comment ça va? Ça va bien."* Just away from the line, a man sporting a natty mustache and a fedora shuffled in very small circles. I stood, dry-mouthed and anxious, in my ridiculous, dusty jeans, and when the shuffling man suddenly looked at me, I had to fight to smile instead of looking away.

The man walked toward me. He was short, maybe in his late fifties. The fedora and his shuffling walk lent him a faint Charlie Chaplin air. He bore the slightest smile.

Look down or no. My eyes went to his name tag.

"Hello, Lloyd," I said.

He kept moving past, taking small, delicate steps, but he smiled.

"Hello, Ken. Welcome to Beverly Hills."

Lunch at All Saints' is served cafeteria style, with volunteers serving the food from large trays. The volunteers wear name tags too, so that, if you wish, you may say, "Hello, Barbara." Today's lunch was chili, spooned onto equally steaming rice, served with cooked vegetables and a choice of lemon pie or chocolate cake. The volunteers smiled and asked me how I was. At the end of the line there was a small table for drinks. Two women—one seated, one standing—had set out a dozen small paper cups of pink lemonade beside a big orange cooler. The seated woman had long hair that matched her long face. Her hair was still dark and thick, but age had brushed it with gray, and weather had turned it brittle.

Hairs curled from her chin. Very softly she said, "Hold the cup from the bottom."

The tables were arranged in a few long rows. The room was not large. All Saints' usually employs a larger room for its lunches, but during my visits the church was undergoing renovations, and that room was among them. A volunteer lets guests into the makeshift dining hall in threes and fours; as folding chairs emptied, more guests were allowed in. Everyone ate with focus, but they took time to talk among themselves and watch newcomers enter the room. I took my self-conscious place at a table and stared hard at my plate.

There was a small commotion behind me. I did not want to appear afraid, though I was.

I heard Michael say, "You can either sit down or leave."
The commotion ended.

I ate as if I was hungry, though no one else did. They declined vegetables, eyed their slice of pie like a jeweler examining a gem before giving it away. They did not scrape their plates clean. All Saints' is not the only good meal in town. Many of the longer-term guests here know this. If you know where the good meals are and you have enough money for the bus, in Los Angeles, at least, you will not starve.

I kept my head down. The man across from me rested a bruised forearm on the table. A hospital bracelet on his wrist read "Jose." Someone said that the new library in Santa Monica had whole lines of computers. A cell phone rang. Two men began discussing the merits of various calling plans. Someone brushed behind me, trailing the smell of mustiness and stale sweat. Another man bumped my chair, and my heart performed its second small leap.

"Excuse me," he said.

I ate quickly and wondered what I thought I was doing.

When I finished eating, I went outside, and as I would do in the following weeks, I sat on a low brick wall just off the court-yard upon which church offices and the makeshift dining hall opened. I felt self-conscious and sneaky. I watched people leave. They came out into the sunshine in groups and alone, smiling and talking, like family making their way to the living room after the Thanksgiving meal. No one hurried. Slowly they collected their belongings, Hefty bags and worn suitcases, and a grocery cart festooned with peace signs and a kazoo.

I sat on the wall feeling hopeless. It is difficult to get to know people without talking to them, but I felt lost, and more than a little afraid. This was not my world. It seemed easy to distinguish between the more troubled guests and those who might be approachable, but no human being is weighed at a glance. Plenty of people had tried to discourage me from spending time with the homeless. Now their words rang in my ears.

Paranoid, mentally ill, drug-addled, unpredictable. My head was down again.

A pair of worn sneakers stopped in front of me. I looked up. I'm afraid my smile was crooked.

Marilyn said, "You have beautiful eyes. What sign are you?" Marilyn didn't give me time to answer.

"I'm Aquarius," she said. "I'm on the cusp."

She leaned on her cane, waiting patiently.

"Cancer," I said.

Marilyn was in her seventies and some of her teeth were missing, but when she was pleased, she produced a young girl's winsome smile.

"Oh, good! I'm looking for a Cancer."

A man stood fifteen yards away. Marilyn looked at him. If it is possible for a scowl to possess fondness, this one did. Marilyn spoke loudly.

"That's Larry," she said. "He's my husband. My fifth one. He talks too much. He's too loud. Everybody pays attention to him. Sometimes he's rude. I have to tell him to watch his mouth. He's forty-seven. We've been married twenty-four years."

The construction workers had put up barriers and a few orange traffic cones to keep people from falling into bits of excavation. Larry picked up a traffic cone and turned it into a megaphone.

"Moooosessssss! Moooosessssss!"

His deep voice, amplified by the traffic cone, boomed about the courtyard. No one but Marilyn paid Larry any mind.

Marilyn said, "Oh, shut up, Larry!"

Larry walked over. His hair was shaved close and he wore a camouflage cap. He gave me a look that was neither friendly nor unfriendly.

It is my experience that compliments are great icebreakers. I attached myself to the one thing I knew about Larry.

"You've got a great voice," I said. "It sounds a little like Jim Carrey's."

He looked a little like Jim Carrey too, and when he gave Marilyn a sneaky little-boy's smile, he looked a lot like Jim Carrey.

Marilyn said, "Oh, no you don't. Don't start," but Larry was already off and riffing. In rapid-fire succession he did impersonations of Jim Carrey, Elvis (with a little body English thrown in), and Bill Clinton ("I did not have sex with that woman"). The impersonations were very good, and when I said so, Larry tossed in Forrest Gump too.

"Life is like a box of condoms! Just pick one!"

"Larry!" Marilyn smacked his arm, but Larry, who had obviously been smacked countless times before, ignored it.

"Larry can tell people's signs. We're a bunch of psychic psychos. What is Ken's sign, Larry?"

"Cancer," Larry said, but he didn't look at me.

"See?" said Marilyn.

"I heard him say it," said Larry.

Marilyn turned her back on Larry.

Marilyn said, "When I was seventeen, I was engaged to the nephew of the publisher of the *Chicago Tribune*. Lots of money. I was very shy. He was like, 'Go into that store and buy anything you like, I'll pay for it.' But to me that didn't seem proper. Chicago was too cold for me. I didn't know any better."

For a moment Marilyn was occupied with her own thoughts.

Then she said, "My mother always said, 'You can't do this, you can't do that.' I was raised to be proper. Sit up straight, be seen and not heard."

Marilyn tapped her cane once. Her smile went away.

Softly she said, "I didn't know any better."

When lunch was over, Michael usually wandered out in the courtyard. Sometimes he simply said goodbye to those who were leaving. Other times he held quiet conversations, for it was also his job to dispense various things people needed—maybe a curling iron, maybe some bus tokens, maybe a little cash. The guests approached him and made their requests. He listened attentively.

Others simply walked past. A woman came out of the dining hall, dragging a suitcase behind her. She walked slowly, the suitcase following her in fits and starts. I recognized her as the woman who had advised me to hold the flimsy paper cup by the bottom.

The suitcase scraped over the pavement. A wheel was missing.

"Hello, Susan," Michael said. "How are you?"

Susan stopped, swaying a little.

She spoke so softly I swayed forward to hear her.

"I'm fine," she said.

"Susan, do you need a new bag?"

Susan nodded thoughtfully.

"That would be helpful. My foot is bothering me."

"You ever try sanding the callus?"

"I'm doing that."

Susan looked at me.

"Did you like the lunch?"

"Very much."

"This came from Target, but the wheel broke," she said.

"I'm sorry," I said, the words ringing useless in my ears.

"It's OK," Susan said. "Goodbye."

We watched her go, bumping along.

I said, "It looks like it's really hard for her to get around."

Michael turned to me.

"She gets everywhere. She takes classes all the time. She goes to every gallery opening she can get to. She calls and makes reservations and finds something semipresentable to wear."

"Is she an art lover?" I asked.

Michael said, "I think she is a lover of anything she can get to."

Before I left, I sat in the now-empty dining hall and talked with Michael. This too would become part of my ritual. Mondays were understandably busy for Michael, but an hour or so after lunch, when the worst of the busyness subsided, he sat down with me. Slouching easily in a folding chair, he answered my questions, always with patience, and sometimes with hesitation. As we talked, he watched me closely. Though he was kind enough never to say so directly, I knew he didn't trust me. Writers had dramatized homelessness before, getting everything wrong at the expense of people he had come to care about.

Homelessness is not a simple picture. In varying ways, during my visits Michael drove this home to me again and again. Sometimes it was subtle, but I had not missed Michael's pointed correction—"She gets everywhere"—or the mild hint of exasperation. He was not impolite. His was more the air of a patient professor grown tired, and a trifle irritable, by the same misguided preconceptions at the start of each semester.

On this afternoon, pots and pans clanging in the kitchen as volunteers finished the last of the cleanup, Michael addressed the broad picture.

"You have to be careful about painting a society that's done something bad," he said. "Many of these people are bright and proud. For one reason or another they've just made a choice to be homeless. It's not an issue of pity. Bad things can happen to good people, but those people can still make decisions about their own lives. It's a shame we live in a society where people have to make the choice to be homeless, but sometimes it is a choice."

One All Saints' regular, who sometimes slept in the church courtyard at night, was eligible for benefits that would have seen him under a roof had he chosen to accept them.

"He won't be on welfare," Michael said. "He refuses many things. He will probably live like this until Social Security kicks in. He made that choice."

Susan, I would learn, had made choices too. When she first advised me to hold my cup firmly, she was living in an assisted-living group home, but in the short span of my visits that would change. Susan collected things, apparently too many things in the minds of the people who ran the home. They told her if she didn't get rid of some of the things, she would have to leave. She gathered what she could, and left. She did not tell Michael she was out on the street. Susan, I learned, rarely communicated directly with Michael. If she needed something badly, more often she made this need known through beautifully written letters. Michael figured out she was out on the street because he noticed that she was losing weight. When he asked her, she told him what had happened. The street can be a very mean place, but the indoors can be no less bitter.

"They got on Susan, and she said, 'I'm not going to live by your rules,' and she left," Michael said.

Someone said something in the kitchen, and Michael turned away for a moment to listen.

Turning back, he said, "If somebody said to you, 'I'm going to give you three meals a day and a dry place to stay, but you'll be in prison,' or else your monthly check would go directly to you and then you could do what you choose, which would you choose?"

I told Michael I would try as hard as I could to get things right.

He was not won over.

"I don't want this sensationalized," he said. "These are people's lives."

Someone who leaves an executive position for social work is not without a heart.

Michael pushed back his chair and stood up. He smiled.

"You think *you're* naive walking in here? I had to learn to cook lunch for one hundred and twenty."

For the most part the guests who eat lunch at All Saints' like the food, and they will tell you so in word and deed.

Nine months back, during lunch, there was a screech of tires. Sirens followed. Michael ran outside. When he reached the accident, his fears were confirmed. He knew the gray head of hair. The paramedics were already working on Charlotte. Blood streamed down her face, but Charlotte was conscious.

When Michael bent over her, she said, "Michael, are you serving meat loaf? Will there be some left for me?" Fifteen minutes later she walked into lunch, paramedic in tow.

The paramedic smiled at Michael. "We bandaged her up, there are no broken bones. She refused to go to the hospital. She wants lunch."

I was raised on meat loaf. I will tell you that All Saints' meat loaf is very, very good.

The guests will also tell you what they don't like. Standing in line one afternoon, a woman said loudly, "Why do we have to have name tags? We're not kids." Inside the dining hall another woman spoke to everyone. "I don't drink the drinks. They're filled with sugar. Diabetes is bad for you."

No one commented on either statement. While eating, people talked less, but outside, before and after the meal, many of the guests carried on animated conversations. They talked about things we all discuss: money, sports, one another. One afternoon I sat on my retaining wall and listened to two men argue about who was the better boxer, George Foreman or Muhammad Ali, a sharp debate that could have taken place on ESPN. As Michael pointed out, "You don't have twenty-four hours a day to listen to the radio and read the paper. Don't talk politics with these folks."

Some of the guests debated with real people, and some didn't.

One afternoon, as we waited in line for lunch, a black man in an Abercrombie & Fitch T-shirt paced alongside the line. His muscles pressed against his shirt. He had a Bluetooth headset affixed to one ear, but I doubted it was working. It looked as if it had gone through the garbage disposal.

He threw his hands in the air. "You didn't?? Well, then, you was trippin'. . . . Ohhhh nooo. Now you'll be in deep shit." He paced beyond earshot, then spun about and came by me again. "What jaded memories I have," he said, and then he added something about his attorney.

Most afternoons, waiting in line, I also saw Lloyd performing his shuffling, but he did so with a benign charm that I quickly came to find pleasing. For some reason, Lloyd was also nice to me. Rarely did he pass by without some pleasant word. "Hello, Ken. Nice to see you, Ken." He was not interested in talking, he kept walking, but he always smiled slightly and looked me right in the eye.

Because All Saints' is a church, and because people affiliated with a church believe in God and his ability to help, All Saints' lunch always offers a brief church service at two forty-five: a few songs, a few psalms, a brief sermon. Only a handful of guests attend the service, and I came to see that often it was the same guests. Lloyd was a regular, but his attendance was always brief. The service began with a song; usually two guitar players were joined by a woman who sang. Lloyd would make his way to the front; as the song echoed in the chapel, Lloyd made his circles on the square brown tiles. When the song was over, Lloyd shuffled down the aisle and out the door.

When I told Michael this, he nodded.

"Lloyd dances and sings along because he believes that it's his job to help bring people closer to God. He doesn't stay and listen to the sermon, because his job is music."

Once, standing in the lunch line, I saw Lloyd making his same tight circles, but Lloyd's face was flushed, and he made sharp movements with his hands. Michael walked over to him. After a few moments Lloyd's circling calmed, like ripples going smooth on a pond. Later Michael told me that the best way to calm Lloyd was to get him to sing. For this I liked Lloyd even more.

Most guests allowed for the idiosyncrasies of others, though a few didn't. One afternoon a woman spoke to someone only she could see. Another woman huffed, "Look at that loony. She's talkin' to thin air."

Standing in line offered a better chance to watch people because looking around in a line seemed less like snooping than looking around when you are sitting at a meal.

My second Monday was a hot day, pushing eighty-five. It was

hotter still in the sheltered courtyard. The man in front of me wore a corduroy jacket with a fur collar. He held a yellow butane lighter tightly in his right hand. His name tag read Jesus. Jesus had shoulder-length dark hair caked with dirt, and ink-black eyes. He was built like a fireplug.

The man behind him said, "You hot in that jacket?"

"Yes," said Jesus.

The line advanced, moving Jesus close to a chair in the shade, until finally he could sit down.

A man came over to him and said, "Led Zeppelin is playing this Friday."

Slouched in the chair, Jesus spoke with drowsy skepticism, but his eyes bored into the speaker.

"The whole group is gonna' be there? I find that hard to believe."

"Well, that's what I heard," the other man mumbled, and moved away.

It is human nature to seek out a friendly face. Standing in line, I saw Marilyn and Larry sitting at one of the tables eating lunch. Marilyn was wearing a jacket too, though she did not have to carry all her clothing on her back: I would learn that she and Larry had a place to live, a small apartment they rented with the help of her retirement checks.

Her eyes were warm.

"There's Ken," she said.

Larry made no comment.

Today's entrée was macaroni and cheese. In the dining area a woman said, "Now, that's not a food you normally see in Beverly Hills. Don't even see it in the delicatessens. It's children's food."

I had missed breakfast. It was two thirty. I was hungry. I polished my plate clean, not as part of my feeble act but because I wanted to. I still kept my head down. I felt out of place because I was out of place.

"Hey."

I looked up.

The man across from me said, "You want my bread?"

"Yes, please."

He stood and held out his plate. I took the garlic bread.

"Take care," he said.

After lunch I went outside and sat on the wall and waited, this time for Marilyn, who had become my friend in the crowd.

Marilyn came out, Larry in tow.

I stood and smiled. Before I could speak, Marilyn said, "Look, he's quiet and a gentleman."

None of us are everything all the time.

"I've got plenty of faults," I said.

It felt good to finally tell the truth.

"Ohhhh, I'll bet you behave yourself most of the time," Marilyn said.

I am afraid I smiled at Marilyn with genuine affection. I was extremely grateful for her simple act of reaching out.

"Why can't you be polite like him?" she said to Larry.

Larry said, "I wrote you poetry one time, remember?"

"I remember."

"We've got to find it," Larry said.

Marilyn turned her back to him as she said to me, "He talks too much."

A man stood close to us. He was young. He looked Middle Eastern. He held a thick textbook. He had piercing blue eyes.

Marilyn said, "Larry, who has prettier blue eyes, this man or Ken?"

"Ken's eyes are green," said Larry, playing the trump card every spouse loves.

Marilyn looked closely at me. Discerning this to be true, she cuffed Larry anyhow.

"That's not an answer," she said.

Larry hesitated. This was his chance to lower me a notch in his wife's mind.

"Ken," he said.

Marilyn said, "I met this man once. He said he was a world traveler. I thought how nice it must be to just get on a plane and go somewhere."

Larry lit up.

"I love planes from World War II," he said. "The other day I saw a B-fifty-two and a B-seventeen fly over Hollywood. You can rent them out at Van Nuys. There's an airport there. It's like a thousand dollars. I like the fighter planes—the P-fifty-one Mustang, the P-thirty-eight, the P-thirty-nine, the P-forty-four. You can rent fighter planes too. Get in a P-fifty-one. That's what I'd like to do. I'd be in heaven."

Marilyn interrupted, but she looked at Larry fondly.

"He went to a Gypsy fortune-teller once. She told him he was a pilot in his last life. A leader of men. He was shot down over the ocean."

"I hate the water," Larry said. "Won't go anywhere near it."

It occurred to me that Larry looked like a fighter pilot.

We stood for a moment, each of us quietly absorbed in our own thoughts: Larry banking and issuing orders through the headset of a P-51, Marilyn imagining life with a leader of men and the travel that would entail. I am making this up of course, but it was easy to imagine. Who among us hasn't daydreamed of another life, even if we are lucky to have a life some people have only in daydreams?

A light breeze blew. The church door swung open of its own accord.

"Look," said Marilyn. "God's coming."

A few minutes later Susan came out into the courtyard, suitcase clattering behind her.

As she passed me, she shook her head apologetically.

"Wheel's broken," she said. "I'm going to get a new wheel next week."

Driving home that afternoon, I wondered if Susan was finding it harder to attend the classes and openings she loved. It is difficult to look even semipresentable without a shower. When many other things are gone, choice remains in our possession. But choice takes away things too.

Some believe we have lost certain essential human values—compassion, understanding, responsibility for ourselves and for others—but I believe we have simply made a choice.

Slowly I noticed certain curious things. Each Monday everyone waited in line without mishap. Michael told me that sometimes there were altercations, but I never saw the slightest ruffle. One afternoon a man arrived late and walked right up to the front of the line. No one said a word.

When I asked Michael about this at our afternoon chat, he said, "No one here is entitled. No one comes in here with what we walk around with every day: *I'm in a hurry at Starbucks because the meter is running.*"

It was an apropos example. Once, I had seen two grown men nearly come to blows in Starbucks because one man had stepped in front of the other man's family. It was an embarrassing thing, because the affronted man was me.

Wait your turn, and sometimes wait a little longer. What does it really matter?

There was something else too. People talked to imaginary lawyers, and danced to tunes only they could hear, and, like the rest of us, complained about the behavior of others, but not once did I hear anyone complain of callused feet, a two-month wait to see a doctor despite onrushing blindness, a year-long wait for dental work. They had reason to complain about these things, for each of these was a very real predicament for one or the other of the All Saints' guests.

This time Michael just shrugged.

"Those just aren't topics of conversation," he said. "I have people tell me about their troubles because they have to; they need bus tokens to get to the doctor's office, that sort of thing. But they only talk about it with me."

Susan didn't even ask Michael for a suitcase. I was fairly certain she would drag the one she had until someone thrust a new suitcase into her hand.

There was plenty of humor too.

One day after lunch, as people made their way back to the streets, one of the guests hustled about the courtyard brandishing a local weekly newspaper. He thrust the full-page ad under various noses.

"Look! It's the grand opening of Johnny Rockets. Mrs. C is going to be there!"

One accosted man looked befuddled.

The man with the paper exclaimed, *"Happy Days*! The TV show! Mrs. Cunningham!"

Recognition dawned on the man's face. He had no hair and so no comb, but he pulled an imaginary comb out of his back pocket and ran it over his shiny pate.

"Heeeeeyyyy," he said.

Larry, standing nearby, said, "I wonder what kind of food they're having."

The Fonz grinned.

"We can't be too particular," he said.

Rarest of all, people weren't offended if the joke was on them.

Making his way to an empty seat in the dining hall, a man in a floral shirt looked down at a seated man.

"Hey! How you been?"

"Pretty good."

"I can tell."

"You can tell?"

"You got fat!"

The seated man smiled down at his paunch.

"Yes, I did."

Not that they didn't get depressed, and they certainly had their troubles. One day Larry surprised me, dropping the impersonations and the traffic-cone bellowings to tell me he was tired of the constant comments about the age difference between him and his wife.

"If I had a dollar for every comment, I'd be wealthy," he said, but he didn't smile.

Marilyn complained heatedly about Larry, but almost always in his presence. Their relationship had plenty of bumps, some substantial and quite dark; Marilyn was startlingly open. The bumps are their business; what marriage is without dark seams? But once, when Larry was out of earshot, Marilyn said to me, "I suppose he is devoted."

Larry did not learn devotion by example. When he was eight, his father dropped him off at an orphanage in Washington State: "Wait here. I'll see you in an hour." Larry is still waiting.

On the day Larry told me this, he and Marilyn attended the church service. As they stepped through the entryway to the chapel, Larry boomed, "Enter Cleopatra!"

Standing in the doorway, I watched them walk together down the aisle. Fewer and fewer animals mate for life anymore.

One of the guitarists announced they would begin the service with a hymn.

"Sing 'Welcome to the Jungle,'" Larry said.

Marilyn cuffed him.

"Shut up! Where's the button to turn him off?"

She was just as loud.

At my last free lunch at All Souls' I gave Susan a new suitcase. It made me uncomfortable, because I still felt like a liar, and, though it likely didn't matter to her, I had deceived this quiet woman who wrote beautiful letters that asked for little. I brought her the suitcase right away, to the small table where she dispensed drinks and advice. I did not wait until after lunch because, despite my experiences at All Saints', I was still afraid someone would steal it if I left it outside.

I also told Marilyn and Larry the truth, that I wasn't homeless, that I was writing a book. Marilyn gave me permission to use their names, and then she smiled at me and said, "I knew you were more than here."

And I thought, *'More' is a matter of opinion.*

Santa Cruz Island

· · · ▪ ▪ · ·

AT ITS CLOSEST POINT, Santa Cruz Island, specifically its eastern end, is only nineteen miles from mainland California. This makes Santa Cruz, and the east-end campground at Scorpion Canyon, the most visited spot in Channel Islands National Park. In summer Island Packers boats scurry out to Santa Cruz three and four times a day, putting ashore hikers in strappy heels and campers toting propane grills only slightly smaller than a Volkswagen (I am not making these things up; a ranger told me so), so that perhaps they may showcase the outer limits of common sense and various sinews.

I knew my opportunity for solitude was coming to an end. Listening to the morning radio report on Santa Barbara Island, I had heard this clearly; Island Packers' boats, filled with nature revelers, were already storming the shores of both Anacapa and Santa Cruz in late April. I was coming to Santa Cruz just before Memorial Day.

Our own vessel was filled with a group of high school students on a day field trip. I was told that two other groups of teens were already on the island; both groups camping for a week.

I did not see this as bad news. I like teenagers; I have two at home. Plus I knew it would be easy to get away from them. Santa Cruz is a very large island; in fact it is the largest island off the west coast of the United States. At ninety-six square miles it is four times the size of Manhattan and slightly bigger than the District of Columbia. If our elected representatives could dodge their constituents, surely I could slip away from two school groups and a smattering of other campers.

Weather permitting, it takes Island Packers' high-speed catamarans roughly an hour to cross the Santa Barbara Channel to Scorpion Canyon. On the ride out I shared a bench seat with a young German couple. Michael and Sonya were already well into a several-week exploration of America's western parks. They had been to Zion, Bryce, and Yosemite, and were much impressed, though they were somewhat puzzled by American life outside of the parks.

"This is one thing we don't like in America!" said Michael. "You don't see anybody walk! In Germany we go shopping in no-driving zones! Here, you have to drive to cross the street!"

Michael was just making friendly conversation, but the bark of his mother tongue made his words sound like either happy declaratives (*I so like glockenspiels!*) or orders (*Moffff ovah in your seat! Your thigh is brushing mine!*). Michael and Sonya were only visiting Santa Cruz for the day. Michael told me they very much wanted to see an island fox.

I told him I had seen the foxes on Santa Rosa, jaunty little apparitions that had morphed out of the mist. I told him how the diminutive foxes had experienced a wondrous comeback from near extinction, a comeback so successful that the previous fall the park service had suspended its captive breeding programs on San Miguel and Santa Cruz, because the foxes in the wild were now doing a fine job of procreating on their own. Still, because they are found only on the Channel Islands, they remain one of America's rarest mammals, perhaps as rare as the American pedestrian.

"Very rare!" agreed Michael.

"Not that rare," I told him, encouragingly. I thought his chances of seeing a fox on Santa Cruz were good. According to park service estimates, there were over three hundred of the little critters on the island, although ninety-six square miles allows for plenty of room to spread out.

Michael caught the spirit.

"Well, then, we will see one!" he barked.

I imagined the foxes on Santa Cruz already scurrying into parade formation at the pier.

When we stepped off the boat and onto the small cement landing pier at the mouth of Scorpion Canyon, there were no foxes, but Lulis Cuevas was there to meet us. Lulis was the ranger, and it was immediately apparent that she had much experience with Americans.

Gathering us for a briefing, she said, "Even if you've been here twenty times, we keep having the same problems, so we just keep telling everybody the same story, because no one reads the bulletin board."

I was familiar with the bulletin boards. I had perused them in detail on the other islands, not because they detailed things that might bite you, stick you, fall out from underneath you, or kill you, but because I'd had a great deal of time. I also read the backs of my oatmeal packets. But it was not hard for me to imagine day-trippers blithely walking past the most recently posted notice. The last boat back to the mainland leaves five minutes after you ignore this bulletin. I love my fellow Americans, but there is no other society that so blithely ignores the most overt warnings and then blithely expects to be rescued and returned home in time for dinner.

After Lulis's briefing, the other campers and day visitors left. I stayed behind. I knew now that I could learn much from the rangers, and maybe even wheedle a dinner invitation.

I told Lulis what I was doing, using the solitude of the islands for reflection, examining our busy world, and our place in it.

She gave me a knowing smile.

"If you look in the back of the book where it says places not to find solitude, Scorpion Canyon is it," she said. "Scorpion to me is like the Yosemite Valley of the Channel Islands."

I have been to the valley floor of America's most popular park, and, odds are, you probably have too. If not, imagine the floor of the stock exchange. Now add RVs and tour buses.

Lulis told me that Island Packers was currently allowed to bring a maximum of 200 day visitors out to Scorpion Canyon. The campground, which rests in the folds of the canyon a half mile from the pier, was allowed a maximum of 240 campers. That is a lot of people drinking Jägermeister and shouting about the paucity of wildlife.

But Lulis knew of a way to escape the crowds.

"Most people don't walk more than a mile away from the campground," she said. "Last Saturday the campground was packed. I went up to Montanon Ridge and I was alone. It's still possible to get away."

I thanked Lulis for her advice.

She nodded.

"I hope you find what you're looking for."

Initially what I looked for were the two small propane canisters I had brought to cook my food. Rooting through my bags at the campground, I quickly realized I had left the canisters on the boat. On boarding we had been asked to put flammable items in a small case. My cannisters were still there. I felt a rising panic. I had packed mostly freeze-dried meals. Without boiled water it is impossible to distinguish these meals from their packaging. I also had brought a jar of peanut butter and a box of Ritz crackers, but now, on close inspection, I saw that the cracker box was nearly empty, allowing me an allotment of roughly six crackers a day. Without cooking gas I would have to club and eat an island fox, turning it inside out so as to lay blame on the golden eagles.

And then I realized, of course, that the boat was coming back, how else would Michael and Sonya get home, so I made it my goal for my first day to be at the dock two hours before the boat's arrival.

This still afforded me time. I set up camp, took a short hike, and then returned to the cobbled beach, where I found Michael and Sonya distinguishing themselves as foreigners by reading a bulletin board.

Michael gave me their fox report.

"We did not see the foxes, but we saw a lot of their shit!"

This struck me as a memory one does not want to carry long, but Michael and Sonya seemed quite happy, in the fashion of young people who will soon be leaving an island and eating hot food cooked in a place that doesn't require propane.

The boat arrived. I made my way with practiced slowness to the pier, while my mind played its last few games. What if one of the other campers had seen my lonely propane still in the case, and taken it? What if a member of Island Packers' staff had a weakness for sniffing gas? What if I weaned myself of the habit of losing something everywhere I go? Each scenario was more ridiculous than the last, but I was nervous nonetheless. At the end of the pier I took a deep breath to steady my nerves; when I looked down, I saw that the container housing my canisters had been off-loaded onto the dock when we arrived. Lifting the lid, I casually procured both canisters, as if, with the foresight of a savvy outdoorsman, I had saved myself a hernia by separating out these six ounces from the rest of my load.

Scorpion Canyon's campground had one glorious item the other campgrounds had lacked—trees. And not just any trees, enormous 120-year-old blue gum eucalyptus that rose high into the blue sky. I would later learn that the eucalyptus had been planted by the ranchers who lived on Santa Cruz Island in the 1880s for shade, fuel, pier pilings, and assorted other building materials. I would also learn that the majestic trees were some of the oldest in California. But I didn't care if they had slept with Ponce de León, I only knew that they offered blessed shelter from a wind that was already rising. I had not forgotten the gusting eddies that ignored the windbreaks at the campground on Santa Rosa and blew out my cooking fires, or the howling train winds on Anacapa that had stomped the roof of my tent against my face. Nay, I had come to greatly respect the wind; sometimes the word's mere mention made me weep.

And now the winds were coming again. Before we had even departed from Ventura Harbor, the talk was all about the weather; namely, how it was expected to fall apart later in the week. Eventually the winds on Santa Cruz were supposed to blow at twenty-five to thirty-five miles per hour, with gusts of forty-five miles per hour. On the exposed islands of Santa Rosa and San Miguel this was still bikini weather, but for Santa Cruz, sheltered by Point Conception, these were high winds indeed. Had there not been other campers in the campground, I would have kissed each and every eucalyptus tree.

During our briefing, Lulis had reminded us of this forecast, advising us not to pitch our tents beneath the trees or else risk being crushed by a trunk-size branch. This warning had been posted on the bulletin board at the entrance to the campground, she told us. But apparently, in our attention-deficient age, a half-mile walk is far too long to hold on to a thought, and of course no one looked at the bulletin board either. Walking back through the campground with my propane, I saw that most of my fellow campers had pitched their tents in the pleasant shade of the great trees.

Scorpion Canyon actually has a lower and upper campground; the upper campground, a bit farther back in the canyon, is reached via a short hike along the dirt road and stream bed (now dry) that wends past both campgrounds. I had booked a site in the lower campground. Both school groups inhabited the upper campground. As soon as I set up my tent, I heard their laughter, funneled as effectively as if by Larry's traffic cone, down the streambed. The noise didn't bother me; in fact, I found it pleasant. Only a curmudgeon or a high school principal would want to deny youth its joyful vigor.

That night I fell asleep to the lovely rustling of wind high in the eucalyptus. When I stepped outside in the middle of the night to inspect the nearby bushes, the full moon was sun-bright, bathing the eucalyptus grove in swaying shadow and silver. Back in my sleeping bag I heard again the familiar roar of approaching wind, but the eucalyptus allowed it only a mild bump against my tent, more of a rocking that lulled me back to sleep.

Youth, of course, does not always possess youthful vigor. The following morning I rose early and, heeding Lulis's advice, made for solitude and Montanon Ridge. The trail I followed led first through the flatlands of the Canyon, but then it rose fairly steeply up a ridge. Having attained higher ground, it continued for a time at a gradual upward cant before turning steep again as it summitted toward the ridgeline.

All the way up, there were sweeping views of ocean, brown-grassed hillsides studded with stands of island scrub oak and coast live oak, soaring ridgelines, and rounded canyons spilling to the sea. My surroundings made me feel small and happy. It felt good to again be under wide sky.

Eventually I turned back; descending, I passed a group of teenagers hiking up. Some moved nimbly, but some did not.

A girl stopped on the trail, and looked plaintively at me.

"How much farther until we see something?" she asked.

With 360 degrees of island panorama surrounding her, this seemed an odd question. Still I wanted to give her some hope in whatever world it was that she was seeing.

"Just over the next ridge," I said.

The boy behind her peeled back his lips so that I could see every inch of his braces.

"You lie!" he spat.

Maybe so, maybe not, but either way I'm leaving you to die.

Before I could give my ugly thoughts proper voice, a teacher came up. Perhaps he had heard his young charge's outburst. Perhaps I was still wiping brace spittle off my sleeve.

"They were supposed to go kayaking," he said to me amiably, "but the wind made it too rough. I'm sure they'd prefer that. This is too much up."

Not long ago I read a newspaper article documenting visitor falloffs at national parks. No doubt hard-bodied Audubon types were still frequenting nature, but according to the article, the young were avoiding the wilds in droves. The article informed me that someone had even written a book on the subject; the title was *Last Child in the Woods: Saving Our Children from Nature Deficit Disorder.*

I did not read the book, that would have been too much work, but I did read the newspaper article all the way through. What it had to say was both amusing and unsettling. Apparently some people were reading posted bulletins. A spokesperson for one national park surmised that today's youth were scared out of the wilds by signs and pamphlets warning them of everything from spiders to bears. "Small wonder they are terrified," the spokesperson said. I read that some parks were using technology to lure youth into their parks; one park had developed a game that simulated activities that could be done at the park. Here we are getting mauled by a bear. Here we slip ourselves into a sleeping bag already occupied by a tarantula. I am joking, but only to keep my spirits up. Simulating nature seemed far more frightening than any mishap that could actually befall one in the outdoors.

But most of the kids I saw on Santa Cruz, with the possible exception of young Hannibal Lecter, were enjoying themselves immensely. By day they hiked impressive distances in the continuously rising wind. At night the campgrounds rang, not with iPod muteness, but with the ring of laughter. This was reassuring to see.

It was fun, too, to eavesdrop on their sweet naiveté, for they were still dew in the world. Hiking past a boy and a girl, I heard the girl begin a story. After the first three words, the boy fairly shouted, "You already told me that story!" No right-minded male over thirty has ever used this phrase, though the opportunity to do so does present itself now and again.

Still, I preferred that my young friends honed their social and nature skills away from me, for I did seek solitude. Plus, I reasoned it would be difficult to happen on an island fox with the Mormon Tabernacle Choir in tow. In Michael and Sonya's honor, I made it my quest to see a fox on Santa Cruz.

But as I hiked about the eastern end of Santa Cruz, they eluded me, though their scat did not. At times it was quite fresh. It was not difficult to imagine the foxes, just off the trail, wiping themselves and snickering in the waist-high grasses.

Lulis was right. You don't have to hike far from the campground at Scorpion Canyon to find solitude and solace. I found mine in Delphine's Grove, a spot as lovely as the name itself. Delphine's Grove is a small stand of cypress pines. The grove is easily reached by a short hike up Smuggler's Road (actually a dirt track). The huddled trees sit on a sloping hillside, high above the water, amid a Serengeti Plain of grass. Like the eucalyptus, they supply dappled shade and protection, but unlike the towering and somewhat lordly eucalyptus, the cypress pines were small and approachable, like a knot of close friends. Each time I stretched out beneath them, I knew I had come to an oasis. It is now one of my favorite places in the world to daydream.

But I'll tell you why I really liked Delphine's Grove. I liked it because it shouldn't be there. Delphine, the oldest child of Justinian Caire (who supervised a ranching operation on the island that began around 1880), planted her fledgling cypress on a slope bereft of water. In my readings I could find nothing telling me why Delphine planted her cypress trees where she did, but anyone's rational guess would be for the view, for the grove looks out to the water, across the Santa Barbara Channel to the mainland, and it is a heart-squeezing expanse of white-caps and hazy blue coastal ranges. For Delphine it may have been something more; this is only speculation, but only a hope-less romantic would plant a tree in a place without water. Hers was a healthy spit in the face to conventional wisdom, a rebuff to the naysayers, and a handshake with belief. It was Father Eleutherius's sequoia, grown tall and strong in the desert.

Father Eleutherius also planted his sequoia with a mind to a view, for the farthest distances fascinate us. They raise a simple yet absorbing question. What is over the ridge, beyond the ho-rizon? The far distances inspire us to explore, to conquer, to migrate. It is the reason many of us are where we are; at some time, one of our ancestors packed up a few things and set out to see what was over there, and now we are over there.

The unseen distances are metaphorical too, places of pos-sibilities and imaginings, and so, bewitching times two. Father Eleutherius might have gazed out across the desert and dreamed of a family. For a young girl on an island the blue mainland might have swum with lovers and a more exciting life, but only Delphine would know. Everyone's distances are different. It's what makes us unique, and often inexplicable, even to those who claim to know us intimately. Husband and wife stand at a ship's railing, fingers intertwined, looking out to secret hori-zons of which they will never speak.

Delphine's Grove is also just a great place to worm off your hiking boots and listen to the wind in the boughs. The sounds are different, depending on the wind and the leanings of your imagination. Sometimes the wind is simply the constant drum of distant breaking surf. Sometimes the wind passes in distinct gusts, like trundling trains passing as you wait at a railroad crossing. Sometimes the boughs themselves creak, making the sound of a porch swing rocking slowly, its occupant riding gravity and memory. Winds can be like songs; they take you back to forgotten moments. But winds can only do this if they are carefully attended to, and this is not easy in a noisy world. Solitude helps one remember, and this is not just an exercise in pleasant memory. Solitude recalls the things that really matter.

Among other amenities, I discovered that if I stood on the end of the pier, I had cell phone reception. That evening I called home. As soon as Kathy answered, I knew it had been a mistake to call. The school year was finishing, and she was overwhelmed.

"I'm really stressed," she said, the edge in her voice making this clear. "It's seven o'clock and I have no idea what we're having for dinner. I haven't had a chance to do any of my schoolwork. It's just too much. I can't really talk now. I'm sorry."

I said goodbye. I stood for a long moment, slapped by the cold wind blowing off the ocean, and then I hiked back up to the cypress trees.

I understood. My wife was alone with two boys and more responsibilities than she could count. I was alone on an island. Her edginess was not aimed entirely at me.

I sat with my back against a tree. Across the water, lights began to flicker in the gloaming. Commuters making their way home, fluorescent convenience stores open 24/7, televisions and microwaves flicking on, computers humming with Internet connections. The world purpled; evening's cool gained weight against my skin.

I understood my wife's distraction, but my heart still ached. I wondered how many gloamings our sons would absorb in their lives. Or will we simply be overwhelmed until we cannot observe anything anymore?

I had hiked on Santa Cruz four years earlier, and I had done so with no small trepidation. At one time Santa Cruz was home to an appreciable number of wild pigs, the unruly descendants of more proper livestock abandoned by ranchers. By the time

I arrived at Scorpion Canyon four years later, the wild pigs had been eliminated from the island, thanks largely to the steady trigger fingers of a group of nearly-as-wild New Zealand pig hunters brought in to rid the island of these rutting scourges.

Animal lovers may decry this eradication, but the wild pigs were destroying Santa Cruz, rooting up everything from rare plant species to nine-thousand-year-old Chumash Indian archaeological sites. The pigs had also played a pivotal role in the drastic falloff of the Santa Cruz island fox. The presence of young piglets suddenly provided a year-round food source for the golden eagles, birds that were once rare visitors to the islands. So the golden eagles settled in on the island, and when they did, they discovered that foxes tasted good too.

On that first visit I camped on the western side of Santa Cruz, and evidence of pigs was not hard to find. Everywhere I hiked I saw great piles of jumbled, dark earth where the pigs had raked at the soil with their sharp hooves, foraging for food. An adult wild pig is no small thing; the animal throws substantial weight behind its razored pawings, and these are further aided by the application of nasty little tusks. At night I heard the pigs outside my tent, snorting and huffing like participants in a pornographic film. Hiking one afternoon, I came around a bend quickly, surprising an enormous pig. To this day I cannot recall if the ensuing squealing belonged to the pig or me, but let's just say that both man and pig can fly.

Now I didn't have to worry about the pigs, but I was beginning to worry about the foxes. Despite the passage of several days, I still hadn't seen one. Perhaps the scat was just a park service ruse perpetuated by a last remaining fox that was being kept captive and fed a daunting supply of laxatives.

When I hiked, I also made a game of scanning my surroundings for my fellow man. Most of the time I saw no one, just the mountain ridges, with their sloping foothills descending into the canyons like lion paws. But sometimes I did spy my fellow campers in the distance, and, no surprise, they looked very small against the vast island, and I thought, *Who would believe that something so insignificant could wreak such havoc?* Tornadoes are touching down in New York City. For the first time in recorded history Canada's fabled Northwest Passage was ice-free. Spring plants bloom weeks ahead of their traditional time. You don't know whether to weep or be astonished by our ability to turn the earth on its ear.

Our treatment of our fellow human beings has not been much better than our treatment of the earth, though there are certainly many oases of goodwill—All Saints' Church is one example. The Chumash who once inhabited the Channel Islands have a saying regarding the world: *I sari wa.* (It will continue indefinitely.) But the Chumash no longer inhabit the islands that were once their home. Smallpox killed them, and when that didn't, the Spanish explorers, the Russian otter hunters, and even the missionaries took up the job. There are those who claim some of the dead still drift about the islands, spectral Indians, sometimes spied on peaks at dawn, crying out to the gods that failed them. I saw no ghosts during my dawns on Santa Cruz, but it is not ghosts that frighten me. "Ghosts fear men much more than men fear ghosts," goes a Chinese proverb. Perhaps with good reason.

One sunny afternoon I hiked out to Smuggler's Cove. The winds had nearly reached their peak, blowing hard enough to force Island Packers to cancel all their boat trips for the following day. I saw the notice, posted no doubt by a skeptical Lulis, on the campground bulletin board. Campers were given the option of going home early or waiting for the next boat, possibly two days later.

Smuggler's Cove was entrancing, a long crescent bay of cobbled beach, bashed by large emerald waves and looked down upon by a tidily aligned grove of olive trees planted by ranchers who at one time saw money in olives.

More recently someone had planted a lemon tree. It grew close to the empty two-story Smuggler's Ranch house that once housed laborers who worked in the olive orchard and a nearby vineyard. The abandoned ranch house sat in a small valley; out of the wind it was hot. I had neglected to bring enough water. By the time I sat down beneath the lemon tree, I was very, very thirsty.

One advancement man should hold on to is the slope-backed wooden chair and bench on which to rest one's feet. I found them both in the shade of the lemon tree. I also found lemons. I have never picked a fruit that did not belong to me, but I picked one of these lemons and ate it; sour-sweet and moist, it was the best lemon I have ever tasted. Because they did not belong to me, I ate only one, but, looking about, I saw numerous rinds in various states of decomposition, left there no doubt by other dehydrated hikers.

I believe that earlier in this book I said that wind makes you feel alive, but it is also true that if the wind blows long and hard enough, it will reduce you to slobbering madness. As I hiked back from Smuggler's Cove, the wind blew directly in my face. Though I walked bent like a crazed hunchback, at times it still stood me upright. Other times it made me stagger like a drunk. I wished I were. Conducting an experiment, I turned my back to the wind and spat. Somewhere in Iowa, a man wiped the back of his neck. Walking into the wind felt like walking through knee-deep snow. Once or twice when the wind screamed its loudest, I screamed back. The wind didn't care. It whipped my potty language off to Iowa too.

When I finally made it back to camp, I was bone-weary. I had planned on hiking up to the bluff at nearby Cavern Point to watch the stars, but I had abandoned that idea halfway back from Smuggler's Cove. Apparently Americans can change their ways, for as I trudged through the campground, I found it pretty much abandoned. All but one of my fellow residents in the lower campground had opted to go home on the early boat. The sole remaining camper was a slender man with snow-white hair and an equally white beard. Before the winds had reached gale force, I had seen him down at Scorpion Beach instructing the high school students in the intricacies of kayaking. Though our campsites were separated by no more than twenty yards, we had only exchanged waves.

Now, the upper reaches of the eucalyptus bobbing violently up and down like dashboard bobble heads, we both quietly went about preparing dinner. At least he did; I was too tired. There were times on the islands when I felt lonely, dirt-encrusted, and depressed, and this was one of them. I plunked myself down at my picnic table, a jar of peanut butter in one hand, a knife in the other, and swallowed hunks of fat and protein I didn't taste. I looked at my watch. Seven fifteen. I glanced over my shoulder. My neighbor was heading for the toilets. As soon as he disappeared inside, I ducked into my tent, zipped the rain flap shut, and went to sleep.

When I stepped out of the tent in the middle of the night, the campground was again a silvery glen. The wind still blew. The moon illuminated the bobbing eucalyptus trees so brightly they appeared to be in near daylight. They looked like beneficent giants, nodding either approval or dismissal.

And so I spent my days hiking back into the canyon, along various ridgelines and, without fail, going back to Delphine's Grove, where there may now be a permanent imprint in the grass that aligns perfectly with my body.

I finally saw Michael's foxes too, though not in the fashion I imagined. Standing up from my picnic table one evening, I nearly fell over one as it dashed through my campsite.

This rare sighting was too much to keep to myself. As I looked around for my white-haired neighbor, I saw another fox, slinking along the outer edge of the campground, a housecat with a thyroid-afflicted tail.

My neighbor's name was Tony Chapman, though when we met, I barely heard him introduce himself, consumed as I was with my need to tell him that unicorns were cavorting all about us.

"Did you see the fox?"

I may have shouted, for Tony raised his white eyebrows.

"You haven't seen one before?" he asked.

This stole some of my thunder.

"Well, no," I said. "At least not here."

"Did you hear the squalling the other night?"

I had. But I had assumed that a branch had fallen on an un-lucky camper.

"That was foxes," Tony continued. "They were fighting for either food or territory. But whatever it was, they were fighting. They're all over the campground." He gestured to a hillside sloping down to the edge of the campground.

"See those cliffs over there? They're filled with holes, and those holes are filled with fox dens."

As if on cue, two small foxes emerged from some bushes near the streambed and moved along the edge of the campground with an odd prancing trot. No more than a minute later, two more appeared, sauntering right down the middle of the road.

Were they mocking me?

To save at least some face, I told Tony that a fox had dashed past me no more than an arm's length away.

Tony shrugged.

"That's not unusual," he said. "They'll come even closer than that."

Well what about this? I thought. *I saw a platoon of foxes marching behind two German tourists, the lot of them bellowing out, "Bier hier, bier hier!" And it was your beer that they were drinking.*

Instead I said, "Oh."

Tony, it turned out, had been coming out to the islands for some forty years. He had seen a few foxes.

Perhaps my transparent deflation caused Tony some pangs, because later he told me a story. Once he served as kayak guide for a group of boisterous Fijians. One night, after consuming ample amounts of liquor, part of the group dragged Tony up to a nearby hillside to sing songs and look at the stars. When they returned, their comrades were stuffed inside a single tent, staring out into the night.

"I asked them why they were in the tent," recalled Tony. His eyes went wide with mock terror. "They're like, 'The foxes!'"

Perhaps we have become a bit too accomplished at distancing ourselves from nature.

That evening I walked up to Cavern Point in the fast falling light. I stood listening to wind and birdsong. Across the Channel, lights came on. Slowly the stars appeared, forming an umbrella that spanned both worlds

I left the island the same morning the school groups did, the kids hauling their coolers and memories down to the pier.

We stood bunched on the pier, waiting to board the Island Packers' boat. In the distance a freighter made its way south, its decks piled high with enormous containers.

Watching the freighter's grinding progress, I recalled the continuous procession of freighters that had steamed past during my week on Anacapa.

Smoke spiraled from the freighter.

The girl in front of me said, "Look at that pollution."

Today's teenagers are both innocent and world-weary.

Her companion said, "That's civilization." And then he added, "The American dream."

Not just the American dream. Much of the world covets flat-screen TVs, and designer clothes, and the ability to get things faster than at any time in the history of the world. But numbers do not make things right.

What if our dreams are a lie?

The World to Come

. . ■ ■ . .

I HAD VISITED ALL of the islands, but I was not finished with my search, so I undertook one more visit. This is how I found myself, on a glaring-white morning, sitting beside my new friend, Alek, who was, at the moment, very concerned about bears. The odds of us encountering a bear were slim. We sat in a sad field of cracked earth, gopher holes, and weeds (a vacant lot, actually) surrounded by busy roads and subdivisions. Alek's classroom was a cracker-toss away. Nonetheless, Alek's head swung about. His fellow picnickers, also readying to leave, huddled together and glanced over their shoulders too.

My friend Alek has close-cropped hair that lifts in front in a small wave. He also has a rapier-sharp mind. He knows what a dormant volcano is·and he intuits things quickly, though it is also true that he thinks a slice of pie costs a nickel.

When he stood up from the blanket, he was only up to my waist. Alek is not yet five.

"Alek," I said. "I've seen bears in the wild. They run away from people. They're more afraid of us than we are of them."

"Uh-huh."

Alek craned his neck.

Many thoughts occur to Alek. One did now.

"Bears growl at you," he said.

"They do that because they're scared of you."

Alek, whom I had just met yesterday, put his hand in mine, but he did not look up at me.

"Do you try to catch them?" he asked.

"Well, that's not really a good idea," I said.

Alek nodded.

"Sometimes bears want to climb up into a mountain where people get tired and can't catch them," he said.

We crossed the field to the parking lot that fronts Children's World Nursery School.

"Do you feel better now that you know bears are afraid of you, Alek?"

"And I know I am afraid of them!"

Even young habits can be hard to shake.

Alek attends Children's World Nursery School in Ventura, California. His teachers are Ronna Streeton and Odette Huber. Mrs. Streeton and Mrs. Huber were also Graham and Cullen's teachers, and for that I am still grateful. Mrs. Streeton and Mrs. Huber have been teaching a long time. They now teach the children of former students. Preschool teachers seem to have the half-life of plutonium. And why not?

"This is a good place to tank up," smiled Mrs. Huber.

And so I spent several days in Mrs. Streeton and Mrs. Huber's classroom (hereafter referred to as S&H's classroom). Along with tanking up, this is the place where things begin, and in the beginning there is always an ample supply of hope. I am a big fan of hope—it can accomplish great things, and sometimes it is all we have to stand on—though it is also important to remember that nursery school is not all popcorn, ice cream, rainbows, and unicorns with wings. One morning I leafed through the menus S&H's class had made for the bakery they operate. I turned one menu over. On the back, written in bold dark marker, it said *No No No No*.

The children in S&H's class are four and five years old. Next year many of them will go to kindergarten, everything they know in tow.

Spend time with preschoolers and you will learn many interesting things. I learned that William's mom has long blond hair and there's a lot of brown under it. I learned why we have two ears and one set of lips. (Hint: which is most important?) I learned what it means to be a family, and what to do if I do something wrong. I learned to see the astonishing in what many see as commonplace. I learned to be grateful. I learned the purpose for living (it's love—seems unfair to make you wait), and the purpose for my notebook. Some of these things I knew before, but it never hurts to be reminded.

Nursery school is not a place of solitude, unless you get sent to Mrs. Levine's office, but I had come to see that solitude was not the only path to deeper understanding. I had learned a great deal from Abbot Francis and Father Eleutherius, from combat veteran Dan Seidenberg, from my fellow campers and my fellow creatures in the wild. Why not Alek, Elise, Fiona, and Luke too?

And so I went back to repeat my own education for a few days.

Mrs. Streeton favors jean jackets. Sometimes she wears bright red tennis shoes. She would like to live in a peaceful world, but she is no pushover. If someone does something wrong, she tells them about it. Mrs. Huber still retains the lovely lilt of her Belgian heritage. She is quieter than Mrs. Streeton, often working in the background. They work together seamlessly, making imprints on child and parent. Once, Mrs. Huber asked the students in her class to list the things that were good for their hearts. She wrote them on a piece of poster board and put it on her classroom door for everyone to see. Cullen wrote, "My family and my shoes." I still remember that.

Mrs. Streeton and Mrs. Huber see a lesson in everything, for life is like that. *Everybody has a teddy bear? Let's line them up against the wall according to size. We're proud of you. What does* proud *mean?* It had been eight years since Graham attended Children's World; ten for Cullen. Eerily, neither woman appeared to have aged. I was happy with this. My hope is that they both live forever, teaching nursery school.

When I returned, Mrs. Streeton and Mrs. Huber were employing a teaching program based on the Reggio Emilia approach. I have no idea what that means officially; I'm sure there is some dry documentation somewhere that outlines its philosophies. But it did entail some wonderful things. The kids weren't taught at, with a specified curriculum; more often, they offered suggestions of what they might do, and the curriculum followed them. If they were curious about bears, well, they might have a teddy bear picnic and talk about how bears have families too. If they were discussing peace, they might decide to collectively write a book on peace, putting it together from start to finish—there would be writers, cover illustrators, people to put together the table of contents. What these teachers did each day was like improvisational theater, powered by ingenuity and creativity that would dumbfound Da Vinci.

"We show the children that their words are heard and valued," Mrs. Streeton told me on my first day. "We want them to know how important they are. Isn't that how it should be? And they'll remember that forever."

She also explained that the classroom operated as a family, a community working together. The families did things outside of school, and the parents were required to spend a certain number of hours in the classroom, and there was a sign on the door that said La Famiglia, in part because Reggio Emilia was developed in Italy.

Mrs. Streeton and Mrs. Huber explained this important concept to me, and they reiterated it again and again to the kids.

"Why do we call ourselves *la famiglia?*" Mrs. Streeton asked the gathering seated on the rug one morning.

"Because we're a family," someone said.

"And what does that mean, that we're a family?" Mrs. Streeton asked. "Are we sisters and brothers?"

"Noooooooo."

"We care about each other and we love each other," Mrs. Streeton said.

"Yeeeeeessssss."

How nice that would be.

Once, around Christmas, the students were understandably wound up. Mrs. Streeton advised they all take a very deep breath. A parent, standing in the classroom, suggested one better. Her father did yoga. Next thing, Grandpa is in the classroom demonstrating yoga. The children can now perform a fairly polished sun salutation, mixed with just the right amount of fidgeting and drooping pants.

Each morning before the class day begins, the lights go off; in the dimness the children get into poses and stretch on the rug while soft classical music or maybe John Lennon's "Imagine" plays. They do not touch one another, for that would be distracting. They try not to go too fast (not always easy). When they are finished, they shout, "Good morning, sun!"

And so I learned a fine way to start the day.

I met Alek in the Bakery. The Bakery isn't a real bakery, or maybe it is, but most adults can't see it. What adults see is a small desk and baskets stacked with plastic bagels and brownies and filled with childishly scrawled menus.

I wanted to make a friend. I bent down to Alek.

"Is the bakery open?" I asked.

The sign affixed to the bakery table said Closed, but, like his classmates, Alek did not cling blindly to convention, or let trivialities stand in his way.

"Oh yes! It is open!"

To illustrate this, Alek promptly began arranging a few things so that they might be better displayed.

"OK, sir. What would you like?"

The wise diner lets the chef select.

"Well, what do you recommend?"

"We have all kinds of things." Alek puffed up slightly. "We have *menus.*"

Alek reached into the jumbled pile of menus and procured one for me. Not by coincidence, I found myself looking at Alek's menu.

Already I admired Alek's spunk, and his magician's ability to pick the right card from the deck. So I ordered the most expensive item on his menu. Spaghetti was a dollar, substantially more than ham, which was a penny. Going through the menus later, I discovered it was a good thing Alek had handed me his menu. On one menu cookies were eighty-nine dollars. There was no danger of price-fixing at the Children's World Bakery.

Alek was thrilled with my selection, but it had nothing to do with profit.

"We get to make spaghetti! First I have to find a bowl."

He did so. Then he turned to the stove, explaining the two red plastic knobs to me.

"These make it hot."

No surprise, the spaghetti was ready instantly.

"Here!"

Alek held out the bowl. That it looked empty to my eyes made me slightly sad. But I lapped up its contents like a Labrador.

Alek didn't wait around for compliments.

"What else?" he asked.

"What else goes with spaghetti?"

"Everything!"

Of course.

So I had ham and eggs and bread and pumpkin pie. I didn't

give a hoot what Jenny Craig thought. The chef's smile was beyond price.

Finished eating, I asked, "How do I pay for this?"

Alek looked puzzled.

Two girls had been watching us. They went over to a plastic cash register, opened it, and paraded past Alek clenching fistfuls of bills.

As I said, Alek has a sharp mind. His face took on a very un-flattering adult expression. A dark cloud passed over the room.

"Money! Money! I'm earning money!"

Mrs. Streeton spoke to him.

"Alek. We don't say that out loud."

If someone asked you to paint like Monet, you'd probably say, "Fine, and why don't I just come up with a solution for global warming with a hunk of silly putty and three dimes?" But if you are four, you would just sit down with your paints and get started.

Almost everything in S&H's classroom begins, continues, and ends with an explanation.

Before everyone started painting, Mrs. Streeton told them that Monet liked to paint outside, and that he often painted the exact same scene many times, only at different times of the day.

"He wanted to see how the sun looked on whatever it was he was painting at different times of the day or even at different times of the year," Mrs. Streeton said.

Monet painted haystacks in autumn and haystacks at the end of the summer, and they are vastly different paintings, though they each possess a subtle glazing of contentment that makes you believe that Monet was happy to be alive.

We sat on the rug. Mrs. Streeton sat in a chair. She held up a book about Monet. The page was opened to *The Japanese Foot-bridge,* a lovely painting of a lily pond, a Japanese footbridge arching over it. No esoteric titles for Mr. Monet.

"Ohhhhhhh," said everybody, including me. I cannot draw a balloon-handed stick figure, but I understood how nature's subtleties had entranced Monet. I had seen evening's shadows crawl up the cliffs of the Channel Islands.

After this brief bout of admiration everyone got down to the business of painting better than Monet.

Like Monet, they sat outside, at desks in the shade.

Mrs. Streeton and I stood behind them, so as not to block their view of the world.

"We do other artists too," Mrs. Streeton said to me. "We did Jackson Pollock."

I am no art history major, but even a nematode knows that Pollock slung paint around, creating something people saw as art.

"That must have been a hit," I said.

"Actually they were kind of inhibited. We just wanted them to fling it against the wall, but it took them a while to realize that was OK."

I understand that it is neither acceptable nor proper to stride into an AARP convention naked, but it also seems to me that our society has become more stringent about what can and can't be done, squeezing us between increasingly confining lines. Political correctness, the corralling of independence, call it what you want. But four-year-olds thinking twice about throwing paint unsettled me.

Claude Monet lived to be eighty-six years old, which is about a billion times older than anything Alek, Elise, Fiona, or Luke know. Here is something else about Monet you might not know: Young Claude had quite the sense of humor. He didn't pay much attention in school. Instead he drew caricatures of his teachers. Often he gave them monstrous noses. No doubt, in return they gave Mr. Monet poor grades. In Monet's time, most painters painted indoors. Throughout his life, Monet continued to follow his own muse, which, in the end, turned out to be a very good thing.

We drew out on the playground at recess too. This wasn't a planned activity. It happened like this: Children's World forms a three-sided square around a large patch of grass (the fourth side is a playground). This is where the children play. One afternoon Alek and Kelsa were driving race cars on a rug someone had dragged out onto the grass. The rug had a road on it, and lakes and barns. Not that anyone paid any attention to the road. Their driving was atrocious. In their hurry to race each other here and there, they drove their cars over everything but the ducks, and they would have run over the ducks if Alek hadn't objected. I joined them, running over everything too. It was good fun driving over the roof of a barn, knowing that, four days later, you weren't going to get a photograph of yourself violating Statute 33686 and fining you $3,361 for your joy ride.

In the classroom, out on the bear-free field, at the bakery counter, I had been taking notes on a yellow steno-pad, scratching away furiously when I witnessed something I thought should be noted. No one paid my scribblings any mind. Being among four-year-olds is a bit like wandering through an insane asylum; no one is judgmental.

Alek stopped driving. He picked up my notebook and my pen. "Can I draw?" he asked.

"You bet."

This, of course, was a siren call. In thirty seconds, a half-dozen small beings were gathered on the rug, clamoring for a chance to draw.

Matters appeared to be on the edge of riot. Someone had to take control. I looked for Mrs. Huber and Mrs. Streeton, but they were nowhere to be seen.

So I said, "Let's play a game."

"What kind of game?"

Everyone got quiet. I had no idea.

To my surprise my own lips said, "A guessing game," and off we went. One person drew, while everyone else but me—having reflexively assumed control, I was now president for life—closed their eyes. When the person drawing finished, they didn't show their drawing. We played twenty questions—or four, or six—the nondrawers asking questions while the artist of the moment did their best to give the answer away. Four-year-olds are not much at keeping secrets.

Still, they managed to hold their tongues for long enough to make the game rollicking good fun.

Alek went first. I sat on the rug. He sat on my lap, legs bent behind him, drawing in my notebook, looking up now and again to cast suspicious glances at his eager audience. Elise and Kelsa sprawled across my legs like sea lions.

When Alek finished, he showed me his drawing. I recognized it immediately, which was not the case with some of the other drawings.

Alek and I exchanged knowing glances.

"OK," I said, "give them a hint," and Alek said, "It's a car that races around a racetrack," and that was it for Alek.

They drew pictures of mermaids, princesses, hot dogs—no wait, it was a dog but the legs were really hard to see—cats, and hamsters.

Elise took her turn. She sketched very slowly, tongue protruding to aid her concentration.

We waited. We waited some more. They were as patient as the guests at All Saints' lunch.

Finally someone observed, "She's taking her time."

Elise did not look up.

"I'm trying to make it perfect," she said.

Francis said, "Everything doesn't have to be perfect," and instantly I knew something about Francis's home life.

What they drew and what I saw on the paper didn't always match. In the very beginning of his wonderful book *The Little Prince*, Antoine de Saint-Exupéry tells the story of a drawing he made at the age of six. It was a boa constrictor, immensely swollen in the middle from having ingested an elephant. But with its nearly square rise in the middle, and two small extensions on either side (the head and tail of the snake), the drawing did look very much like a hat. When little Antoine showed the drawing around, every adult said so. Antoine kept the drawing. Now and again, over the course of his life, he would show the picture to a grown-up he thought was particularly wise and clear-sighted. They, too, said it was a hat. And so his imagination lived alone, among sensible people.

We played the guessing game for the rest of recess, the lot of us sprawled about the rug, and, as with the guessing games that followed in subsequent recesses, on this day there were many boa constrictors that had ingested elephants, though I saw only hats.

Just before recess ended, Mrs. Huber walked by.

"Well," she smiled. "Aren't you the Pied Piper?"

It was the nicest compliment I have ever received.

I have always tried to see the elephant inside the boa constrictor. Some sensible adults claim that this gets harder and harder as imagination seeps out of you. Even if you see the distended boa in the beginning, eventually it will just be a hat. I prefer not to think of it as lack of imagination. I think it means there is never just one answer.

One day, instead of playing at recess, I stood on the lawn and talked with Mrs. Levine, of "Mrs. Levine's office" fame. Marion Levine is the director of Children's World Nursery School, but actually it is quite rare that someone gets sent to her office, for this is not high school, where it's standing-room only at detention. Here the teachers handle most matters swiftly and on their own.

Marion and I talked adult talk. Instead of drawing a jellyfish on a roller coaster and saying, "Guess what this is?" I asked her serous writerlike questions, such as what had she learned from children?

Marion had been a teacher for thirty years. She spoke warmly about the children's innocence and unconditional love, and I wondered why it is we grow into lovers who always expect something in return.

"They help me refocus on what the important things in life

are," she said, as small bodies careened about us. "Just stopping and watching them, noticing what they're looking at and what they find awesome and beautiful."

We talked a bit longer, and then she said a curious thing.

"The kids that really interest me are the quiet ones," she said. "Why aren't they laughing and enjoying the games alongside everyone else? I wonder if they have already been coached not to act up."

I saw those few children now, watching sober-eyed from the periphery. It seemed to me they already knew something of solitude. Whether this was good or bad, I didn't know. Maybe it was neither. Maybe they were just being quiet. It is very hard not to foist our beliefs and thoughts on others. I recalled Hamlet's wise words: "There is nothing either good or bad, but thinking makes it so."

There was much talk of peace in S&H's classroom. A sign on the door of another teacher's room proclaimed it The Happiest Place on Earth. But we are imperfect, even in our innocent unconditional form.

One day I caught the tail end of a small uproar. Someone had pushed Alek to the ground as he was getting a drink from the water fountain. At almost the same instant two girls were in the bathroom, one urging the other to follow her lead, which she did, both of them plunking their hands in the toilet. When it rains, it pours.

So immediately *la famiglia* came into the classroom to discuss things. First we lay on the rug and listened to "Imagine" ("Imagine all the people, living life in peace . . ."). Then the children sat up. Mrs. Streeton sat in her chair in front of the class.

"I have some things to talk about," Mrs. Streeton said. "Remember how we said we're all a family? Well, I'm unhappy with some members of our family right now. It doesn't make me happy when members of my family are doing things that are very, very wrong."

Everybody waited quietly.

Mrs. Streeton continued.

"You have to treat others with respect. And you have to know how to make good choices. When somebody says something to you that you know in your brain is wrong, you need to be adult and make the right choice."

Of course Mrs. Streeton, Mrs. Huber, and I all knew that adults don't always make the right choices, but we kept that secret. They would figure this out soon enough.

"I'm very, very sad now," Mrs. Streeton said, "because right now it isn't peaceful in our home. And only you can make that change. We are going to work really hard to be a peaceful classroom. We need to do peaceful things."

Someone asked, "Will you tell us when we do something peaceful?"

Mrs. Streeton shook her head, and there was a short murmuring of surprise.

"You won't have to ask. You'll know."

There was nothing but breathing.

Peace is easy to practice in stillness; the real challenge is practicing peace at the height of the storm.

I hadn't seen Alek pushed, but I had witnessed the immediate aftermath, Mrs. Streeton moving quickly over to the pusher and reprimanding him in no uncertain terms. And then she took his hand.

That afternoon, after school was over, Mrs. Streeton looked tired. She stood in the doorway, the room now quiet.

"Sometimes I think the world is mostly good," she said, "and sometimes I don't. I try to believe, but it's hard."

Her shoulders slumped a touch beneath her jean jacket, and she tugged on her fingers. Hands never lie.

I thought, *In thirteen years they, too, can go off to war.*

The next morning when I arrived at Children's World, the boy who had pushed Alek was presenting him with a card. Apparently this was a matter of both forgiveness and practicality. He said to Alek, "Keep it. That way if I push you again, you already have a card."

Mrs. Streeton and the mother continued discussing the event, while the boys played together on the playground.

Elise came up to me.

"Good morning, Elise," I said.

Elise skipped the formalities.

"I want you to stay here forever," she said.

I couldn't stay. My sons were not in nursery school anymore, and soon Alek and Elise wouldn't be either. One day the scruffy, bear-haunted field will be gone. Alek and Elise will be in charge, and if things are done right now in little worlds like this one, maybe the bigger world will one day be a better place. This is oversimplifying, but what harm is there in that? We could do with more simplicity.

I walked to my car. It was parked by the dusty field. I opened the door, but I did not get in. I paused to relive a memory or two, now shockingly distant, of when my sons went here—life has always moved at a pace beyond belief. But instead of getting lost in these memories, I saw the empty field. There were still no bears, but gathering clouds had softened the light so that the flowers erupting from the weeds assumed their brightest yellow, and now, above the cracked earth and weeds and gopher holes, butterflies danced.

Monet saw. The world comes in every hue, and we are fortunate to dwell in them all.

ABOUT THE AUTHOR

Ken McAlpine is an award-winning travel writer whose work has appeared in *Sports Illustrated, Outside, Reader's Digest*, the *Los Angeles Times*, and other publications. He is the author of *Off-Season: Discovering America on Winter's Shore*, a chronicle of the author's travels through beach towns from Florida to Maine after the seasonal vacationers have gone. He lives in Ventura, California. For more information, or to contact the author, visit www.kenmcalpine.com.

Peter Muz